Migration, Diasporas and Citizenship Series

Series Editors: **Robin Cohen**, Former Director of the International Migration Institute and Professor of Development Studies, University of Oxford, UK and **Zig Layton-Henry**, Professor of Politics, University of Warwick, UK.

Editorial Board: **Rainer Baubock**, European University Institute, Italy; **James F. Hollifield**, Southern Methodist University, USA; **Jan Rath**, University of Amsterdam, the Netherlands

The Migration, Diasporas and Citizenship series covers three important aspects of the migration progress. Firstly, the determinants, dynamics and characteristics of international migration. Secondly, the continuing attachment of many contemporary migrants to their places of origin, signified by the word 'diaspora', and thirdly the attempt, by contrast, to belong and gain acceptance in places of settlement, signified by the word 'citizenship'. The series publishes work that shows engagement with and a lively appreciation of the wider social and political issues that are influenced by international migration.

Also published in Migration Studies by Palgrave Macmillan

Bridget Anderson and Isabel Shutes (*editors*)
MIGRATION AND CARE LABOUR
Theory, Policy and Politics

Rutvica Andrijasevic
MIGRATION, AGENCY AND CITIZENSHIP IN SEX TRAFFICKING

Floya Anthias and Mojca Pajnik (*editors*)
CONTESTING INTEGRATION, ENGENDERING MIGRATION
Theory and Practice

Claudine Attias-Donfut, Joanne Cook, Jaco Hoffman and Louise Waite (*editors*)
CITIZENSHIP, BELONGING AND INTERGENERATIONAL RELATIONS IN AFRICAN MIGRATION

Grete Brochmann and Anniken Hagelund (*authors*) with Karin Borevi, Heidi Vad Jønsson and Klaus Petersen IMMIGRATION POLICY AND THE SCANDINAVIAN WELFARE STATE 1945–2010

Gideon Calder, Phillip Cole and Jonathan Seglow
CITIZENSHIP ACQUISITION AND NATIONAL BELONGING
Migration, Membership and the Liberal Democratic State

Michael Collyer
EMIGRATION NATIONS
Policies and Ideologies of Emigrant Engagement

Enzo Colombo and Paola Rebughini (*editors*)
CHILDREN OF IMMIGRANTS IN A GLOBALIZED WORLD
A Generational Experience

Huub Dijstelbloem and Albert Meijer (*editors*)
MIGRATION AND THE NEW TECHNOLOGICAL BORDERS OF EUROPE

Thomas Faist and Andreas Ette (*editors*)
THE EUROPEANIZATION OF NATIONAL POLICIES AND POLITICS OF IMMIGRATION
Between Autonomy and the European Union

Thomas Faist and Peter Kivisto (*editors*)
DUAL CITIZENSHIP IN GLOBAL PERSPECTIVE
From Unitary to Multiple Citizenship

Katrine Fangen, Thomas Johansson and Nils Hammarén (*editors*)
YOUNG MIGRANTS
Exclusion and Belonging in Europe

Martin Geiger and Antoine Pécoud (*editors*)
THE POLITICS OF INTERNATIONAL MIGRATION MANAGEMENT

John R. Hinnells (*editor*)
RELIGIOUS RECONSTRUCTION IN THE SOUTH ASIAN DIASPORAS
From One Generation to Another

Ronit Lentin and Elena Moreo (*editors*)
MIGRANT ACTIVISM AND INTEGRATION FROM BELOW IN IRELAND

Catrin Lundström
WHITE MIGRATIONS
Gender, Whiteness and Privilege in Transnational Migration

Ayhan Kaya
ISLAM, MIGRATION AND INTEGRATION
The Age of Securitization

Majella Kilkey, Diane Perrons and Ania Plomien
GENDER, MIGRATION AND DOMESTIC WORK
Masculinities, Male Labour and Fathering in the UK and USA

Amanda Klekowski von Koppenfels
MIGRANTS OR EXPATRIATES?
Americans in Europe

Marie Macy and Alan H. Carling
ETHNIC, RACIAL AND RELIGIOUS INEQUALITIES
The Perils of Subjectivity

George Menz and Alexander Caviedes (editors)
LABOUR MIGRATION IN EUROPE

Laura Morales and Marco Giugni (editors)
SOCIAL CAPITAL, POLITICAL PARTICIPATION AND MIGRATION IN EUROPE
Making Multicultural Democracy Work?

Eric Morier-Genoud
IMPERIAL MIGRATIONS
Colonial Communities and Diaspora in the Portuguese World

Aspasia Papadopoulou-Kourkoula
TRANSIT MIGRATION
The Missing Link Between Emigration and Settlement

Ludger Pries and Zeynep Sezgin (editors)
CROSS BORDER MIGRANT ORGANIZATIONS IN COMPARATIVE PERSPECTIVE

Prodromos Panayiotopoulos
ETHNICITY, MIGRATION AND ENTERPRISE

Shanthi Robertson
TRANSNATIONAL STUDENT-MIGRANTS AND THE STATE
The Education-Migration Nexus

Olivia Sheringham
TRANSNATIONAL RELIGIOUS SPACES
Faith and the Brazilian Migration Experience

Evan Smith and Marinella Marmo
RACE, GENDER AND THE BODY IN BRITISH IMMIGRATION CONTROL
Subject to Examination

Vicky Squire
THE EXCLUSIONARY POLITICS OF ASYLUM

Anna Triandafyllidou and Thanos Maroukis (editors)
MIGRANT SMUGGLING
Irregular Migration from Asia and Africa to Europe

Vron Ware
MILITARY MIGRANTS
Fighting for YOUR Country

Lucy Williams
GLOBAL MARRIAGE
Cross-Border Marriage Migration in Global Context

Migration, Diasporas and Citizenship Series
Series Standing Order ISBN 978–0–230–30078–1 (hardback) and 978–0–230–30079–8 (paperback)
(outside North America only)

You can receive future titles in this series as they are published by placing a standing order. Please contact your bookseller or, in case of difficulty, write to us at the address below with your name and address, the title of the series and the ISBN quoted above.

Customer Services Department, Macmillan Distribution Ltd, Houndmills, Basingstoke, Hampshire RG21 6XS, England

Race, Gender and the Body in British Immigration Control

Subject to Examination

Evan Smith and Marinella Marmo
Flinders University, Australia

First published 2014 by
PALGRAVE MACMILLAN

Palgrave Macmillan in the UK is an imprint of Macmillan Publishers Limited, registered in England, company number 785998, of Houndmills, Basingstoke, Hampshire RG21 6XS.

Palgrave Macmillan in the US is a division of St Martin's Press LLC, 175 Fifth Avenue, New York, NY 10010.

Palgrave Macmillan is the global academic imprint of the above companies and has companies and representatives throughout the world.

Palgrave® and Macmillan® are registered trademarks in the United States, the United Kingdom, Europe and other countries.

ISBN 978–1–137–28043–5

This book is printed on paper suitable for recycling and made from fully managed and sustained forest sources. Logging, pulping and manufacturing processes are expected to conform to the environmental regulations of the country of origin.

A catalogue record for this book is available from the British Library.

Library of Congress Cataloging-in-Publication Data
Smith, Evan, 1981–
    Race, gender and the body in British immigration control : subject to examination / Evan Smith and Marinella Marmo, Flinders University, Australia.
        pages cm. — (Migration, diasporas and citizenship)
    Summary: "Race, Gender and the Body in British Immigration Control provides the most detailed account of the virginity testing controversy in the late 1970s, and demonstrates that this abusive practice, which was endured by South Asian women for more than a decade, was part of a wider culture of mistreatment and discrimination that occurred within the immigration system authorized by the state. Using recently opened government documents, Smith and Marmo offer a unique insight into this matter and uncover the extent to which these women were scrutinized, interrogated and subject to physical examination at the border. Combining cutting edge criminological theory and historical research, this book proposes that the contemporary British immigration control system should be viewed as an attempt to replicate colonial hierarchies upon migrants in the post-imperial era. For this reason, the abuses of human rights at the border became a secondary issue to the need of the post-imperial British nation-state to enforce strict immigration controls"—Provided by publisher.
    ISBN 978–1–137–28043–5 (hardback)
    1. Women immigrants—Government policy—Great Britain—History—20th century. 2. Women immigrants—South Asia—History—20th century. 3. Great Britain—Emigration and immigration—Government policy—History—20th century. 4. South Asia—Emigration and immigration—History—20th century. 5. Virginity—Political aspects—Great Britain. I. Marmo, Marinella. II. Title.
JV7684.S65 2014
325.41—dc23   2014019773

To the voiceless and faceless victims of the practice of virginity testing and other human rights abuses by the British immigration control system over the decades

Contents

Acknowledgements

This book started as a small project, a sidenote in a study of UK responses to the victims of human trafficking, and grew into a bigger project as we developed a broader understanding of its far-reaching implications in its historical, as well as contemporary, contexts. We would like to thank the Faculty of Education, Humanities and Law at Flinders University for providing funding on two occasions to develop this project and helping us obtain the newly released National Archives documents, which allowed us the scope to write this book. The School of International Studies and the School of Law at Flinders both provided publication support funding as well. The support we have received from our colleagues in the School of International Studies and the Flinders Law School is also much appreciated.

We would like to thank the staff at the various archives that we visited for their assistance: the National Archives at Kew, the Hull History Centre, the Black History Library at the Institute of Race Relations, the Race Relations Archive at the University of Manchester, the Black Cultural Archives and Adriano Gonçalves at the United Nations Library in Geneva.

We have both been fortunate to present on our research internationally and, among others, we would like to thank in particular the Department of Human Geography at the University of Sheffield (organised by Margo Huxley) and the Prato Roundtable on Transnational Crime (organised by Jude McCulloch and Sharon Pickering) for providing these opportunities to present our research findings. Thanks are also due to Tiziana Torresi and Rebecca La Forgia for organising the Migration Roundtable at the University of Adelaide, which also allowed us to present our work at the local level.

The Guardian Home Affairs editor Alan Travis and journalist Huma Qureshi should also be thanked for their kind assistance in publicising our research findings in 2011.

We are grateful to a number of people who have read earlier versions of our work and provided much-needed feedback: Margaret

Davies, Matthew Fitzpatrick, Andrekos Varnava, Catherine Kevin, Lucy Mayblin, Derek Dalton and Leanne Weber.

We would like to express our sincere gratitude to Julia Farrell who helped with the editing and formatting of the manuscript and who performed an exceptional task under hectic conditions.

We would like to thank all our friends and family for their support over the lifetime of this project, in particular David Hercock, Laura Butterworth and Mark Siebert, Richard and Margaret Meredith for their hospitality, as well as Aliese Millington and Denni Meredith, Peter and Felicity Nixon, Robert and Helen Smith. Evan would most importantly like to thank Zenna Nixon and Remy and Honor Nixon-Smith for their love and support.

All the errors remain ours.

If you wish to contact us regarding this project, please do so via emails: evan.smith@flinders.edu.au or marinella.marmo@flinders.edu.au

Introduction

The practice of virginity testing at Britain's national and international borders first received national attention through a story published by *The Guardian* newspaper on 1 February 1979. This case involved a 35-year-old Indian woman who had arrived at Heathrow Airport on 24 January 1979, wishing to enter Britain to marry her fiancé, a British resident of Indian descent. The British legal regime at the time stipulated that people entering Britain to marry their fiancées/fiancés did not require an entry clearance or visa in those cases in which the marriage would take place within three months of their arrival. This woman, however, was subjected to an extensive investigation, which included a rudimentary gynaecological examination. Internal Home Office documents, disclosed only recently, state that the Immigration Officer in this case acted on the belief that her purported engagement status was not in line with her age group and that, in fact, she had already been married. Based on this view, the Immigration Officer 'asked the doctor to determine whether she had had children'.[1] A male doctor performed the examination and certified that the woman's hymen was intact. This outcome meant that the woman's story was deemed to be reliable and she was given conditional leave to enter Britain. This book takes this episode and places it within a wider historical and socio-economic context to look at the events that preceded, accompanied and followed it. The year 1979 becomes a point in time that delineates the brutality of the immigration regime of postcolonial Britain that existed to fulfil the needs and desires of a modern Britain, with appalling implications for the powerless. What will become evident throughout this book is that virginity testing was part of a systematic method of filtering black migrants from the Indian subcontinent based on the assumption that people from this region are not trustworthy and that evidence to substantiate the truth of their claims needs to be obtained elsewhere, in particular from scrutinising the body of the migrant. The normalisation of virginity testing at the border – a practice that reportedly began in 1968 and officially ended in February 1979 – is the epitome of an attitude of racial superiority and dominance over the black 'other' rooted in Britain's colonial past. This is evident in the fact that the test was not reserved for those holding the status of fiancée, who did not require a visa, but extended to teenage girls claiming to be under the age of 16 and to married women.[2] Further, this practice was taking place at both onshore and offshore points of departure,[3] with most of the available (albeit limited) data suggesting a higher number of such examinations occurring at British High Commissions in South Asia, which would indicate an attempt to keep the practice hidden from the view of the British public.

The main methodological approach adopted for the research underpinning this book was archival research based on recently opened Home Office and Foreign and Commonwealth Office (FCO) files held at the National Archives in London (released to the public between 2004 and 2012). This approach allowed us to capture the internal voice of authority – the one that we know exists but often cannot be reached – representing the secretive side of the state that excludes us unless there is a leak of information (as recent cases linked to Wikileaks and Edward Snowden would suggest). Thus, we must wait an inordinate number of years to access such information, should any trace of it remain. In the case of the virginity testing controversy, we had to wait 30 years to access this side of the story, for more details of what occurred to be released. This practice must also be understood within a wider context of a series of human rights abuses conducted by British state institutions in the 1970s and 1980s (with the relevant files being released in the same timeframe), such as the actions of the British forces in Northern Ireland, the death of Blair Peach at the hands of a police officer in 1979, the policing of the Brixton riots and the response to the Hillsborough disaster in 1989. We see in black and white the recurrence of the typical cycle of government evasion of accountability, which usually starts with denial, and is followed by the adoption of a minimisation approach and 'othering' strategies. The crude reality of what is known and not shared publicly conveys a sense of uneasiness, and of unbalanced power between those who govern and those who are governed, which can be readdressed by the opening of the archival record.

Therefore, alongside public material, internal documents help us to reconstruct the events by adding those unheard voices. In relation to the Heathrow case, the two statements below suggest the power of accompanying the public story with the internal 'voice' of the government. The first quotation is the description of what happened at Heathrow Airport on 24 January 1979 as provided by the woman to *Guardian* journalist Melanie Phillips and published on 1 February 1979; the second, also dated 1 February 1979, is an account of the doctor's examination of the woman. The emotional language of the woman's testimony is juxtaposed with the clinical description given by the Home Office:

He was wearing rubber gloves and took some medicine out of a tube and put it on some cotton and inserted it into me. He said he was deciding whether I was pregnant before. I said that he could see that without doing anything to me, but he said there was no need to get shy.[4]	[P]enetration of about half an inch made it apparent that she had an intact hymen and no other internal examination was made. The doctor then examined her chest with a stethascope [sic], but she was not asked to remove her blouse or bra for this. The only time she was bare chested was for the X-ray examination.... The doctor told the immigration officer [sic] verbally that the lady had not had children and she was then given conditional leave to enter for 3 months as a fiancee [sic].[5]

While the doctor confidentially provided his testimony to the authorities, the Home Office made a public declaration that no internal vaginal examination had taken place, stating that 'there was no internal examination and that [the medical officer] very quickly and decently established that she was virgo intacto'.[6] Further, this act of denial assumed a new significance one year later when the Home Office could no longer deny that many other cases had been taking place, and yet symbolically this first publicly known case was the impetus for the government to assume a defensive strategy, with the Immigration and Nationality Department of the Home Office suggesting that '[t]he doctor himself denied that the examination was internal, and... that [this] will re-open controversy about the exact nature of the examination'.[7]

Examining the disclosed material, we share the opinion of the Commission for Racial Equality (CRE) (see chapters 4 and 6) that the practice of virginity testing was clearly not solely undertaken at the discretion of individual Immigration Officers in Britain or their equivalent abroad, Entry Clearance Officers (ECOs). Rather, there is sufficient evidence to sustain the argument that the practice was known of and tolerated, if not condoned, by the upper echelons of the Home Office and the FCO. We also argue that the procedure had broader functions for the benefit of the receiving society. Unlike migrant men or migrant women from other regions who had an immediate economic value as skilled or unskilled labour, the South Asian woman was seen as a useful resource only in terms of her contribution to the building and maintenance of 'good race relations' through her potential to form a heterosexual, nuclear family within her migrant community (and thereby prevent South Asian men from entering into relationships with 'white' women). Hence, the preferential treatment given to wives-to-be within Britain's entry regime enabled the identification of women of supposed strong moral background, deemed to be a suitable party to marry to a South Asian man who would then supposedly stop searching for companionship or fulfilment of their sexual needs within the white community. This scenario was based on colonial ideas about race and sexuality developed during the Victorian era and the colonisation of India, as discussed in Chapter 3.

With the colonialist assumption that South Asian women could not be trusted and that their integrity needed to be physically verified, the female migrant had to succumb to the scrutinising gaze of the British immigration authorities. In order to demonstrate that she was a 'genuine' wife or wife-to-be, this scrutiny went beyond her oral testimony and the verification of her supporting documents. In the virginity testing cases, the authorities sought 'signs of marriage' (which meant physical signs of sexual activity or of bearing children), such as the absence of the hymen, enlarged breasts and stretch marks, to confirm or deny the veracity of a woman's claims on her application. The integrity of the female body was checked through a humiliating procedure which also served the purpose of reaffirming the low status of the newcomer within the established race and gendered hierarchical order of the destination country. In these circumstances, the South Asian woman became the undesired-but-needed migrant whose social function was to contribute to the British vision of good race relations through her attachment to men from the same ethnic community. Breaching her human rights came to be a point to consider only when Britain was called before the United Nations Commission on Human Rights (UNCHR) (see Chapter 5) or its amendments to the policy on dependants were deemed to contravene the European Convention on Human Rights (see Chapter 6 for the case through the European Court of Human Rights). Normally Britain was a defender of such supra-national bodies and treaties as they upheld the values of Western liberal democracies, but both the UNHCR and the European Court of Human Rights found that Britain was in violation of these democratic values through its treatment of migrants. Not wishing to be seen as a state that ignored the value of human rights, the British authorities first sought to hide the abuses that were committed within its immigration control system and then to justify them with the argument that the British border was a special 'zone' where discriminatory and invasive procedures had to take place to protect British society from the threat of the 'undesirable' migrant. This book uses the overt physical scrutiny of the migrant woman in the virginity testing procedure as a microcosm of how women from the Indian subcontinent were objectified and compartmentalised by the British immigration control system and how the body was deferred to as a signifier of 'the truth', as the South Asian woman could not, in the eyes of the British authorities, be completely trusted.

Although under great pressure from sections of the Parliament, the Home Office, the FCO, the tabloid media, anti-immigration groups and wider British society to restrict immigration into Britain, the British government has not been able to stop immigration completely. Competing factors have had to be balanced, with the government under both Labour and the Conservatives having to negotiate the economic requirements of postcolonial Britain, amid fears over the threat to the 'whiteness' of its society, and in consideration of its humanitarian obligations and the need to maintain its reputation in the international community. As this book will demonstrate, priority is given to what is perceived to be more important at any given point in time. The virginity testing controversy, the way in which the government (first under Labour and then under the Conservatives) negotiated its conflicting priorities and its ferocious justification of the immigration control system following the Heathrow incident in 1979 represent how the government tried to balance its anti-immigration agenda with its other socio-economic, political and diplomatic concerns.

We have chosen to focus on the treatment of South Asian women by the British immigration control system in the 1970s and 1980s for three main reasons. First, the 1970s saw the beginning of what we now know as the modern immigration control system in Britain. Passed in 1971 and implemented in January 1973, the Immigration Act 1971 is the cornerstone of Britain's immigration control policy which distinguishes between those who have an ancestral connection to the UK (and thus are allowed to enter, reside and work in the country without restriction) and those who do not (and who thus fall foul of the system). The 1971 Act greatly restricted labour migration from the Commonwealth but coincided with Britain joining the European Economic Community (EEC), which allowed the free movement of people into Britain from other EEC countries. Second, the largest demographic group that migrated to Britain in the 1970s and 1980s were from the Indian subcontinent and were predominantly women coming to join their male family members who had migrated to Britain prior to 1973 in search of work. Third, it was South Asian women, as the largest migrant group flowing through the immigration control system during this period, who bore the brunt of the system's scrutinising gaze and the invasive procedures used to detect 'bogus' migrants.

A historical review of the British border control system across those years helped us to reconstruct how the regime became increasingly strict and obsessed with control – a process the results of which are in clear view today. The profiling of fraudulent, untrustworthy migrants is the aim of the Home Office, based on the belief that the composition of a healthy society can be established via a mathematical formula that can be applied at the border. As the Home Affairs Committee has stated, '[f]irm immigration control is essential to achieve good community relations'.[8] Over the past 40 years, the border has assumed a new and fortified connotation, as not only the filter for a good, 'mixed' society but also its mirror: what takes place at the border is after all for the greatest benefit of the vast majority of 'white' British people and is therefore tolerable. In the eyes of the British authorities, if the migrant's subordinate status is established at the border, this will help them to accept the dominant 'British values', and thus contribute to good race relations as defined by the political elites, who have condoned an anti-immigrationist agenda since the 1960s. As Kristen Phillips has written:

> The modern state...can tolerate and 'cultivate' a population which includes even bodies of a 'different race' as long as ordering mechanisms for managing this difference (for which an idea of nation in racial terms remains a central defining trope) are upheld. Of key importance is the fact that migrants enter the nation-state under the control and surveillance of that biopolitical state, and can be known, categorised and positioned in the social hierarchy effectively.[9]

In line with this, we propose that the findings of our research are important on two levels. On one level, our research has uncovered internal government documents that show that the extent of the practice of virginity testing was far greater than the government publicly acknowledged in the 1970s and even more so than what we found in 2010–2011, when *The Guardian* publicised our preliminary findings of around 80 cases.[10] A handwritten note, discussed at length in Chapter 4, reveals that in 1980 the government knew that there had been over 120 cases of virginity testing conducted at British High Commissions across the Indian subcontinent in the 1970s – higher than the 80 cases referred to in an internal memo to Labour Prime Minister James Callaghan that we uncovered in 2010 and much higher than the 34 cases mentioned by Labour MP Jo Richardson in Parliament in 1979. But on a broader level, our research reveals the underlying racist and sexist prejudices harboured within the British immigration control system in the 1970s and 1980s and how these prejudices informed the manner in which non-white migrants trying to enter the country were treated by immigration officials. Internal government documents show the extent to which the government, under both Callaghan's Labour and Thatcher's Conservatives, prioritised maintaining the strict measures of the immigration control system and how the revelations of abuses in the 1970s and 1980s did not change the outlook of the government on whether strict immigration controls were worth the human cost.

Existing literature on the virginity testing controversy

Other scholars have written about the practice of virginity testing within the British immigration control system. We refer to their work in this book and build on their knowledge with reference to the archival material. Their work can be separated according to different themes. Some authors have explained how these practices stem from institutional racism inherent to immigration law and its aim to restrict the entrance of non-white migrants.[11] Other scholars took this case study as further evidence to expose the patriarchal nature of British law and its constant infringement of women's rights.[12] We embrace an intersectional approach, a concept first developed by Kimberle Crenshaw[13] and later applied by Rachel A. Hall and Amrit Wilson to British immigration control.[14] As such, we argue that virginity testing was a product of a number of intersecting factors – not only did race and gender determine what took place, but so did other elements such as nationality, marital status, age, socio-economic class, education level and sexual conduct. Intersectionality has been employed by other scholars in relation to the intertwining relationship between race, gender and class in the lives of non-white women in Britain; however, to date, it has not been fully extended to explore the phenomenon of immigration control.[15]

Biopolitics and the focus on the body

The analysis of the immigration control system in this book is informed by the theory of biopolitics as developed by Michel Foucault, then taken up by other scholars, such as Giorgio Agamben and Mark Kelly, amongst many others. Biopolitics, as described by Foucault in his lectures at the College de France in the late 1970s, explains two processes that began in the 20th century: first, the intervention of the state in *all* aspects of life, including the body (what Foucault described as 'basic biological features... [becoming] the object of a political strategy');[16] and second, the desire of the state to order mass populations, often based on these 'biological features'. In *Society Must Be Defended*, Foucault describes this 'biological and centralized racism' as 'state racism'.[17]

Mark G. Kelly has written that 'biopolitics is deployed to manage population; for example, to ensure a healthy workforce'[18] and the concept of 'biopolitical state racism'[19] gives us an understanding of how the British immigration control system has operated since the 1960s. Through this system, the individual migrant became part of a wider scheme to 'manage' British (that is, so-called white) society and the influx of non-white Commonwealth citizens. The oft-repeated maxim that 'good race relations' stemmed from 'strict immigration control', by limiting the numbers of foreign 'others' and applying strict conditions to their entry, demonstrates the desire to create order amongst large populations based upon racial difference. Ensuring the 'health' of British domestic society and 'healthy' race relations was the desired outcome of the biopolitical agenda of the British authorities.

The process of biopolitics – the focus on the biological body – has become increasingly important in shaping how we understand the workings of the British immigration control system over the past 50 years. Agamben's work on the *bios* in biopolitics is key to understanding this development and the scrutiny placed upon the body of the migrant within this system. Agamben works from the concept that under restrictive systems of government (or authority in the context of immigration control),[20] the body becomes the focus of determining 'value' and citizenship. Taking the concept of *habeus corpus* as the concept that is fundamental to modern liberal democracy, Agamben writes that the body becomes central to the 'politico-juridical terminology' of Western democracy:

> the root of modern democracy's secret biopolitical calling lies here: he [sic] who will appear later as the bearer of rights and ... as the new sovereign subject ... can only be constituted as such through the repetition of the sovereign exception and the isolation of *corpus*, bare life, in himself [sic]. If it is true that law needs a body in order to be in force, and if one can speak, in this sense, of

'law's desire to have a body', democracy responds to this desire
by compelling law to assume the care of this body.[21]

Explaining how the biopolitical state creates the basis for the management of mass populations, Agamben argues that governments have
worked from the premise that bodies are to be considered *zoes* (bare
life) until they are proved to be politically and economically valuable
to the dominant society and thus become *bios* (political life). Citizenship is thus acquired through the value ascribed to the body of
the individual, or group, passing what Agamben calls the 'threshold
of articulation between nature and culture'.[22] However, the criteria
for passing the threshold are continually changing in line with the
desires of the nation-state, and as we see with the British immigration
control system, the authorities have placed ever-increasing restrictions on who qualifies for entry into Britain. As Agamben states,
'[o]ne of the essential characteristics of modern biopolitics... is its
constant need to redefine the threshold in life that distinguishes and
separates what is inside from what is outside'.[23]

In line with Agamben, we argue that biopolitics operates on two
levels within the British immigration control system. First, it works
at a broad level in 'managing' the relationship between the 'British'
population and the migrant 'other', whereby the individual is relegated by the abstract concept of maintaining societal order (in this
case, so-called good race relations) through large-scale demographics,
with the racialised 'minority' always kept in check by the 'majority'. Second, it works on a microlevel by placing the migrant body
under intense scrutiny and determining the value of the migrant
for the host society on the basis of their physicality. The 'health'
of the migrant body and its economic value – increasingly important under the pretext of neo-liberalism (which has, for the most
part, risen in tandem with the development of the modern immigration control system) – are used to decide whether the migrant may
enter the host society. Taking the concepts of 'states of being (human
life)' and 'states of belonging (political life)' from Imogen Tyler (via
Agamben),[24] we can say that migrants *exist* within the immigration
control system, but that the state decides whether they are allowed
to *belong* to the destination country.

Under the logic of the biopolitical state, citizenship is thus determined by the integration of the individual body into the 'healthy'

society. Drawing from the work of Julia Kristeva and the concepts of the 'abject/other', we assert that if the individual body is thought to be detrimental to the 'health' of the host society, the individual must be repelled or expelled. In the immigration control system, this means either rejection of the potential migrant in their home country or at the port of entry, or deportation from Britain if the 'undesirable' migrant has been found to have penetrated the border. The border thereby becomes an 'object' that distinguishes between the desired and the undesired (the 'abject').[25] Informed by the work of Kristeva, Tyler argues that the state creates 'abject subjects' in order to 'constitute itself and draw its borders'[26] – and that post-imperial British society is defined in relation to the colonial 'other' and 'British values' are defined by what they reject. Thus Tyler claims:

> British citizenship has been redesigned to abjectify specific groups and populations.... Abjection... is a design principle of British citizenship, in the most active and violent sense of the verb, 'to design'.[27]

We also take from Agamben the idea of the 'state of exception' and 'the camp' – the (not necessarily physical) space in which those considered 'undesirable' can be subjected to extreme scrutiny and, if this 'undesirability' is confirmed, a space in which human rights and the rule of law can be ignored. Originally evoked by governments as a suspension of the rule of law in the face of 'an external and provisional state of factual danger',[28] the state of exception can be extended as long as the nation-state perceives itself to be under threat. 'The camp' is the space in which the state of exception is allowed to perpetuate itself and those who enter the camp therefore 'remain outside the normal order'.[29] As Agamben writes, '[t]he camp is the space that is opened when the state of exception begins to become the rule'.[30] In this book, we conceptualise the immigration control system as a version of the camp, in which the state of exception is applied – where the potential migrant submits (either willingly or by coercion) to physical scrutiny, via gynaecological examinations, examinations of the genitals and/or breasts, x-rays and other tests, in order to prove their value to British society. As evidenced in Chapter 6, in the face of criticism from domestic and international bodies, the British government argued that the suspension of (some) human rights was necessary to maintain a definitive line between 'white' British society and the postcolonial 'other'. Without this state of exception and the strict implementation of immigration controls, it was claimed that migrants would threaten the fabric of British society and undermine the 'British way of life'.

We acknowledge that the concept of biopolitics as advanced by Foucault and Agamben has been criticised for its lack of consideration of the role of gender and the assumption made by both theorists that biopolitics affects men and women in the same way.[31] On this point, we have taken inspiration from the work of Kristen Phillips, who has conducted research on the immigration detention centres in Australia and the containment of refugee women, and highlighted that 'male and female bodies are reduced to bare life in different ways, and are treated differently as bare life'.[32] Phillips argues that, when reduced to bare life, women are seen as merely 'reproductive bodies'.[33] However, in the British context and particularly in the case of the virginity testing, the South Asian woman was not reduced to a reproductive body, but a body that could perform sexually and contain the sexual desires of men from the same ethnic community – her ability to reproduce was not deemed necessary by the British authorities, but her ability to be used, for sex and marriage, by the South Asian male, was. With one of the panics about South Asian migration being the differing birth rates between South Asian and 'white' Britons, there was no 'value' for the British nation-state in the South Asian woman's ability to have children; instead, her value was determined by her use by other men from the same ethnic background. As Jordanna Bailkin has argued, the British authorities wanted non-white migrant men and women to cohabit and marry, but their children were seen as troubling to the white British nation-state.[34]

The structure of the British immigration control system

The British immigration control system is not just a single entity that exists at the ports of entry into the UK, but is a sprawling network of agencies and sites that together create 'the border'. Although the system has expanded and become more technologically proficient, it has had essentially the same structure since the 1970s. Since 1968, when the FCO was established as a merger between the Foreign

Office and the Commonwealth Office (formerly the Colonial Office), immigration has been regulated by both the FCO and the Home Office. The Home Office is nominally in charge of all immigration control policy and is also responsible for the operation of passport and border control in the UK at ports of entry. Immigration Officers are those personnel who deal with migrants at these ports of entry into the UK, predominantly at airports and seaports, and fall under the direct control of the Home Office.

The British immigration control system, as we argue in this book, works by keeping a clear distance between domestic British society and the alien – colonial 'other'. This is achieved by requiring people attempting to enter the country to obtain a visa or entry clearance in their home country prior to travelling to the UK. Entry clearances were similar to visas, provided only to Commonwealth migrants, and supposedly reduced the likelihood of lengthy questioning once the migrant had arrived in Britain. Although migrants were not technically obligated to obtain entry clearances before arriving in Britain, it was strongly recommended by immigration officials in Britain that these be obtained to prevent delays.

Entry clearances were (and still are) to be obtained from the Migration and Visa Department of the FCO, which operates through the British High Commissions that exist in Commonwealth countries (British Embassies only exist in non-Commonwealth countries). In South Asia, High Commissions are present in the capital cities of India (Delhi), Pakistan (Islamabad), and after it gained independence in 1971, Bangladesh (Dacca), as well as other major cities, such as Bombay (Mumbai), Calcutta (Kolkota) and Jaipur in India and Karachi and Lahore in Pakistan.

As is revealed in this book, the process of obtaining an entry clearance certificate usually involves a detailed application form, combined with the presentation of necessary documents and an extensive interview. This is conducted by an ECO, who, as the first point of contact with the immigration control system, is responsible for ascertaining whether those applying for entry clearances are 'worthy' of gaining entry into the UK. People enter the immigration control system in their home country as 'potential' migrants (a term that we use in this book) because their ability to move (or migrate) may be inhibited by ECOs before they even reach the UK.

Contradicting the government's view of South Asian women

The focus of this book is on how the British authorities, through the immigration control system, treated South Asian women who attempted to enter the country between the 1960s and the 1980s. The British view of South Asian women, created through centuries of colonialism, was (and still is) racist and sexist, and incorporated a belief that these women are meek and submissive.[35] In the interaction between the South Asian woman and the immigration control system, the power imbalance between the state and the migrant woman is asserted through the scrutiny placed upon her by the state, ensuring that she aligns with the categorised 'desires' of the British nation-state. As we argue in this book, this process attempts to strip the migrant woman of her identity and focuses solely on what her body can offer the host society. In the files of the Home Office and the FCO, the female victims of the virginity testing practice and other human rights abuses are rarely named.

However, many of the South Asian women who came to Britain during the period under study challenged this racist and sexist view of them harboured by the authorities and the stereotyping and discrimination they faced. As Pratibha Parmar wrote in 1982:

> Despite the force of racist stereotypes Asian women do not experience the racism from which they suffer in a passive way. They have developed their own forms of resistance, articulate their own ideas about British society, and rely on their own historical cultural traditions as a means of support.[36]

As we demonstrate in this book, South Asian women were vocal in their challenges to the discrimination they suffered at the hands of the immigration control system, forming groups like the Organisation of Women of Afro-Caribbean and Asian Descent, Awaz or the Friends of Anwar Ditta. As shown in Chapter 6, Anwar Ditta, with the help of others, conducted a four-year campaign to convince the British government that her children were indeed hers and that they needed to be in Britain with her and her husband. Through the work of a wide range of migrants' rights, trade union, left-wing and feminist groups, the hard-won success of the Anwar Ditta campaign, as Anandi Ramamurthy recently wrote, is 'testament to the possibilities of joint action'.[37]

Activism by South Asian women was not relegated only to campaigns against racist immigration laws but was also evident in many other areas of struggle. For example, the Grunwick strike, which lasted from 1976 to 1978, was led by Ugandan Asian women, such as Jayaben Desai[38]; while the mayhem caused by the police at the demonstration against the National Front in April 1979 led to the formation of the Southall Black Sisters, who campaigned against racism and spoke up for women's rights.[39] In these campaigns, but also in other day-to-day struggles, South Asian women defied the stereotypes and assumptions made about them and sought to overcome the racism and sexism they experienced in Britain. It would be wrong to conclude that, although they suffered immensely under the discriminatory practices of the British state, they had no agency.

The following excerpt from a 2011 article by Huma Qureshi in *The Guardian*, writing about her mother's experience of the virginity testing procedure, highlights the contradictions around South Asian women's agency and their interaction with the British immigration control system:

> My mum didn't meet the stereotype of a 'submissive' or 'meek' south Asian woman back then, any more than she does now. She arrived in the UK with a master's degree in politics and strong-minded views, fluent in three languages, confident and excited about what the future here would hold. My parents had already proved their marriage to British officials, submitting the marriage certificate and my mum also already had a visa, allowing her entry into the UK.
>
> So why, then, considering she had all the correct legal documentation required to enter the country, did she still have to go through this degrading test?
>
> 'I don't know,' she says. 'Maybe it was the colour of my skin and where I came from. They didn't do it to the women coming from Europe or Australia or America, did they? I suppose it was just to prove that they had power in their hands.'[40]

Book structure

This book is separated into six chapters that examine the history of the British immigration control system, the way in which racial and sexual biases have informed immigration control practices and the treatment of South Asian women within the system. Chapter 1 outlines the development of immigration control legislation in Britain since the end of the Second World War, revealing that the road to immigration controls was not as straightforward as commonly perceived. As the chapter demonstrates, both Labour and the Conservatives tried to prevent large-scale immigration unofficially at first and only started thinking in terms of legislative change in this area from 1955. Yet even then, those drafting the legislation had a series of economic, political, social and diplomatic considerations they had to negotiate. However, since controls for Commonwealth citizens were established in 1962, the bipartisan consensus between the major parties has been that 'good race relations' require strict immigration controls.

Chapter 2 examines this consensus further and explains how the British border functions as an 'object', in line with the aforementioned work of Kristeva and Tyler. In this chapter, the border is described as a barrier between 'white' British society and the colonial 'other', which attempts to maintain a distance between the metropole and the periphery as it existed in the colonial era. As the post-imperial era and the emergence of globalisation have seen the collapse of this colonial system, the border acts to reinforce the colonial relationship in the era of postcolonialism. It acts as a filter to allow in only those Commonwealth migrants who are deemed 'useful' or 'desirable' to the host society and who are then subject to the political and economic whims of the modern British nation-state. Chapter 2 also reveals how this filter worked in practice and the pressure placed upon immigration officials in Britain and its High Commissions overseas to detect and 'weed out' so-called bogus migrants.

Chapter 3 explains how this emphasis on 'weeding out' suspected 'bogus' migrants, combined with the racist and sexist assumptions held by immigration officials about South Asian women, led to the practice of virginity testing. The chapter traces these racist and sexist beliefs about South Asian women back to the Victorian era when India was a British colony and finds precedent in the British Contagious Diseases Acts of the 1860s and 1870s, when the British authorities imposed their scrutinising gaze upon the South Asian female body in order to ascertain 'the truth' of her purity. It explores the reasoning behind the virginity testing practice and the concern amongst immigration officials that South Asian women, mostly claiming to be fiancées, were defrauding the system. In Chapter 3, it is argued that the authorities were in favour of fiancées coming to Britain to form monogamous nuclear families with men from the same ethnic community, but felt that these women first had to be determined to be 'genuine' wives-to-be, thus resulting in the gynaecological examinations on migrant women.

Chapters 4 and 5 look at the fallout of the virginity testing controversy after it was made public in *The Guardian* in February 1979, both domestically and internationally. The chapter outlines how the British government, first under James Callaghan and then under Margaret Thatcher, attempted to deny the extent of virginity testing and hindered any investigation into this and any other discriminatory practices employed within the immigration control system. Internal Home Office and FCO documents are cited to show that the government had prior knowledge of this practice and sought to portray it as something that only occurred overseas, away from the control of the government in London. Both Labour and the Conservatives also attempted to shut down an investigation by the CRE into the immigration control system, arguing that discrimination was necessary for the effective control of migration. Chapter 4 concludes with a discussion of an additional controversy over the use of X-rays in South Asia for age assessment purposes, news of which emerged at the same time as the media coverage of virginity testing.

Chapter 5 looks at how the virginity testing controversy played out on the international stage, particularly the damage it caused to Anglo-Indian relations. India used the forum of the UNCHR to criticise Britain and called for condemnation by the UN, yet this did not occur. Instead, Britain offered a half-hearted apology to the victims of virginity testing and tried to deflect criticism by arguing that other non-Western countries (such as Cambodia) were engaged in worse human rights abuses.

Chapter 6 demonstrates that although the practice of virginity testing officially ended in early 1979 and the use of X-rays to assess the age of children ceased in 1982, the British immigration control system still focused on the body to determine whether a migrant was telling 'the truth', but in other ways. The chapter highlights the story of Anwar Ditta, a Pakistani-British woman who sought to bring her children to the UK to join her, but whose request was denied by the British government for four years. Only after Granada Television paid for extensive blood tests to be carried out, were Ditta's children allowed to join her in the UK. By the mid-1980s, migrants' rights groups were hopeful that the introduction of DNA testing would allow more family reunification applications to be successful, but the findings of such tests have since then been used to keep families apart and disprove kinship rather than to facilitate family reunion. These developments occurred against a background of further restrictions on migrant women being introduced by the Conservatives in the early 1980s. Chapter 6 shows that, despite criticisms from both the CRE and the European Court of Human Rights (ECHR), the Tories maintained their adherence to strict immigration control procedures, establishing the framework for further legislative restrictions under both John Major and Tony Blair.

Through these chapters, we hope that a better understanding can be achieved of how 'race', gender and the body have intertwined in the application of immigration controls in Britain since the 1970s. We believe that this book is important because it argues that the restrictions placed upon migrant women were largely based on the idea of the woman as a 'commodity', and on how she can be used as a body rather than a human being, to meet the societal needs of the destination country. The book also adds to understanding of the techniques used at the border to filter undesirable immigrants, shedding light on how the British immigration control system has functioned since the introduction of the Immigration Act in 1971. This is relevant insofar as it contributes to our understanding of contemporary immigration practices. This book explores the important links that can be found between historical processes and modern practices and institutions within the British immigration control system. In the past and more recently, successive British governments have claimed that their immigration policies have been fair and non-discriminatory. However, our examination of the government's internal documents has provided much material to counter these claims, and the similar arguments that can be found in current discourses on the function of immigration control, particularly in regard to the debates surrounding asylum seekers and human trafficking.

Notes

1. Letter from Mr Hillary to Mr Flesher, 1 February 1979, HO 418/29, National Archives, London (hereafter NA).
2. Amrit Wilson, *Finding a Voice: Asian Women in Britain* (London: Virago Press, 1985) pp. 72–76; Huma Qureshi, 'Passport, Visa, Virginity? A Mother's Tale of Immigration in the 1970s', *The Guardian*, 13 May 2011, http://www.theguardian.com/lifeandstyle/2011/may/13/virginity-tests-uk-immigrants-1970s (accessed 11 January 2014).
3. *The Guardian*, 2 February 1979, p. 24; p. 1; *Hansard*, 21 March 1979, col. 672w.
4. *The Guardian*, 1 February 1979, p. 1.
5. Letter from Mr Hillary to Mr Flesher, 1 February 1979.
6. *The Guardian*, 1 February 1979, p. 1.
7. Immigration and Nationality Department, 'Review of Overseas Medical Examinations for Immigration Purposes: Comments by the Immigration and Nationality Department and the Foreign and Commonwealth Office', January 1980, p. 1, FCO 50/676, NA.
8. Cited in Vaughn Bevan, *The Development of British Immigration Law* (London: Routledge, 1986) p. 164.
9. Kristen Phillips, 'Immigration Detention, Containment Fantasies and the Gendering of Political Status in Australia', unpublished PhD thesis, Curtin University, 2009, p. 123, http://espace.library.curtin.edu.au/R?func=dbin-jump-full&local_base=gen01-era02&object_id=129031 (accessed 11 January 2014).
10. See Alan Travis, 'Virginity Tests for Immigrants "Reflected Dark Age Prejudices" of 1970s Britain', *The Guardian*, 9 May 2011, http://www.theguardian.com/uk/2011/may/08/virginity-tests-immigrants-prejudices-britain?intcmp=239 (accessed 11 January 2014). This newspaper report was based on our articles: Evan Smith and Marinella Marmo, 'Uncovering the "Virginity Testing" Controversy in the National Archives: The Intersectionality of Discrimination in British Immigration History', *Gender & History*, 23/1, April 2011, pp. 147–165; Marinella Marmo and Evan Smith, 'Is There a Desirable Migrant? A Reflection of Human Rights Violations at the Border: The Case of "Virginity Testing"', *Alternative Law Journal*, 35/4, December 2010, pp. 223–226.
11. See Gideon Ben-Tovim and John Gabriel, 'The Politics of Race in Britain, 1962–1979: A Review of the Major Trends and of Recent Debates', in Charles Husband (ed.), *'Race' in Britain: Continuity and Change* (Hutchinson, London, 1982) p. 146; Peter Alexander, *Racism, Resistance and Revolution* (Bookmarks, London, 1987) p. 40; Keith Tompson, *Under Siege: Racial Violence in Britain Today* (Penguin, London, 1988) p. 70.

12. Deborah Cheney, 'Those Whom the Immigration Law Has Kept Apart – Let No-one Join Together: A View of Immigration Incantation', in Delia Jarrett-Macauley (ed.), *Reconstructing Womanhood, Reconstructing Feminism: Writings on Black Women* (Routledge, London, 1996) pp. 58–84; Steve Cohen, *Immigration Controls, the Family and the Welfare State* (Jessica Kingsley Publishers, London, 2001); Helena Wray, 'An Ideal Husband? Marriages of Convenience, Moral Gate-keeping and Immigration to the UK', *European Journal of Migration and Law*, 8, 2006, pp. 303–320.
13. See Kimberle Crenshaw, 'Demarginalizing the Intersection of Race and Sex: A Black Feminist Critique of Antidiscrimination Doctrine, Feminist Theory and Antiracist Politics', *University of Chicago Legal Forum*, 1989, pp. 139–168; Kimberle Crenshaw, 'Mapping the Margins: Intersectionality, Identity Politics, and Violence against Women of Color', *Stanford Law Review*, 43/6, July 1991, pp. 1242–1300.
14. Wilson, *Finding a Voice*, pp. 72–86; Rachel A. Hall, 'The Interaction of Gender and Ethnicity: An Exploration of British Immigration Control, Focusing on the Experiences of South Asian Women in West Yorkshire', unpublished PhD thesis, University of Huddersfield, 2006; Rachel A. Hall, 'When Is a Wife Not a Wife? Some Observations on the Immigration Experiences of South Asian Women in West Yorkshire', *Contemporary Politics*, 8/1, 2002, pp. 55–68; Amrit Wilson, *Dreams, Questions, Struggles: South Asian Women in Britain* (London: Pluto Press, 2006) pp. 76–78.
15. Notable exceptions include: Hall, 'The Interaction of Gender and Ethnicity'; Avtar Brah, *Cartographies of Diaspora: Contesting Identities* (London: Routledge, 1996); Nira Yuval-Davis, Floya Anthias and Eleonore Kofman, 'Secure Borders and Safe Haven and the Gendered Politics of Belonging', *Ethnic & Racial Studies*, 28/3, March 2005, pp. 513–535.
16. Michel Foucault, *Security, Territory, Population: Lectures at the College de France 1977–1978* (Houndmills: Palgrave Macmillan, 2009) p. 1.
17. Michel Foucault, *Society Must Be Defended: Lectures at the College de France 1975–1976* (New York: Picador, 2003) p. 82.
18. Mark G. Kelly, 'Racism, Nationalism and Biopolitics: Foucault's *Society Must Be Defended*, 2003', *Contretemps*, 4 September 2004 p. 59.
19. Kelly, 'Racism, Nationalism and Biopolitics', p. 67.
20. Although Agamben, referring to the work of Karl Löwith, highlights the slippage between liberal democracies and dictatorship and the potential of democratic forms of government to become undemocratic and restrictive: 'The contiguity between mass democracy and totalitarian states…does not have the form of sudden transformation.' Giorgio Agamben, *Homo Sacer: Sovereign Power and Bare Life* (Stanford, CA: Stanford University Press, 1998) pp. 71–72.
21. Agamben, *Homo Sacer*, p. 73.
22. Ibid., p. 102.
23. Ibid., p. 77.
24. Imogen Tyler, *Revolting Subjects: Social Abjection and Resistance in Neoliberal Britain* (London: Zed Books, 2013) p. 20.

25. Julia Kristeva, *Powers of Horror: An Essay in Abjection* (New York: Columbia University Press, 1982) p. 4.
26. Tyler, *Revolting Subjects*, p. 4.
27. Ibid., p. 14.
28. Agamben, *Homo Sacer*, p. 96.
29. Ibid.
30. Ibid.
31. For feminist critiques of Foucault, see Jana Sawicki, *Disciplining Foucault: Feminism, Power and the Body* (New York: Routledge, 1991); Lois McNay, *Foucault and Feminism* (Cambridge: Polity Press, 1992); Caroline Ramazanoglu (ed.), *Up against Foucault: Explorations of Some Tensions between Foucault and Feminism* (London: Routledge, 1993); Susan J. Hekman (ed.), *Feminist Interpretations of Michel Foucault* (Pennsylvania, PA: Pennsylvania State University Press, 1996); Angela King, 'The Prisoner of Gender: Foucault and the Disciplining of the Female Body', *Journal of International Women's Studies*, 5/2 ,2004, pp. 29–39. For feminist critiques of Agamben, see Phillips, 'Immigration Detention, Containment Fantasies and the Gendering of Political Status in Australia'; Anna Marie Smith, 'Neo-eugenics: A Feminist Critique of Agamben', *Occasion: Interdisciplinary Studies in the Humanities*, 2, 20 December 2010, http://occasion. stanford.edu/node/59 (accessed 11 January 2014); Allaine Cerwonka and Anna Loutfi, 'Biopolitics and the Female Reproductive Body as the New Subject of Law', *Feminists@Law*, 1/1, 2011 pp. 1–5.
32. Phillips, 'Immigration Detention, Containment Fantasies and the Gendering of Political Status in Australia', p. 20.
33. Ibid.
34. Jordanna Bailkin, *The Afterlife of Empire* (Berkeley, CA: University of California Press, 2012) pp. 164–170.
35. Pratibha Parmar, 'Gender, Race and Class: Asian Women in Resistance', in Centre for Contemporary Cultural Studies, *The Empire Strikes Back: Race and Racism in 70s Britain* (London: Hutchinson, 1986) p. 245.
36. Parmar, 'Gender, Race and Class', p. 239.
37. Anandi Ramamurthy, *Black Star: Britain's Asian Youth Movements* (London: Pluto Press, 2013) p. 105.
38. See 'Grunwick Strike: The Bitter Lessons', *Race Today*, November/December 1977; 'Grunwick (2)', *Race & Class*, 19/3, 1978; Wilson, *Finding a Voice*, pp. 59–70.
39. See: Rahila Gupta, *From Homebreakers to Jailbreakers: Southall Black Sisters* (London: Zed Books, 2003); Gita Sahgal, 'Secular Spaces: The Experience of Asian Women Organizing', in Gita Sahgal and Nira Yuval-Davis (eds), *Refusing Holy Orders: Women and Fundamentalism in Britain* (London: Virago Press, 1992) pp. 163–197.
40. Qureshi, 'Passport, Visa, Virginity?'.

1
Decolonisation and the Creation of the British Immigration Control System

Since the introduction of immigration controls in Britain in the early 20th century, racially and sexually discriminatory practices have been used by the British authorities to filter incoming migrants according to their level of desirability to the state. This chapter charts the introduction of immigration control legislation in the UK and the development of discriminatory policies that have become more restrictive since the first legislative Act was introduced in 1905. It will be argued that the purpose of controls has been to restrict entry for those considered 'undesirable' to the British nation-state and that these controls have imposed rigorous scrutiny upon potential migrants. At the same time, the chapter will show that, despite the aspiration of the authorities to screen and carefully select the migrant intake, the path towards development of the modern immigration control system, with its cornerstone being the Immigration Act 1971, has not been so straightforward and that the legislative process, negotiating between populist anti-immigrant sentiment and other socio-economic, legal, diplomatic and humanitarian concerns, has been haphazard. However, the end result of this has been a bipartisan consensus between the Conservatives and Labour that good race relations can only be maintained through strict immigration control. As Labour MP Roy Hattersley stated in Parliament in March 1965, 'I believe that unrestricted immigration can only produce additional problems, additional suffering and additional hardship unless some kind of limitation is imposed and continued.'[1]

Decolonisation, immigration and the British 'citizen'

The aim of all of the controls on immigration established by the British government has been to create a legislative cover to filter so-called undesirable migrants entering Britain, predominantly at the cost of other social, economic and humanitarian concerns.[2] The first modern piece of immigration control legislation passed in Britain was the Aliens Act 1905, which applied to those migrants outside the British Commonwealth, and was based on the primary aim of excluding Eastern European Jews.[3] Further legislation followed this Act during the First World War and in the inter-war period in response to concerns that non-naturalised Europeans (predominantly Germans and Austro-Hungarians, but also Italians and other nationalities) presented a security problem. Legislation with a limited scope, focusing on the African, Asian and Caribbean crews (from non-British colonies) that docked in Liverpool, London, Cardiff and Bristol, was passed in the mid-1920s under the Special Restriction (Coloured Alien Seaman) Order of 1925. Laura Tabili has referred to this Order as 'the first instance of state-sanctioned race discrimination inside Britain to come to widespread notice'[4], but by this time, the Aliens Act had already been in effect for 20 years.

With the non-white colonial population of Britain being limited to between 10,000 and 30,000 people and living only in the major cities, there was not much concern about migration from the colonies during the inter-war period. However, this changed with the introduction of the British Nationality Act in 1948 and the influx of migrants from the Caribbean, West Africa and South Asia to fill the post-war labour shortage. From the late 1940s to the early 1960s, there was an ongoing debate in Parliament, in the media and amongst the broader British society over the social, economic and political impact of colonial migration upon Britain, with a strong push by many for limits to be placed upon non-white migration.

The end of the Second World War and its destructive wake left Britain with the massive challenge of post-war reconstruction, which demanded a large increase in labour. The labour shortage, intensified by the large-scale emigration of British residents to Australia, Canada, New Zealand, South Africa and Rhodesia,[5] was filled primarily by immigrants. Although many women in Britain had been mobilised into war production during the Second World War, the increased employment of women in the workforce was rejected in favour of migrant labour, which was a 'far cheaper way of meeting the demand for labour'.[6]

In the first years after the war, most of the immigrants who entered Britain were from Europe and Ireland. This included workers recruited from Central and Eastern Europe, many of whom were from displaced persons camps, prisoners of war who remained in Britain or, as in the case of Poles, were from the Polish Army that was stationed in Britain at the time. Most of the recruitment was executed in cooperation with the British government's Department of Labour as a series of restrictions were placed on immigrants from outside the British Commonwealth.

From June 1948 onwards, Britain experienced large-scale immigration of non-white workers from the Commonwealth. The docking of the *SS Empire Windrush* on 22 June 1948 at Tilbury, carrying 492 (mostly male) West Indians, has come to be recognised as a symbol of the commencement of large-scale black immigration, in turn marking the beginning of a multicultural Britain.[7] The process of migration from the colonies to Britain was simplified with the British Nationality Act 1948, introduced by the Labour government to highlight the supposed importance of the British Commonwealth. This Act justified the free entry of Commonwealth citizens into Britain, declaring that '[e]very person who...is a citizen of the United Kingdom and Colonies or...is a citizen of [Canada, Australia, New Zealand, South Africa, Newfoundland, India, Pakistan, Southern Rhodesia and Ceylon] shall by virtue of that citizenship have the status of a British subject',[8] retaining the legal and unconditional right to enter, settle and work in Britain.[9] Conservative MP Sir David Maxwell Fyfe declared, 'we must maintain our great metropolitan tradition of hospitality to everyone from every part of our Empire'.[10] The early period of large-scale immigration into Britain had been portrayed by earlier scholars as 'an age of innocence and lack of concern about black immigration'.[11] However, the British Nationality Act also meant a fortified position for Britain to continue its privileged socio-economic relationship with its former colonies. Lydia Lindsey suggests that '[t]here was general agreement among British officials that colonial workers were not preferred in the country',[12] but such concerns were offset by the economic advantages for Britain and its labour market of engaging immigrant labour. This led to a massive number of colonial migrants coming to Britain to seek work. Between 1948 and 1962, when the Commonwealth Immigrants Act was introduced, over 279,000 West Indians, over 79,000 Indians and over 68,000 Pakistanis travelled to Britain, alongside nearly 19,000 West Africans and nearly 24,000 Cypriots, as well as the massive, but unrecorded, number of Australian, New Zealand, Canadian, Rhodesian and South African migrants.[13]

In response to this influx, almost immediately emerged an 'increasingly racialized debate about immigration...focusing on the supposed social problems of having too many black migrants'.[14] It is evident that reversed migration flows were allowed only in the interests of Britain's white society. As Robert Miles noted, '[w]hile no one questioned this principle [of free entry] during the debate', both sides of government privately agreed that the 'metropolitan tradition of hospitality could only be sustained if the "non-white races" could be persuaded not to partake of it'.[15]

As Kathleen Paul wrote, the British government was 'never "liberal" with regard to "race and immigration" and indeed tried very hard to prevent the migration of people of colour to the United Kingdom'.[16] During the early 1950s, the government introduced informal controls as the 'solution' to its unrestricted immigration policy.[17] Before its defeat in 1951, Labour had 'instituted a number of covert, and sometimes illegal, administrative measures designed to discourage Black immigration', which were taken up wholeheartedly by the Conservatives once they assumed power.[18] As a study into the reaction of Churchill's Conservative government to immigration observed, 'these ad hoc administrative measures had their limitations and, indeed, some were of questionable legality'.[19] And, as the efforts to prevent further Commonwealth immigration were failing, by the mid-1950s some in government had started to 'favour restrictive legislation'.[20]

The road to the Commonwealth Immigrants Act 1962

Early academic studies on race and immigration in post-war Britain, such as E. J. B. Rose's *Colour and Citizenship* published in the late 1960s, argue that the government was unwilling to impose restrictions upon Commonwealth citizens. The Notting Hill riots that occurred in September 1958, when over 300 white youth (many of them referred to as 'Teddy Boys') attacked West Indians and their property in the London borough,[21] were portrayed as a turning point in 'race relations' which required intervention by the government. Yet a closer historical look at the political reaction to Commonwealth immigration would suggest that, with the arrival of the *Empire Windrush* in 1948, the British government already had concerns about the influx of non-white Commonwealth subjects.[22] For example, in June 1948, Labour MP William Griffith was raising questions about West Indian immigration and its association with unemployment and welfare abuse, asking Minister of Labour Ness Edwards:

> Is my right hon. Friend aware that there are a considerable number of unemployed coloured men in the City of Manchester; and in view of the difficulty they are facing in securing employment, will he do everything possible to dissuade these irresponsible people who are sending shiploads of West Indians to this country without there being any jobs here waiting for them?[23]

Yet immigration from the former colonies of the Commonwealth was considered a favourable option by some within government and British industry since it would reduce the labour deficit. This was primarily because there were no restrictions on these immigrants' right to enter, settle and work in Britain, whereas European immigrants incurred costs (paid for by the government and employers) in relation to reception, employment, accommodation and welfare through their recruitment in government schemes.[24] 'Individual British subjects who [came to Britain] on their own initiative' were deemed not to need any assistance, such as the provision of welfare or housing facilities; and 'beyond directing them to the local employment exchanges, nothing further needed to be done'.[25] For the British government, two competing interests were juxtaposed by immigration from the Commonwealth: the interest of regenerating the British economy through migrant labour and the interest of maintaining some form of homogeneous British culture.

It is clear that the government wished for a sanitised importation of 'bodies' to be injected into those industries deemed to be most in need. This was seen as a favourable compromise in seeking to meet Britain's economic needs, including the maintenance of the

Commonwealth system. Nevertheless, this exercise had to be balanced against fears of a damaging social impact caused by reversed colonial migration.[26]

Thus, the 'cheapness of Commonwealth labour [was] always contrasted with its putative social and political cost'.[27] And the economic dimension of the immigration debate gave way to a 'rather different agenda of nationhood and cultural politics' that created the 'foundations of the "numbers game" equating immigration concentrations with social problems'.[28] This led to the problems faced by anti-racists, especially those on the Marxist left, as racism was not simply about economics and class, but was also tied to notions of cultural and social identity. The balancing arguments and labour needs were not sufficient to calm MPs, who increasingly voiced their concerns over Commonwealth immigrants. In the early 1950s, questions were raised in Parliament over the number of immigrants from the West Indies arriving in Britain and their impact upon British society. There was apprehension about immigration based on the economic grounds that employment opportunities were being taken away from British workers as well as on a concern over immigrants' use of social services. However, concerns were also raised in Parliament about the 'dangerous social problems' supposedly being brought to Britain by Commonwealth immigrants,[29] alongside objections that these immigrants could enter Britain 'regardless of their health, means of subsistence, character record, habits, culture, education, need for them economically ... or of the wishes of the British people'.[30]

As mentioned above, the suggestion that the 1958 riots caused the Conservative government to consider implementing some form of immigration control is not an accurate portrait of a mood that was already lingering in sections of the white population. Zig Layton-Henry states that the riots 'propelled the issue of black immigration onto the front pages of the newspapers and television and made it a national issue, rather than a series of independent local issues'.[31] However, the British government was not provoked by the riots alone into implementing greater immigration control measures, as negative attitudes towards non-white Commonwealth immigration already existed within both major parties.

As parliamentary debates throughout the 1950s demonstrate, there was apprehension amongst MPs from both parties about the social impact of Commonwealth immigration. However, the problems

faced by newly arrived migrants in relation to employment, housing and racial prejudice were never considered. And as Kathleen
Paul states, 'notably absent...was any suggestion of possible ways
to improve or solve the "problems" allegedly caused by migrants'.[32]
Before the 1958 riots, Labour MP Fenner Brockway's Private Members' Bill for the prohibition of racial discrimination was brought
to Parliament for debate three times yet defeated each time, with
Conservative MP Bernard Braine describing it as 'so inconsistent and
ill-conceived that it is almost an insult to the House to consider
it further'.[33] For those who advocated for immigration control, the
riots 'provided phenomenal evidence of the inevitability of conflict
between "races"', but had a wider impact by constituting the 'terrain
upon which politicians were able to racialize British politics'.[34]

Peter Fryer has observed that '[b]etween 1958 and 1968 black set-
tlers in Britain watched the racist tail wag the parliamentary dog'.[35]
This involved not only Conservative and Labour politicians progressively pandering to a small racist minority but also an increasing
acceptance by both parties of the need for a stricter border control
regime. It has been suggested by some authors that to 'press for any
kind of border control' in the immediate aftermath of the 1958 riots
was 'politically impossible' because it would have 'suggest[ed] that
the government was pandering to a racist populace'.[36] However, as
Robert Miles states, 'the immigration control solution was...not only
immediately proposed' but, more importantly, 'was also systematically reported' in the media.[37] For example, in a parliamentary debate
in the months following the Notting Hill riots, right-wing Labour MP
Frank Tomney stated that 'we must face the fact – and it would be idle
not to face it – that for the first time Great Britain has a colour problem at home'.[38] Similarly, two months earlier, Conservative MP Cyril
Osborne had announced in Parliament that there was an 'urgent need
for a restriction upon immigration into this country, particularly of
coloured immigrants'.[39] These debates were exacerbated by immigration figures which, after a slight decline in 1959, rose in 1960, most
notably an increase in the number of West Indian migrants from
16,400 to 49,650.[40]

In February 1961, backbencher Osborne put forward another Bill
that, 'in view of the enormous increase in immigration in recent
years...and the serious social problems that are consequently arising', urged immigration controls requiring every immigrant to have

proof of a 'guaranteed job; adequate housing accommodation; a clean bill of health; a clear criminal record and a cash deposit... to repay their return fare if they become a charge on public funds'.[41] For Osborne, immigration was the 'most difficult, the most dangerous and most delicate problem' facing Britain at the time and, 'speaking as an Englishman for the English people', he felt that 'the problem of immigration must be tackled, and tackled soon'.[42] In the same debate, Norman Pannell declared that non-white Commonwealth immigration was the main problem because 'coloured immigrants... come in greater numbers', and that many of the immigrants from the Commonwealth 'come from countries... [where] there is a standard of civilisation which is lower and there are acquired habits and inclinations which conflict with the accepted pattern of [Britain]'.[43] Although some disagreed with Osborne's proposals, the consensus that Commonwealth immigration was a problem was being reached by the government. As Nigel Fisher, another Conservative MP, stated, 'I do not deny that the steep increase in West Indian immigration in recent years... [has given] rise to problems in this country'.[44]

On 1 November 1961, the Conservative government first presented the Commonwealth Immigrants Bill to 'make temporary provision for controlling the immigration into the United Kingdom of Commonwealth citizens'.[45] The 'indefinite continuance of virtually limitless immigration' had to be controlled, according to the government. It declared, 'at present there are no factors visible which might lead us to expect a reversal or even a modification of the immigration trend', although Home Secretary R. A. Butler did acknowledge that immigration numbers fluctuated with rises and dips in the British economy.[46] Increased immigration, according to the Home Secretary, posed the 'real risk that the drive for improved conditions will be defeated by the sheer weight of numbers',[47] putting the blame for the Conservative government's failure to meet national housing requirements onto newly arrived immigrants. Despite assurances that the Bill treated all Commonwealth citizens (including Australians, New Zealanders and Canadians) equally, its true nature as intended to control Commonwealth immigration was demonstrated by Home Secretary Butler's statement that:

> It cannot be denied that the immigrants who have come to this country in such large numbers have presented the country with an

intensified social problem. They tend to settle in communities of their own, with their own mode of life, in big cities. The greater the numbers coming into this country the larger these communities and the more difficult will it be to integrate them into our national life.[48]

That this view underpinned the Bill was confirmed in 1968 by William Deedes, a Conservative Minister at the time of the Commonwealth Immigrants Bill's passing, who, reflecting back on those events, admitted, 'The Bill's real purpose was to restrict the influx of coloured immigrants. We were reluctant to say as much openly.'[49]

The debate around the 1962 Act symbolises the beginning of the 'numbers game', and the formation of an ideal that 'good race relations' could only be achieved by a strict immigration control system. Support for this notion is demonstrated by Butler's statement that 'if the numbers of new entrants are excessive, their assimilation into our society presents the gravest difficulty'.[50] However, the numbers game also immediately revealed its contradictory elements. '[T]he argument about numbers is unwinnable because however many you decide upon there will always be someone to campaign for less and others for whom one is too many', wrote Robert Moore. If one has 'admitted that black people are a problem in themselves', Moore argued, 'it is impossible to resist the argument for less [sic] of them'.[51]

The Bill, with reservations from the Labour Party, was passed on 27 February 1962 and the Commonwealth Immigrants Act came into effect on 1 July 1962. The Act introduced a voucher system that divided applicant immigrants into three different groups – A, B or C – depending on 'skill' and 'experience' levels. According to 'political and economic considerations', the total number of vouchers granted was not fixed; but as Kathleen Paul wrote, 'the voucher system significantly reduced primary migration to Britain', with 66,941 vouchers issued between July and December 1962, which was reduced to 16,046 by December 1965 when the C category was abolished.[52] The C category was designated for unskilled labour, which comprised the bulk of applicants from the Commonwealth, while a higher proportion of applicants from Australia, New Zealand and Canada were successful in obtaining 'skilled' category A and B vouchers.[53] For the Conservatives who designed the legislation, the Act could be presented as non-discriminatory even though in practice 'its restrictive effect [was] intended to, and would in fact, operate on coloured people almost exclusively'.[54] The Act significantly reduced the number of immigrant workers from the Commonwealth, but no restrictions were placed on immigrants from Ireland.

While the Commonwealth Immigrants Act greatly reduced the number of non-white Commonwealth immigrants entering Britain after 1962, therefore to a certain extent placating the racist wing of the government, the number of immigrants who attempted to 'beat the Act' was significantly higher than the numbers who had entered in the previous decade. In 1960, the total number of immigrants had been 57,700, but this number leapt to 136,400 in 1961 and another 94,900 in the first six months of 1962 before the Act became enforceable.[55] As Ruth Brown has observed, 'the racism of Britain's Tory government led them to destroy in one single act the almost perfect symmetry which had previously existed between levels of migration into Britain and the level of demand for labour there'.[56]

Two forms of citizenship: Labour and the Commonwealth Immigrants Act 1962–68

Throughout the 1950s, the *official* position of the Labour Party on immigration control was one of consistent opposition. When the Commonwealth Immigrants Bill was debated in Parliament in November 1961, the Labour Party opposed it on the same grounds it had presented in 1958. Gordon Walker, Labour MP for Smethwick, contended that the Conservative Home Secretary R. A. Butler 'advocates a Bill into which race discrimination is now written – not only into its spirit and practice but into its very letter'.[57] Labour's opposition to the introduction of the Commonwealth Immigrants Act was based on both political and economic arguments.[58]

Politically, the Labour Party favoured a more benevolent British Commonwealth and defended the right of free entry for Commonwealth citizens, attacking the Conservatives for 'having rejected the Commonwealth' and what it supposed were 'the principles on which it was founded'.[59] The Labour Party opposed the Commonwealth Immigrants Bill on the *principle* that it was racially biased, and 'consistently accused the government of implementing racism'.[60] During the Bill's second reading, Walker declared that Labour would 'bitterly oppose the Bill and will resist it' as it was 'widely and rightly regarded as introducing a colour bar into our legislation'.[61] Labour's economic argument was that the flow of migration had been regulated by the demands of the British economy, with leader Hugh Gaitskell stating that 'the rate of immigrants into this country is closely related and...will always be closely related, to the rate of economic absorption'.[62] As Gaitskell explained, throughout the 1950s until 1959, there was 'an almost precise correlation between the movement in the number of unfulfilled vacancies...and the immigration figures'.[63]

Some authors, in particular Paul Foot and Peter Alexander, have emphasised the principled opposition of Gaitskell, as leader of the Labour Party, who presented an official, unified, formal position on the concept of immigration control for Labour.[64] Foot wrote that Gaitskell understood 'much better than his colleagues the general principles behind the international migration of labour', and believed in the British Commonwealth as a 'world-wide multi-racial community network'.[65] In Parliament, Gaitskell declared that the Bill was 'a plain anti-Commonwealth Measure in theory and...a plain anti-colour Measure in practice',[66] and Denis Healey, Labour's spokesperson on colonial issues, pledged at a meeting of immigrant and Commonwealth organisations that a Labour government would repeal the Act if elected.[67]

However, the Labour Party's official position changed soon after Gaitskell's death in early 1963, when Harold Wilson became leader of the party. Whereas previously Labour's opposition to immigration control had been officially 'unconditional', now Wilson claimed that the party 'supported and...do support certain provisions of the Act'.[68] Wilson announced that '[w]e do not contest the need for control of immigration into this country' and accepted the continuation of the Commonwealth Immigrants Act.[69]

Wilson's statement that Labour accepted the concept of immigration control was the beginning of a growing consensus between the two major parties that non-white immigration from the Commonwealth was a problem. The defeat of Labour MP Gordon Walker to Conservative candidate Peter Griffiths in the 1964 general election, primarily fought on the issue of immigration, made many within the Labour Party move towards an acceptance of strict immigration controls, believing that opposition to controls could be cited by the Conservatives as a sign of Labour's weakness. Griffiths used the issue of immigration, supported by the Conservative Association, local anti-immigration advocates and fascist groups, to disrupt the traditional support for the Labour Party in Smethwick. The most notorious and infamous aspect of this campaign was the slogan, 'If you want a nigger neighbour, vote Labour', about which Griffiths commented, 'I would not condemn anyone who said that. I regard it as a manifestation of popular feeling.'[70] The Labour Party's interpretation of the loss of Smethwick (a loss of 7.2 per cent against an average swing across the nation to Labour of 3.5 per cent)[71] was, according to Labour Minister Richard Crossman, that '[e]ver since the Smethwick election it has been quite clear that immigration can be the greatest potential vote-loser for the Labour Party'.[72]

Despite the official front, the Labour Party had been internally divided on the issue of immigration for many years. The official position on unconditional right of entry had seemingly only been held together by the leadership qualities of Hugh Gaitskell.[73] The notion of the Labour Party yielding in the face of racist public opinion has been well documented in the history of race relations in Britain. Yet, as Kathleen Paul has observed, the concept of a 'hostile public push[ing] an otherwise liberal administration toward ever greater "immigration" control' is the 'picture presented by policy makers themselves'.[74] Both Labour and the Conservatives had adopted unofficial means to prevent Commonwealth immigration into Britain in the late 1940s and throughout the 1950s. While the traditional history views the Smethwick result as impetus for Labour's acceptance of restrictions upon non-white Commonwealth immigration, Kathleen Paul's assertion that these measures were 'driven not by the explosion of "race and immigration" into the electoral arena but by imperatives internal to the governing elite' is far more convincing.[75]

In March 1965, Wilson stated that the Commonwealth Immigrants Act was 'not working as was intended', recommending that 'a fresh examination of the whole problem of control is necessary'.[76] The result of this re-examination of immigration policy was the White Paper *Immigration from the Commonwealth*, published in August 1965. The White Paper suggested that the problem involved how to 'control the entry of immigrants so that it does not outrun Britain's capacity to absorb them'.[77] The emphasis of the Labour government's platform on immigration during this period was on the notions of 'integration' and 'absorption' of Commonwealth immigrants, but the government believed that integration could not occur without immigration controls. Labour MP Roy Hattersley summarised this by declaring that, 'without integration, limitation is inexcusable; without limitation, integration is impossible'.[78] To this end, the White Paper made two main proposals: the discontinuation of the Category C vouchers and a large reduction in the number of vouchers issued.[79] Category C vouchers had been the most issued voucher since their introduction, with 42,367 issued between July 1962 and September 1964.[80] More importantly, the total number of vouchers was to be reduced from around 20,000 a year to just 8500 a year, with 1000 reserved for citizens of Malta and 'not more than 15 per cent of the vouchers issued in Category A will go to any one Commonwealth country'.[81] Effectively this meant that Old Commonwealth countries, such as Australia and New Zealand, which had fairly small populations, were entitled to the same number of vouchers as the more populous Commonwealth countries like India and Pakistan. Regarding the Labour government's fears of 'evasion' of control, the Paper also proposed stronger powers for Immigration Officers to refuse entry to those who were not considered '*bona fides*'.[82]

The result of the White Paper's release was that consensus was reached within government circles that Commonwealth immigration was undesirable and threatened social cohesion in Britain. As Roy Hattersley stated in Parliament in March 1965, 'I believe that unrestricted immigration can only produce additional problems, additional suffering and additional hardship unless some kind of limitation is imposed and continued.'[83] Previously speaking as 'a passionate opponent of the Act', Hattersley came claimed in 1965 that, 'with the advantages of hindsight, I suspect that we were wrong to oppose the Act'.[84]

The Labour government's policy of integration featured heavily in the White Paper, which recommended the implementation of tighter restrictions on Commonwealth immigration while tackling racial discrimination in the domestic sphere. This led to the introduction of the first legislation against racial discrimination in late 1965 to 'complement' the White Paper. The Race Relations Act 1965 was introduced to 'prohibit discrimination on racial grounds in places of public resort' and was enacted in November 1965,[85] but was a much weaker Act than had been proposed by MPs such as Fenner Brockway since the mid-1950s. While reservedly welcomed by both progressive and immigrant organisations, the Race Relations Act was inherently tied to the notions of integration and restriction. As Dilip Hiro wrote:

> Taken together, the 1965 White Paper and the 1965 Race Relations Act signalled the convergence of the two major political parties on the issues of immigration control and racial justice. An advance, albeit minor, on the front for ethnic minorities was conceded by the Conservatives in exchange for a retreat by Labour in the matter of immigration restrictions.[86]

The Labour government believed that immigration control and the Race Relations Act would ease the process of integration for non-white immigrants from the Commonwealth into the 'British way of life'. This process of integration, reinforced by legislation against the most overt forms of public racial discrimination, would help 'stamp out the evils of racialism'.[87] As Peter Alexander wrote, '[i]mmigration control was expected to reduce racism. The reverse happened. And with increased racism came further controls'.[88]

While the number of colonial migrants on work vouchers decreased through the mid-1960s, other colonial migrants (on British passports issued overseas) started to increase in numbers, especially after Kenya won independence in 1963. This point in time symbolises the beginning of an 'Africanisation' campaign that 'prompted many [Kenyan South Asians] to migrate to Britain rather than face continued discrimination' in Kenya.[89] A 'steady flow' of Kenyan South Asians migrated to Britain between 1965 and 1967. In 1967, the Kenyan government passed a law under which these British citizens of South Asian descent could reside and work in Kenya only on a temporary basis. This created an increase in migration to Britain and prompted demands from sections of the media and Conservative MPs, such as Enoch Powell, that restrictions be applied to these Kenyan South Asians.[90] Powell claimed that the number of South Asians arriving from Kenya would reach a total of 200,000, but the reality was a much smaller 66,000 out of a potential 95,000, with 29,000 already settled in Britain by February 1968.[91] In late February 1968, the Labour government 'steamrollered through Parliament in three days of emergency debate' the Commonwealth Immigrants Act 1968 with the 'sole purpose of restricting entry into Britain of Kenyan Asians holding British passports'.[92] According to this Act,

British citizenship was determined by the birth of a person or of one of their parents or grandparents in Britain. This effectively excluded the Kenyan South Asians, or any other non-white citizens of the Commonwealth, from British citizenship. Despite the rhetoric that the 1968 Act was impartial and not racially biased, the reality underpinning this amendment was the Labour government's intention to prevent further non-white immigration to Britain.

Zig Layton-Henry described the 1968 Act as the 'logical outcome of appeasement that the Labour government had adopted in order to achieve the bipartisan consensus with the Conservatives and to reduce the electoral salience of the issue'.[93] However, this was more than merely a pragmatic issue of Labour attempting to not appear 'weaker than the Conservatives on the issue of immigration controls',[94] but was the result of a deeper reassessment of the idea of British nationality as Britain's colonial empire collapsed. White British citizens born abroad were 'never referred to as "immigrants" under any circumstances'. The term 'immigrant' was reserved for non-white Commonwealth migrants, and by the late 1960s the equation of 'immigrant' with 'black' had become the prevailing attitude.[95] The Labour Party had originally opposed immigration controls on the grounds of the ideal of the free movement of people and trade throughout the Commonwealth. However, the right to enter and live in Britain without restriction did not mean that Commonwealth immigrants were 'regarded as British in any other sense'.[96] For Labour, the 'Commonwealth ideal had never been intended as a defence of [unrestricted] black immigration to Britain'. And, as Caroline Knowles has stated, the increasingly tougher controls on immigration seen in the 1960s demonstrated that Labour 'reconstructed immigration away from Commonwealth and labour needs', perceiving immigrants as 'an invasive and oppositional political community to indigenousness'.[97]

In 1968, Robert Moore wrote that '[r]acialists have nothing to lose and everything to gain by pressing the Labour government even harder'.[98] The long-term effect of the Commonwealth Immigrants Act 1968 was to create a distinction between the predominantly white British citizenry who could claim lineage within Britain and the predominantly non-white Commonwealth citizenry who could no longer claim to be 'British', which in turn barred the Commonwealth immigrant from entering Britain. In this we can trace the beginning of the double standard citizenship rule which divides 'desirable' and 'undesirable' migrants according to country of origin.

Closing the door on the Commonwealth: The Immigration Act 1971

After winning the 1970 general election, Conservative leader Edward Heath stated that his party had been 'returned to office to change the course and history of this nation, nothing else'.[99] Rallying against the mixed economy of the Wilson era and the 'permissive society' that allowed the explosion of cultural radicalism and industrial militancy, Heath launched a campaign for a less-restricted market economy, while strengthening state structures against the 'enemy within'.[100] The political radicalism and industrial militancy of the late 1960s created a perception amongst the Conservatives that, in order to prevent British society from drifting into 'violence' and 'disorder', a transition towards a more repressive role for state institutions was needed.[101] The introduction of the Immigration Act 1971, therefore, needs to be viewed in the wider context of the Conservative government introducing legislation to ensure greater control by the state over those who were deemed to be threats to 'the nation'.

During the 1970 general election campaign, influenced by the rise of 'Powellism', the Conservatives promised that there would be 'no further large scale permanent immigration'. Reiko Karatani wrote, '[i]n the end, the purpose of the IA [Immigration Act] 1971 never became clear during parliamentary debates, except that the Conservative government wished to fulfil an election pledge'.[102] And, accordingly, under the Act, 'primary immigration [of new workers] was effectively halted'.[103] This was done by creating a distinction between 'patrial' and 'non-patrial' migrants. A 'patrial' migrant was:

(a)...a citizen of the United Kingdom and Colonies who has that citizenship by birth...in the United Kingdom

(c)...a citizen of the United Kingdom and Colonies who has at any time been settled in the United Kingdom and Islands and...been ordinarily resident there for the last five years or more.[104]

Any Commonwealth citizens who could not prove their status according to the above criteria, as well as any non-Commonwealth aliens, thus came to be considered 'non-patrials' and, with the exception of EEC migrants, were restricted in their entry into the country, conditional on their obtaining an annually renewable work permit.[105] Non-patrials could only be granted permission to stay in Britain once their annual work permit had been renewed four times and the type of employment in which they were engaged approved by the government.[106]

The Immigration Act 1971 was intended to prevent migrants from obtaining the right to residency through a work voucher. This was believed to cut down significantly on the number of male Commonwealth migrants entering Britain; hence, the legislation stopping labour migration from the Commonwealth was enacted with the purpose of containing a perceived social problem. However, the Act did not cut labour migration completely. In fact, Britain entered the EEC on 1 January 1973, which allowed the free movement of labour within the borders of the EEC. The desirability of EEC workers was in part because they could freely enter and leave Britain with the rise and fall in labour demand, there was no formal recruitment campaign and, thus, no need for government expenditure to transport or accommodate EEC workers.

Alongside the tightening of controls on entry, state officials, such as Immigration Officers at ports of entry and the police, were given a 'wide range of discretionary powers, including...the right to deport people and to refuse entry'.[107] Those suspected 'with reasonable cause' to have entered Britain illegally or overstayed their time could be arrested without warrant under the new discretionary powers enabled by the Act.[108] While the former immigration controls had primarily been attempts to restrict non-white immigration, the Immigration Act 1971 also focused on controlling those who already lived in Britain. 'The problem was...the black labour that was already here', wrote A. Sivanandan, 'with laws and regulations that kept families apart, sanctioned police harassment [and] invited fascist violence', the Conservatives 'generally made life untenable for the black citizens of Britain'.[109]

After the 1971 Act effectively ended the permanent migration of Commonwealth workers, the attention of the British government turned to the relatives, such as wives, children or parents, of those immigrants who were already resident in Britain before the Act came into effect on 1 January 1973. However, those classified as non-patrials, who had obtained work vouchers under the Immigration Act 1971, in most cases were unable to bring their families to Britain. The family reunification of Commonwealth migrants became the next big item in the migration agenda. This caused a major backlog of applications, particularly in South Asia where the process often took up to 18–24 months to complete. With the application process for family reconciliation taking so long and the large number of people applying, the British government was fearful that people would attempt to sidestep the process and seek to enter Britain under false pretences. This suspicion of migrants, especially women and children from South Asia, is key to understanding the scrutiny and level of examination placed upon potential migrants in the 1970s and 1980s. The category of the 'desirable' migrant grew smaller and smaller and the category of the 'undesirable' migrant grew larger and larger – to prove one's desirability meant undergoing an exhaustive (and often humiliating) process that determined whether a person fit into the scheme of the host society. The humanity of the migrants was stripped away and only their 'value' to the British nation-state was assessed – a process that is discussed further in Chapter 2.

Conclusion

By the mid-1970s, the British immigration control system as we now know it had been established. The Immigration Act 1971 severely restricted the number of non-EEC migrants coming to Britain and labour migration (mostly by men) from the Commonwealth came almost to an end. Instead, the number of women and children seeking to join their male family members who had already travelled to Britain for work prior to 1973 rose dramatically. However, a vast control apparatus had been created to ensure that only those who could prove a familial connection to someone living in Britain would gain entry. This was the result of a long legislative process that sought to implement ever more restrictive controls upon Britain's migrants from the Commonwealth. While the British government was happy with the economic benefits that Commonwealth migrants brought in the late 1940s and throughout the 1950s as they filled an acute labour shortage in certain industries, scholars have shown that since the mid-1950s the authorities had also been devising ways to first discourage, then prevent Commonwealth migrants from making the journey to Britain. This chapter has outlined that path to what Robert Miles and Annie Phizacklea have called 'the racialization of British politics'[110] and the introduction of the Commonwealth Immigrants Act 1962. But it has also shown that both Labour and the Conservatives still felt that migration needed to be further restricted and spent much of their time following 1962 attempting to implement stricter controls.

Notes

1. *Hansard*, 23 March 1965, col. 380–381.
2. For a good overview of the history of British immigration policy, see Peter Fryer, *Staying Power: The History of Black People in Britain* (London: Pluto Press, 1984); Kathleen Paul, *Whitewashing Britain: Race and Citizenship in the Postwar Era* (Ithaca: Cornell University Press, 1997); Ian R.G. Spencer, *British Immigration Policy Since 1939: The Making of a Multi-Racial Britain* (London: Routledge, 1997).
3. Discussion of the exclusionary debates surrounding the Aliens Act 1905 can be found in Steve Cohen, *It's the Same Old Story: Immigration Controls against Jewish, Black and Asian People, with Special Reference to Manchester* (Manchester: Manchester City Council, 1987); Colin Holmes, *John Bull's Island: Immigration & British Society, 1871–1971* (Houndmills: Macmillan, 1988); Robert Winder, *Bloody Foreigners: The Story of Immigration to Britain* (London: Abacus, 2006) pp. 250–275.
4. L. Tabili, *'We Ask for British Justice': Workers and Racial Difference in Late Imperial Britain* (Ithaca, NY: Cornell University Press, 1994) p. 60.
5. According to Kathleen Paul, over 1.5 million British residents emigrated between 1946 and 1960. Paul, *Whitewashing Britain*, p. 25.
6. Ruth Brown, 'Racism and Immigration in Britain', *International Socialism*, 2/68, Autumn 1995, p. 12.
7. See Mike Phillips and Trevor Phillips, *Windrush: The Irresistible Rise of Multiracial Britain* (London: HarperCollins, 1998).
8. British Nationality Act 1948, 1 (1).
9. Solomos, 'The Politics of Immigration Since 1945', in Peter Braham, Ali Rattansi and Richard Skellington (eds), *Racism and Anti-Racism: Inequalities, Opportunities and Policies* (London: Sage Publications, 1992) p. 9.
10. *Hansard*, 7 July, 1948, col. 411.
11. Solomos, 'The Politics of Immigration Since 1945', p. 10.
12. Lydia Lindsey, 'Halting the Tide: Responses to West Indian Immigration to Britain, 1946–1952', *Journal of Caribbean History*, 26/1, 1992, p. 63.
13. Figures calculated from those given in Dilip Hiro, *Black British, White British: A History of Race Relations in Britain* (London: Paladin, 1992) p. 331 and *Hansard*, 18 March 1965, col. 311–312w.

14. Solomos, 'The Politics of Immigration Since 1945', p. 10.
15. Robert Miles, 'The Racialization of British Politics', *Political Studies*, 38, 1990, pp. 281–282.
16. Paul, *Whitewashing Britain*, p. 132.
17. Kenneth Lunn, 'The British State and Immigration, 194551: New Light on the *Empire Windrush'*, in Tony Kushner and Kenneth Lunn (eds), *The Politics of Marginality: Race, the Radical Right and Minorities in Twentieth Century Britain* (London: Frank Cass, 1990) p. 172.
18. Bob Carter, Clive Harris and Shirley Joshi, 'The 1951–55 Conservative Government and the Racialization of Black Immigration', *Immigrants and Minorities*, 6/3, November 1987, p. 336.
19. B. Carter, C. Harris and S. Joshi, 'The 1951–55 Conservative Government and the Racialization of Black Immigration', p. 337.
20. Carter, Harris and Joshi, 'The 1951–55 Conservative Government', p. 337.
21. For further information about the 1958 Notting Hill riots, see Robert Miles, 'The Riots of 1958: Notes on the Ideological Construction of "Race Relations" as a Political Issue in Britain', *Immigrants & Minorities* 3/3, 1984, pp. 252–275; Edward Pilkington, 'The West Indian Community and the Notting Hill Riots of 1958', *Racial Violence in Britain in the Nineteenth and Twentieth Centuries (Revised ed.)* 1996, pp. 171–184.
22. Lindsey, 'Halting the Tide', p. 62.
23. *Hansard*, 15 June, 1948, col. 224.
24. S. Joshi and B. Carter, 'The Role of Labour in the Creation of a Racist Britain', *Race & Class*, 25/3, 1984, p. 58; *Hansard*, 24 June, 1948, col. 1555.
25. *Hansard*, 24 June, 1948, col. 1555; Joshi and Carter, 'The Role of Labour in the Creation of a Racist Britain', p. 58.
26. See Joshi and Carter, 'The Role of Labour in the Creation of a Racist Britain'; Shamit Saggar, 'Integration and Adjustment: Britain's Liberal Settlement Revisited', in David Lowe (ed.), *Immigration and Integration: Australia and Britain* (London: Bureau of Immigration Multicultural and Population Research/Sir Robert Menzies Centre for Australian Studies, 1995) pp. 105–131; M.D.A. Freeman and Sarah Spencer, 'Immigration Control, Black Workers and the Economy,' *British Journal of Law & Society*, 6, 1979, pp. 65.
27. Joshi and Carter, 'The Role of Labour in the Creation of a Racist Britain', p. 59.
28. Saggar, 'Integration and Adjustment', p. 115.
29. *Hansard*, 13 June 1951, col. 2278.
30. *Hansard*, 16 December 1954, col. 190.
31. Zig Layton-Henry, *The Politics of Immigration: Immigration, 'Race' and 'Race' Relations in Post-War Britain* (Oxford: Blackwell, 1992) p. 38.
32. Paul, *Whitewashing Britain*, p. 156.
33. *Hansard*, 24 May 1957, col. 1607.
34. Robert Miles, 'The Riots of 1958', pp. 269, 272.
35. Fryer, *Staying Power*, p. 381.

36. Paul, *Whitewashing Britain*, p. 157; Spencer, *British Immigration Policy Since 1939*, p. 101; Robert Winder, *Bloody Foreigners: The Story of Immigration to Britain* (London: Little, Brown, 2004) p. 280.
37. Miles, 'The Riots of 1958', p. 264.
38. *Hansard*, 5 December 1958, col. 1589.
39. Ibid., 29 October 1958, col. 195.
40. Ibid., 18 March 1965, col. 311–312.
41. Ibid., 17 February 1961, col. 1929.
42. Ibid., col. 1930.
43. Ibid., col. 1963.
44. Ibid., col. 1993.
45. Ibid., 1 November 1961, col. 161.
46. Ibid., 16 November 1961, col. 687; col. 689.
47. Ibid., col. 695.
48. Ibid., col. 694.
49. William Deedes, *Race without Rancour* (London: Conservative Political Centre, 1968) p. 10.
50. *Hansard*, 16 November 1961, col. 694.
51. Robert Moore, *Racism and Black Resistance in Britain* (London: Pluto Press, 1975) p. 27.
52. Paul, *Whitewashing Britain*, p. 166; Figures calculated from *Control of Immigration Statistics 1 July 1962–31 December 1963* (London: HMSO, 1965) p. 15–16; *Control of Immigration Statistics 1965* (London: HMSO, 1966) p. 11.
53. Peach, 'West Indian Migration to Britain', p. 44.
54. Cited in Paul, *Whitewashing Britain*, p. 166.
55. *Hansard*, 18 March 1965, col. 311–312.
56. Brown, 'Racism and Immigration in Britain', p. 16.
57. *Hansard*, 16 November 1961, col. 706.
58. Robert Miles and Annie Phizacklea, *White Man's Country: Racism in British Politics* (London: Pluto Press, 1984) p. 42.
59. Miles and Phizacklea, *White Man's Country*, p. 42.
60. Ibid.
61. *Hansard*, 16 November 1961, col. 1716.
62. Miles and Phizacklea, *White Man's Country*, p. 42; *Hansard*, 16 November 1961, col. 793–794.
63. *Hansard*, 16 November 1961, col. 794; R. Miles and A. Phizacklea, *White Man's Country*, p. 42.
64. Foot, *Immigration and Race in British Politics* (Harmondsworth: Penguin, 1965) pp. 174–175; Peter Alexander, *Racism, Resistance and Revolution* (London: Bookmarks, 1987) pp. 34–35.
65. Foot, *Immigration and Race in British Politics*, p. 175.
66. *Hansard*, 16 November 1961, col. 799.
67. Foot, *Immigration and Race in British Politics*, p. 173; M. Sherwood, *Claudia Jones* (London: Lawrence & Wishart, 1999) p. 99.
68. Cited in Foot, *Immigration and Race in British Politics*, p. 170; *Hansard*, 27 November 1963, col. 365.

69. *Hansard*, 27 November 1963, col. 367.
70. Cited in Miles and Phizacklea, *White Man's Country*, p. 49. The origins of this slogan are not clear. Gordon Walker announced in July 1963 that during the municipal elections that occurred in May that year, children had been organised to chant this slogan. Most histories claim that this slogan was resurrected during the 1964 general election campaign. Foot, *Immigration and Race in British Politics*, p. 44.
71. Miles and Phizacklea, *White Man's Country*, p. 50.
72. Richard Crossman, *The Diaries of a Cabinet Minister, Vol. 1: Minister of Housing 1964–1966* (London: Hamish Hamilton, 1975) pp. 149–150.
73. See Foot, *Immigration and Race in British Politics*, pp. 161–175.
74. Paul, *Whitewashing Britain*, p. 177.
75. Ibid., pp. 177–178.
76. *Hansard*, 9 March 1965, col. 249.
77. *Immigration from the Commonwealth*, Cmnd. 2739, (London: HMSO, 1965) p. 2.
78. Cited in Miles and Phizacklea, *White Man's Country*, p. 57.
79. *Immigration from the Commonwealth*, p. 6.
80. Figures calculated from *Control of Immigration Statistics 1 July 1962–31 December 1963*, HMSO, London, 1965, pp. 15–16; *Control of Immigration Statistics 1964*, HMSO, London, 1965, p. 11.
81. *Immigration from the Commonwealth*, p. 6.
82. Ibid., p. 8.
83. *Hansard*, 23 March 1965, col. 380–381.
84. Ibid.
85. Race Relations Act, 1965.
86. Hiro, *Black British, White British*, p. 211.
87. David Ennals, 'Labour's Race Relations Policy', *Institute of Race Relations Newsletter*, November/December 1968, p. 437.
88. Alexander, *Racism, Resistance and Revolution*, p. 34.
89. Paul, *Whitewashing Britain*, p. 179.
90. John Solomos, *Race and Racism in Britain* (Houndmills: Palgrave, 2003) p. 60; D. Hiro, *Black British, White British*, p. 213.
91. Alexander, *Racism, Resistance and Revolution*, p. 36; Hiro, *Black British, White British*, p. 214.
92. Fryer, *Staying Power*, p. 383.
93. Zig Layton-Henry, *The Politics of Immigration: Immigration, 'Race' and 'Race' Relations in Post-War Britain* (Oxford: Blackwell, 1992) p. 79.
94. Layton-Henry, *The Politics of Immigration*, p. 79.
95. Ann Dummett and Andrew Nicol, *Subjects, Citizens, Aliens and Others: Nationality and Immigration Law* (London: Weidenfeld and Nicholson, 1990) p. 201.
96. Caroline Knowles, *Race, Discourse and Labourism* (London: Routledge, 1992) p. 94.
97. Knowles, *Race, Discourse and Labourism*, p. 96, 103.
98. Robert Moore, 'Labour and Colour – 1965–1968', *Institute of Race Relations Newsletter*, October 1968, p. 390.

99. Cited in David Butler and Dennis Kavanagh, *The British General Election of February 1974* (London: Macmillan, 1974) p. 10.
100. John Solomos, Bob Findlay, Simon Jones and Paul Gilroy, 'The Organic Crisis of British Capitalism and Race: The Experience of the Seventies', in Centre for Contemporary Cultural Studies, *The Empire Strikes Back: Race and Racism in 70s Britain* (London: Hutchinson, 1986) p. 23.
101. Solomos, Findlay, Jones and Gilroy, 'The Organic Crisis of British Capitalism and Race', p. 25.
102. Reiko Karatani, *Defining British Citizenship: Empire, Commonwealth and Modern Britain* (London: Routledge, 2003) p. 165.
103. Spencer, *British Immigration Policy Since 1939*, p. 143.
104. Immigration Act, 1971, Part 1, 2, (1).
105. Solomos, *Race and Racism in Britain*, p. 63.
106. Hiro, *Black British, White British*, 223 (italics added).
107. Miles and Phizacklea, *White Man's Country*, p. 69.
108. A. Sivanandan, *A Different Hunger: Writings on Black Resistance* (London: Pluto Press, 1982) p. 27.
109. Sivanandan, *A Different Hunger*, p. 28.
110. Miles and Phizacklea, *White Man's Country*, p. 38.

2
The Border as a Filter: Maintaining the Divide in the Post-Imperial Era

The border has been described by some scholars as an exceptional space where human rights are given less priority than the aims of state sovereignty.[1] Border control practices have been based on the assumption that migrants with less desirable socio-cultural and economic backgrounds are willing to evade or deceive the system in order to gain access to the host country.[2] This narrative reinforces the idea that such migrants are not trustworthy, and that they are not who they claim to be when interacting with immigration officials.[3] Furthermore, border control staff have historically had significant powers (with much discretion attached to them), which over time have increasingly led to stricter and less humanitarian practices. This chapter looks at how the British border control system has functioned as a discretionary *and* discriminatory system since the 1960s.

In 1992, looking back at the history of immigration control in Britain, John Solomos suggested that the British government had wrongly judged the connection between strict immigration controls and 'good race relations':

> If the main rationalisation of the immigration controls and the race relations legislation was the objective of producing an atmosphere for the development of 'good race relations' and integration, it needs to be said that they failed to depoliticise the question of 'race' as such.[4]

As demonstrated in the previous chapter, the purpose of the immigration control system, although tempered by other socio-economic and political concerns, was to protect the 'whiteness' of the British people and prevent large numbers of former colonial migrants from entering the country. This chapter explores how the UK immigration control system, based on the legislation outlined in the previous chapter, has functioned in practice and how it has been used to maintain a divide between 'white' domestic Britain and the colonial 'other'. Drawing on the work of Roxanne Lynn Doty and Paul Gilroy, we argue that the operation of immigration controls since the 1960s reveals a 'desire for order' and an attempt to reassert Britain's past colonial dominance in the post-imperial era. Using archival documents, the chapter shows how this desire for order informed the ways in which border control was performed and the level of suspicion that surrounded all migrants from the former British colonies. Focusing on the period following the introduction of the Immigration Act 1971, we see that women and children from South Asia – the largest category of migrants to enter Britain during the 1970s – were placed under extreme scrutiny and only allowed to enter if they could *prove* their 'value' to the British nation-state. The chapter explores how the body became a marker of worthiness and 'value' as part of this process of intense scrutiny and establishes the framework for chapters 4 and 5, in which a more detailed analysis of the human rights violations (virginity testing and X-rays) will be undertaken.

The purpose of immigration controls: The 'desire for order' in the postcolonial world

Borrowing from the work of Gilles Deleuze and Felix Guattari, Roxanne Lynn Doty has argued that the push for immigration controls, or 'anti-immigrationism', has acted as a means of control and revealed 'a desire for order'.[5] This imposition of control is particularly important and reinforced in the context of an increasingly globalised and postcolonial world, in which there is a palpable sense of fragmentation of centralised power due to shifting economic demands. Control at the border is a way to filter access, and therefore to deem a subject as 'desirable' according to various economic and non-economic purposes, even when such purposes may be contradictory. Doty's work shows us 'a way of thinking about statecraft as a dynamic, contradictory, and tension-filled process' which 'move[s] in various directions, towards certain practices and policies'.[6] As mentioned in the previous chapter, immigration control practices and policies are shaped by contradictions between economic, political, legal and diplomatic motives, but at the same time, the state seeks to override these contradictions. As Deleuze has written elsewhere (with Claire Parnet):

> the apparatus of the State has no meaning...it is the abstract machine which organizes the dominant utterances and the established order of a society, the dominant languages and knowledge, conformist actions and feelings, the segments which prevail over the others. The abstract machine of overcoding segments *ensures the homogenization of different segments*, their controvertibility, their translatability. (Emphasis added)[7]

Doty, using the language of Deleuze and Guattari, describes the actions of the state to override its internal contradictions, primarily through its repressive apparatuses, as a 'desire for order'. Our argument is that the British immigration control system is a primary example of how a desire for order is sought to overcome the contradictions inherent to the idea of nationhood and the identity of the former imperial power in the post-imperial era.

The British immigration control system, an expression of what Paul Gilroy has described as 'postcolonial melancholia', allows the post-imperial British authorities to impose their desire for order. In doing so, they reform and perpetuate the power dynamics inherited from the colonial era, and help the post-imperial British state to find a sense of unity and purpose. The border therefore is not a rigid barrier, but a fluid entity that shifts and morphs to perform according to the state's needs. The border is not just a line that marks territoriality, but also represents in this case the sovereignty of a country that, over the course of a century, has gone from the heights of being the world's leading imperial power to becoming a post-imperial nation in a progressively globalised world.

As argued in the previous chapter, the modern immigration control system in Britain was born out of a wave of decolonisation which coincided with large-scale migration from the Commonwealth to Britain. With the Second World War and Britain's peacekeeping efforts in the aftermath draining its resources, the country simply did not have the finances to maintain the administration of the British Empire (by then the British Commonwealth) or the human resources to administrate it. Between the late 1940s and the mid-1960s, most of Britain's former colonies became self-governing. Benjamin Grob-Fitzgibbon, in his book *Imperial Endgame*, has demonstrated that most of the literature regarding British decolonisation has characterised it as a 'mismanaged disaster', 'paralyzed by uncertainty, inaction, and a general lack of direction',[8] but argues that although its struggles were not as bloody as those of French, Dutch and Portuguese decolonisation, Britain did not willingly give up its rule in every former colony. Grob-Fitzgibbon states:

> The British government developed a concerted imperial strategy designed to secure the colonies for the Commonwealth in an orderly transfer of power while maintaining British influence in the region and strengthening overall Western dominance in the Cold War world.[9]

Grob-Fitzgibbon primarily focuses on the counter-insurgencies that occurred across the British Commonwealth between the end of the Second World War and the 1960s, but these military campaigns were part of a wider strategy developed by successive British governments that was 'carefully calculated to allow decolonization to occur on British terms rather than those of the indigenous people'.[10] This strategy can be understood as an example of the desire for order that the British authorities sought to satisfy in the era of decolonisation, whereby the traditional colonial hierarchies were threatened by the former colonies seeking independence. As the British colonial administration withdrew from various colonies across the globe during the post-war era, many felt embittered at the loss of Britain's 'greatness' and the desire for order was expressed in those areas in which the British still retained control – in this case, the immigration control system that was now in charge of regulating migration from the former colonies to the 'mother country'.

Controlling the migration process has thus allowed the British government to reinforce pre-existing colonial beliefs and prejudices. The immigration regime is an attempt at social control, to stretch further Doty's theory in this area.[11] Through what Deleuze and Guattari describe as 'deterritorialization' and 'reterritorialization',[12] the border acts as a reclaimed space that nurtures colonial ideals that had been deconstructed by the process of decolonisation. The influx of Commonwealth immigrants presents an opportunity for the British state in the era of decolonisation to reaffirm principles of dominance.

The desire for order allows unity in purpose – a purpose to control and conform that prevails over all the other of the state's objectives. This is of significance in the context of Britain's history of decolonisation, and also because of the globalisation process which has established different economic imperatives, especially via the EEC. As the imperial power diminishes, the desire for order becomes closely associated with a power to exclude. And this desire is an attempt to ensure homogenisation and translatability which become ever more out of reach for Britain. As Teresa Hayter points out:

> Nation-states have lost some of their powers in the face of so-called 'globalisation'. They cling to one of their last prerogatives: their power to exclude from their territories the persecuted and the poor.[13]

We propose that the excluded are not necessarily the 'persecuted and the poor'. The process of exclusion follows an underlying logic aimed at imposing a scrutiny that filters out the 'undesirable' colonial migrant. In this rests an assertion of colonial power despite the decolonisation process which has defined the 'melancholic' state of postcolonial Britain.[14] As Gilroy wrote:

> The immigrant is now here because Britain, Europe, was once out there; that basic fact of global history is not usually deniable. And yet its grudging recognition provides a stimulus for forms of hostility rooted in the realization that today's unwanted settlers carry all the ambivalence of empire with them. They project it into unhappy consciousness of their fearful and anxious hosts and neighbors. Indeed, the incomers may be unwanted and feared precisely because they are the unwitting bearers of the imperial and colonial past.[15]

The postcolonial immigration control system can be seen as a filter that supports the distinction between the traditionally white domestic sphere and the traditionally colonial 'other'. The immigrant, as bearer of a colonial past, is a reminder to sections of British society of a loss, a time when this country dominated the other – and this is a memory that has to be rewritten in order to limit the damage. Thus, to this end, the non-white immigrant is filtered in or out to allow the nation-state to reclaim part of its imperial power. Rebalancing its position over the people of its former colonies through border control is the ultimate objective. This cannot be achieved totally, as some non-white migrants are allowed into the country to enable Britain to fulfil some of its requirements, including filling labour shortages, to be seen to be responding sympathetically to migrant communities or wider humanitarian concerns. Further, it allows Britain to maintain its international obligations within the global society, which has created more external onlookers who can scrutinise the behaviour of states, such as the various bodies of the UN.

The postcolonial immigration control system has been used to establish an ideal *mixed* society, in which minorities remain as such. The aphorism attributed to Labour MP Roy Hattersley sums up this attitude: 'Without integration, limitation is inexcusable; without limitation, integration is impossible.'[16] This view was echoed in Margaret Thatcher's 1978 remarks in which she summarised the conservative view on 'good race relations':

> people are really rather afraid that this country might be rather swamped by people with a different culture. . . . So, if you want good race relations, you have got to allay people's fears on numbers. . . . Every country can take some small minorities and in many ways they add to the richness and variety of this country. The moment the minority threatens to become a big one, people get frightened.[17]

This desire to maintain an unequal balance between the 'white' host society and the non-white migrant minority in Britain meant that the potential migrant was seen through the lens of worthiness to the host nation, which often manifest in extreme measures imposed by immigration control officers. In the process of entering the destination country through the immigration control system, the migrant was subjected to examination and scrutiny to determine their utility for the host society. The government's desire for control therefore takes precedence over individual rights and citizenship, creating what

Giorgio Agamben has referred to as a 'state of exception'.[18] This state is 'a space devoid of law, a zone of anomie in which all legal determinations... are deactivated',[19] where the migrant's rights will never be comparable to those of the citizen. In this state of exception the threat of state intervention becomes normalised. The passage across the border is conditional on submission to an unequal social contract, the exceptional state of affairs that must be accepted. For this migrant, the fundamental right to human dignity is suspended in time and space. The border is thus used to imprint this state of exception onto the migrant, not only to select based on the socio-economic values and needs of the host society. The border can also be seen as a point in time when the migrant is exposed to the aggression and dominance of the state, which will be perpetuated after they are allowed into the country. In a 1975 report of an inspection in Dacca, Ian Martin, working for the Joint Council for the Welfare of Immigrants (JCWI), confirmed this:

> It is a curious prescription for good race relations that future British residents and citizens should have as their first experience of UK Government practice the suspicion, harsh interrogation, prevarication and humiliation which characterises the present system.[20]

As they enter the border control system, the migrant has no inherent 'value' to the host society and can be described (using the terminology of Giorgio Agamben) as representing 'bare life'. At the border, this bare life is qualified and defined by the needs of the receiving country, and if these needs intersect with what the migrant can offer, the migrant reaches what Agamben refers to as *bios* – a politically qualified life.[21]

The British immigration control system is constructed as fundamental to good race relations. As other scholars have discussed,[22] the discourse on immigration has continually wavered between highlighting the economic benefits of migration and the alleged sociopolitical problems that non-white migration brings. The border is the rite of passage to reach socio-economic benefits as much as it assigns an identity, of perennial outsider, to the non-white migrant. However, as we have described so far, while the main aim of the immigration control system has been to maintain a majority/minority ratio

between 'white' British society and the colonial 'other', this is compromised at times by Britain's other economic and socio-political
needs and tempered by other social, political, legal and diplomatic
restraints.

Weeding out the 'bogus' and 'illegal'

After non-skilled and semi-skilled male labourers from the British
Commonwealth were allowed into Britain, women, especially from
the Indian subcontinent, were considered under a scheme of family
reconciliation. The purpose of this scheme was to forge a 'man-
ageable' minority composed of homogeneous nuclear family units
of migrants who were economically productive yet socio-politically
reserved. The pressure built over the 1960s based on a common perception that migrants were claiming status that they did not hold,
by entering under false pretences, falsely declaring their intentions
in entering the country or providing false documentation, forced the
government to consider establishing categories of migrants deemed
more likely to be 'bogus' – a task achieved in 1978 by the Select Committee on Race Relations and Immigration, discussed further below.
Conservative MP Nigel Fisher claimed that '[e]vasion, mainly . . . by
students, is running at the rate of about 5,000 a year',[23] while Norman
St John-Stevas declared that '[b]ogus dependants must be checked
and weeded out'.[24]

After years of expressing dissatisfaction about the inefficiencies of
immigration policies in relation to 'bogus' and 'illegal' migration,[25]
the British Parliament passed the Immigration Act 1971. This Act
gave Immigration Officers the power to interview anyone who had
arrived in Britain for any purpose. On the part of an arrival, refusing
to be interviewed, refusing to 'furnish or produce' documentation,
offering a 'statement or representation which he [sic] knows to be
false or does not believe to be true' or producing any document
'which he [sic] knows or has reasonable cause to believe to be false'
gave Immigration Officers the power to refuse entry or impose a
£200 fine and up to six months imprisonment.[26] Such discretionary
powers contained in the Act represented a new strategy to deliver
results heavily dictated by a postcolonial ideology based on a sense of
superiority. Further, immigration officials were expected to produce
tangible outcomes, which translated into a high number of refusals
and rigorous screening of arrivals.

For most of the 1970s, entering the country under false pretences did not make someone an 'illegal entrant', and people who arrived in the country in this manner were protected by British common law and the legal concept of *habeas corpus*. An 'illegal entrant' was someone who had bypassed controls altogether and under the 1971 Act the state, through its Immigration Officers and other agencies, had the use of extraordinary powers of arrest, detention and deportation in relation to these entrants. As Kristin Couper and Ulysses Santamaria have suggested, under the Act suspected illegal immigrants '[had] no safeguards and [could] be arrested by an immigration officer or a police officer without a warrant and sent out of the country at any time'.[27] This changed in 1978 when the Select Committee on Race Relations and Immigration expanded the definition of what constituted an 'illegal entrant' to incorporate the 'bogus' migrant and acts of entering the country under false pretences. Evasion by seeking to enter under false pretences was considered by the Select Committee to be a form of illegal entry into Britain and was defined as per the following:

> applicants for settlement when applying for entry clearance may apply on the basis of false documents; applicants may achieve entry at air and sea ports by presenting forged passports or entry clearances; immigrants...enter[ing] the country covertly; immigrants who have entered the country legally on a short-term basis may overstay.[28]

This new definition of 'illegal' immigration gave the immigration control system, as well as the other institutions of the state, greater scope for 'weeding out' migrants who were suspected of falling foul of the Immigration Act and the scrutiny imposed upon migrants grew more severe.

Despite the strict nature of Immigration Act 1971, the tabloid press and other anti-immigration groups, such as the National Front, raised concerns that not enough was being done to stop illegal migrants from entering Britain.[29] In their 1978 work *Policing the Crisis*, Stuart Hall et al. described this as 'black panic' around what was perceived by many to be part of an insurmountable crisis facing the British people – an 'arena in which complex fears, tensions and anxieties, generated by the impact of the totality of the crisis...can be most conveniently and explicitly projected'.[30] The British government, clearly needing to be seen to be acting on such concerns, adopted a concerted response[31] that included the establishment of the Illegal Immigration Intelligence Unit in 1970, which operated in tandem with the police, the National Health Service and the Department of Social Security. The aim was to track down suspected illegal immigrants, via crosschecks, random passport inspections and raids on houses and workplaces.[32]

While this was occurring, Conservative Home Secretary Robert Carr denied in Parliament that a 'witch-hunt' was taking place.[33] This politics of denial also served the government's interest in reassuring Commonwealth partners in relation to doubts about the success of mixed 'race relations' raised by isolated extremists, such as members of the National Front, the National Party and the British Movement. For example, when Evan Luard, Under-Secretary of State for Foreign Affairs, visited Pakistan in 1976, his message on 'race relations' in Britain was one of bridge-building: '[w]e naturally deplore the doctrines of the National Front and the National Party... It is a mistake to give them too much prominence'.[34] However, the actual situation in Britain was that negative sentiment concerning immigration was spread throughout British society and the government both created this anxiety (through the rhetoric surrounding legislation such as the Immigration Act 1971) and responded to the anxieties expressed by the anti-immigration lobby (such as Thatcher's 1978 remarks that she understood why people voted for the National Front). The 'witch hunt' rhetoric was reinforced by the pervasive sense of mistrust surrounding the migrant at the border. The authenticity of documents was often doubted, especially if carried by people from certain countries. As a direct consequence, the number of refused immigrants escalated – '[f]rom a yearly average of 140 between 1973–1976... to 1,250 in 1980'.[35] The following section discusses the practices employed by immigration control staff that led to this rise in refusals.

Those to be mistrusted: Dependants and students from South Asia

The 1978 Select Committee on Race Relations and Immigration identified key demographic groups towards which the government's mistrust was directed. First, the Indian subcontinent was identified as the main region of origin for 'illegal' or 'bogus' migration. Second, the Committee identified dependants (such as wives and children) and students as a further category. In relation to the first category, Dudley Smith, Conservative MP and Select Committee member, claimed that, 'on reasonably good authority' obtained during a recent investigative trip to Bangladesh, 'something like 80 per cent of all documents and papers that are submitted by applicants of whatever category are forged or false'.[36]

In the Committee's report, citing the FCO, teenage dependants and students were stated to be those who 'most frequently' attempted to enter using false documents.[37] Students were also cited as those who more commonly overstayed their visa, clearly a different matter to producing false or forged documents or attempting to enter the country under false pretences. While the case of students is interesting, the next section will focus predominantly on dependants. This group includes children aged 18 or under, wives, husbands and fiancées/fiancés. The dependants originating from the Indian subcontinent fit both category one and category two.

The 'problem' of dependants needed to be addressed in a comprehensive and visible manner to placate public opinion. Responding to populist pressure to prevent mass migration from the Commonwealth countries, some within the government and immigration control system suggested the creation of a list of all possible dependants who could enter Britain from South Asia, primarily India, Pakistan and Bangladesh. In 1976, a Ministerial Group comprised of Lord Franks, Conservative MP Mark Carlisle and Labour MP Sydney Irving (known as the 'Franks Group' or 'Franks Committee') discussed the feasibility of a register of dependants coming from the Commonwealth – an idea that had been floated by Willie Whitelaw and others in the Conservative opposition. However, both the Home Office and the FCO opposed such a register, partially on economic grounds. In an internal briefing document from the FCO, in arguing against the proposed register the Migration and Visa Department stated that the 'cost of setting up and administering a Register would be substantial and possibly the money could be better spent on improving existing machinery'.[38] In a communication from Home Secretary Merlyn Rees to Prime Minister James Callaghan, Rees similarly argued against a register, stating that 'it would cost several million pounds which we could ill-afford to find'.[39] The cost of immigration control measures also became a point of contention when officials at High Commissions on the Indian subcontinent complained that effective (that is, strict) border controls required an increase in staffing yet the current budget did not allow for this.[40] Some have argued that the backlog in applications for entry clearances to the UK created by this under-staffing was an intentional aspect of the immigration control system, aimed at discouraging potential migrants from applying.[41] But at the same time (as will be discussed in Chapter 5) a number of Home Office and FCO officials were worried that the backlog would sour relationships with migrant communities in Britain and with their countries of origin, particularly the governments of India, Pakistan and Bangladesh.

The idea of a dependants register was seen by the Migration and Visa Department not only as a costly but also an impractical idea. The department doubted its usefulness, except as a popular response, as proved by the statement '[i]n the present state of public opinion it seems to be highly desirable to arrive at some figure to show the size of our commitment towards dependants'.[42] In an internal document Evan Luard wrote to Shirley Summerskill, Under-Secretary of State for Home Affairs, in June 1976 he explained that disclosing to the public a definite number of dependants accepted could be a reassuring tactic:

> It is, I believe, the uncertainty about the number of potential immigrants which, as much as anything, stimulates public apprehensions, and intensifies public clamour, on this subject. If we could obtain clear evidence that the commitment, at least in relation to direct dependants, was a definite and known dimension, and would be completely fulfilled within a certain number of years, that public feeling would without doubt be very relieved.[43]

Nevertheless, Luard also doubted the value of such a strategy insofar as the public might consider the actual number to be too large, exposing the government to criticism. In this regard, discretion could be the better tactic:

> Of course it remains the case that the total revealed by such a process might be larger than we hope, and larger than we

would like to admit to the public... it is arguable that the longer
uncertainty remains... the greater the strength of public feeling
which will arise and the more serious the political difficulties for
the Government.[44]

The tactic of obscuring the real number of dependants from public
view was embraced by Merlyn Rees in his advice to the Prime Minister
on the register of dependants, who, however, urged for the adoption
of an alternative scheme to announce for the upcoming elections:

> To set aside the register without showing good evidence of some
> kind of alternative Government response would be to invite
> renewed attacks on the scale of immigration and the adequacy
> of our control – *and this during a time of impending by-elections*.[45]
> (Emphasis in original)

Despite the reluctance of the government to create a register of
dependants or impose a cap on the number of dependants allowed
into Britain, these documents reveal that the government and those
in charge in the Home Office and the FCO were highly suspicious
of dependants from South Asia. This suspicion and the targeting
of those considered most likely to enter the country under false
pretences resulted in the discriminatory treatment by immigration
officials towards women and children from South Asia. This was
the result not only of lower-level staff indulging in inappropriate
behaviour, but also of a culture of discrimination and suspicion that
flowed from the highest levels of the administration.

Upper echelon of Home Office in determining categories

The belief that discriminatory practices were required to ensure the
efficient administration of immigration control was not confined to
the system's frontline staff, but was endemic throughout the system
and stemmed from directives issued (and racist assumptions held)
by the upper echelons of management. The CRE outlined this in a
document, *Proposal for a Formal Investigation of Immigration Control*,
drafted in 1979 after the virginity testing controversy broke (discussed in Chapter 3). The Proposal recommended an investigation

into whether certain nationalities and ethnicities were being unfairly targeted to detect suspected 'bogus' migrants. In particular, the CRE sought to investigate four general allegations concerning the regulation of migrants at the point of border control:

(i) that passengers from Pakistan, New Commonwealth countries and other 'third world' countries, whether in possession of prior entry clearance or not, are subjected to closer examination than passengers from developed countries;

(ii) that such passengers are significantly more likely to be refused leave to enter than passengers from developed countries;

(iii) that stricter conditions are placed on such passengers when admitted than are applied to passengers from developed countries; and

(iv) that such passengers are frequently subjected to unnecessary delays and various forms of demeaning treatment.[46]

Basing its initial investigation on previous reports produced by the Runnymede Trust (a non-government organisation dedicated to promoting 'good race relations' in Britain) and immigration lawyer Sarah Leigh, the CRE stated that: 'New Commonwealth, Pakistani and other "third world" passengers [are] particularly likely to be seeking to gain admission fraudulently or to be intending to breach the conditions on which they are admitted'.[47] As a consequence, the CRE stated, Immigration Officers 'regard[ed] it as their duty to be particularly alert in detecting ... evasions or attempted evasions of the control'.[48] This point was supported by the finding of a Runnymede Trust study that ECOs appeared to 'place little faith in the documentation', and thus 'documentary evidence was treated as a starting point for questioning rather than as evidence'.[49] This state of affairs was caused by the 'fabrication of documents and presentation of false documents by a few [and] inevitably brought all applicants under suspicion', as the 1978 Select Committee on Race Relations and Immigration explained in a document cited by the CRE.[50]

The CRE cited a study by the Runnymede Trust that concluded that 'refusal rates may be considerably higher than the true number of fraudulent or ineligible applications'.[51] The CRE, as well as the Runnymede Trust, also provided evidence indicating that migrants from Pakistan and the New Commonwealth countries were being subjected to closer scrutiny by ECOs and Immigration Officers than other migrants.[52] And such scrutiny was in part the result of parliamentary and extra-parliamentary pressure on 'bogus' migrants:

> the development of immigration legislation and the social and political context in which the 1971 Act was passed and public discussion of immigration ... may have led many ECOs and Immigration Officers to perceive it as their duty to go to special lengths to prevent 'evasion' of the controls by coloured people. On the other hand, the entry of whites, even by strictly illegal means, is not perceived as presenting the same 'dangers' and need not therefore be so tightly controlled.[53]

The CRE cited figures produced by Sarah Leigh from 1977 that proved that the filter at the border was producing the following results: Bangladesh (one refusal for every 30 migrants, or 1:30), India (1:40), Ghana (1:51), Pakistan (1:54) and Tanzania (1:89). She also produced data for white migrants, proving the immense difference in treatment: Canada (1:5953), Australia (1:3980) and New Zealand (1:3678). Further, no restrictions on entrance were placed on visitors from Canada, Australia, New Zealand and the USA, in contrast to the reception of visitors from the Commonwealth countries of the Indian subcontinent, Africa and Pakistan, who were admitted only with strict conditions placed upon their entry.[54]

Most importantly, decisions to over-scrutinise migrants from select countries were not being made at the individual level. Immigration officials acted under instruction from their superiors in the Home Office and the FCO, as records from the CRE's investigation prove. The CRE concluded that 'this practice is so common as to suggest that it is based on a standing instruction to Immigration Officers',[55] further stating that '[s]pecific instructions are known to be issued to ECOs' concerning the detection of 'bogus' migrants, but admitting that 'it is not known what instructions are given to Immigration Officers'.[56] However, the recently opened files of the Home Office at the National Archives have provided an example of such instructions taken from Immigration Service documentation from 1974, which confirm the claims made by the CRE in 1979. The 1974 document instructed officials to be on the look-out for a particular kind of 'bogus' migrant, stating:

> many Commonwealth citizens have evaded the immigration control by contravening their conditions of admission and remaining in the country after gaining entry in the guise of a visitor.[57]

And as a more specific example of the targeting of nationalities, another instruction that we located in the National Archives states:

> The majority of such attempted deceptions have involved the holders of Indian and Pakistani passports or persons of Indian or Pakistani origin holding United Kingdom passports.[58]

It is now a well-established fact that the over-policing of ethnic communities produces higher numbers of arrests and imprisonment of their members.[59] At the time, this phenomenon was less well understood, but clearly its application at the border was not uncommon. Over-policing is often conducted according to an assumption of guilt that requires pre-emptive action, even if guilt cannot be proven. The following instruction is an example of such:

> The Immigration Officer should be on his [sic] guard to ensure that persons from countries where there is pressure to emigrate do not obtain leave to enter as visitors when their real purpose is employment or settlement.[60]

However, one would question precisely *how* an Immigration Officer might be given to know when a person is lying about the reasons for their visit. Further, it is clear that instructions such as those shown above put pressure on Immigration Officers to produce results. Indeed, instructions from senior management of the Home Office set a tone, and established a mentality that was very often not questioned (and sometimes embraced wholeheartedly) by the lower ranks.

The directive that Immigration Officers should conduct more comprehensive checks of migrants 'from countries where there is pressure to emigrate' was further qualified by the Chief Immigration Officer B.A. Smith in a 1982 document titled 'Evasion of the Immigration Control'. In this document, Smith cited people from countries in the Indian subcontinent and other nationalities such as Turks, Palestinians, Algerians and South Americans as requiring extra attention. This document states that 'countries from which there is pressure to emigrate' refer directly to 'countries undergoing economic, social or political hardship', and that these countries were predominantly from 'the Indian sub-continent, West Africa, the Caribbean, the Levant and North Africa, South America and the Iberian peninsula'.[61]

Smith also explained that misleading applications from India, Pakistan and Bangladesh are the product of the 'system for recording births, marriages and deaths' in these countries, which is 'ineffective and patchy'.[62] However, rather than blaming the institutional disorganisation, there is a sense that the blame rests with individuals who exploit gaps in the system which offers 'ample scope [...] for fraudulent attempts at entry'.[63] Smith pointed the finger at Pakistan and Bangladesh as the main sources of forged or falsified documents: 'some nationalities, in particular Pakistanis and Bengalees [sic], attempt to enter as returning residents with passports bearing forged or falsified embarkation stamps'.[64] And further:

> Forgeries were first discovered in large numbers during the late 1950s and early 1960s in the hands of groups of Asians from the Indian sub-continent, and from 1967 a steady flow of Bengalees [sic] and Pakistanis seeking entry as either returning residents or dependants were refused admission holding falsified passports bearing substituted photographs or forged endorsements.[65]

In addressing the categories of migrants most suspected of false entry, Smith stated that 'the principal source of fraudulent applications for settlement entry clearances as dependants is the Indian sub-continent'.[66]

Designed to fail, designed to demoralise: The immigration 'queue' and the bureaucratic maze

In her 2010 article, Imogen Tyler argued that the British Nationality Act 1981 created categories of citizenship through which sections of the population (namely, nationals from the former colonies) were to be 'controlled and fashioned'. Tyler wrote that '[t]his Act instituted a "citizenship gap" within the British state...as large numbers of British nationals found they had been *designed out* of citizenship'.[67] She further claimed that this was 'not an accident or flawed design, but foundational...to British citizenship', and that since 1981, Britain's border control legislation has 'been *designed to fail* specific groups and populations' through its strict parameters.[68] However, we would argue that this was also the aim of earlier legislation, particularly the Immigration Act 1971, with the high threshold set for non-white migrants specifically designed to ensure applicants would fail to satisfy the conditions for entry clearance and would thus be rejected by the British authorities. The purpose of the immigration control system, as we have contended, was to maintain a divide between 'white' British society and the colonial 'other', and there was great pressure on immigration control staff to ensure that this divide was upheld. Therefore, where the Immigration Rules allowed for the possibility of successful entry into the UK, they also gave control staff a high level of discretionary power to determine whether or not an application was to be successful. With pressure to keep people out, the discretionary powers of immigration officials acted as a 'safety valve' for the British authorities to ensure that a certain cross-section of applicants *failed* or were demoralised by the system's bureaucratic maze.

Immigration Officers would generally base their decision over whether to question migrants further on an assessment of 'a passport, the answers to a couple of questions and a passenger's appearance and demeanour'.[69] This means that officers had significant discretionary powers to decide when to proceed and to assess a case in more detail. Inevitably, this suggests that internal instructions would be applied using a stereotyping system based on nationalities and ethnicities combined with the expectations of border officials regarding how a genuine traveller should look and behave. The overall initial screening was designed to create a second class of migrants, comprised of people from nations that were listed in broad economic terms as poor or socio-politically disadvantaged. However, it is also evident that at the base of this economic rating system were prejudices closely linked to the belief that some countries were the source of most fraudulent migration requests. In a document outlining statistics on 'illegal entrants and deportees', the Home Office suggested that only six nationalities accounted for 57 per cent of all illegal entrants detected and only seven nationalities accounted for over 55 per cent of all deportation orders.[70] Even if it is not clear how these statistics were collated, such data have been constantly referred to as evidence of a mistrust of the genuineness of travellers from certain nationalities. On this point, the Home Office stated that '[e]xperience of the categories of passengers from whom evasion has most commonly been detected in the past is bound to influence the immigration officer as to the passengers he [sic] selects for closer examination'.[71] Yet this screening was both superficial and ferocious in its intent.

Further, the pressure placed upon Immigration Officers to maintain the system should not be underestimated. Even if P.J. Woodfield argued in a letter to other Home Office officials that 'officials do not act like robots but take account of historical and background information which may indicate that more careful scrutiny is required of some cases than of others',[72] the pressure not to question instructions was palpable. And such pressure rose in line with the impression that Britain was increasingly becoming the ideal destination country for many disadvantaged people. The level of this pressure is evident in the concluding remarks of Chief Immigration Officer B.A. Smith in *Evasion of the Immigration Control*, in which he reminds his staff of the need to be ever vigilant:

> There is no reason to believe that the incidence of evasion will decrease to any marked extent, for while the pressure the emigrate for economic reasons from Third World countries remains, developed countries will continue to be subjected to determined efforts at settlement by unentitled potential immigrants. It follows therefore that the UK Immigration Service cannot afford to relax its vigilance, now or in the foreseeable future, if evasion is to be thwarted, and that a firm on and after entry control must be maintained.[73]

It is reasonable to believe that Smith, being in charge of the immigration portfolio, is passing on to his staff the instructions he has received from the higher echelons of the Home Office, as the following 1981 note below attests:

> The effect of immigration control properly operated is that a minority of passengers are likely to be questioned intensively or to be refused not because of their race, colour or religion but because they come from poor or unsettled countries or from areas where

there is much evidence of organised evasion of the immigration control.[74]

It is remarkable how economic rationality, statistical data and so-called practical experience are used as logical explanations for the creation of second-class migrants based on a discriminatory stereotyping system. And yet, internal documents reveal a level of awareness that, in order to be functional, the system had to be based on a degree of discrimination. The Home Office exposed itself by stating that the aim of immigration control was to 'discriminate between those who are qualified for admission and extension or variation of stay and those who are not'.[75] And that immigration system had an 'essentially discriminatory nature',[76] with the Home Office frustrated with the CRE for not accepting the basic facts: 'it is a well-known fact' that immigration laws 'discriminate on their face between nationalities' and 'a greater proportion of citizens of some countries fall foul of the control'.[77]

The burden of proof

One of the central criticisms of the bureaucratic maze created by the immigration control system was that the requirements of Immigration Officers and ECOs were difficult to satisfy and that applicants found it hard to provide enough evidence to 'prove' that they were 'genuine' migrants. In a memorandum submitted by the FCO to the Select Committee on Race Relations and Immigration in 1978, the standard of proof required by ECOs to issue entry clearances was that they were 'required to satisfy, *on the balance of probabilities* [emphasis added]...the bona fides of the applicant'.[78] This had been the 'official' stance since 1972, when Lord Chief Justice Widgery held that the Immigration Rules did not need to 'contemplate proof beyond dispute, or even proof beyond reasonable doubt'.[79] However, in its 1978 report *Appeal Dismissed*, the Runnymede Trust found that 'the standard of proof demanded was...*beyond reasonable doubt*', which was 'a standard of proof far beyond what is required by law'.[80]

After the release of a 1975 report by the Trust, Alex Lyon, then Minister for Immigration and Race Relations, and the FCO both stressed that the burden of proof required was 'on the balance of probabilities'. During a visit to South Asia, Lyon told ECOs that the Immigration Rules 'required them to accept the civil, not the criminal, standard of proof', explaining that this meant that 'they should decide cases on the broad possibilities and not try to satisfy themselves "beyond reasonable doubt" '.[81] An internal document outlining Lyon's visit bluntly stated, '[i]n effect, Mr Lyon advocated controlled lowering of the standard of proof of identity currently required by ECOs', noting that in Dacca and Islamabad 'ECOs still feel that they are likely to be swamped by hordes of applicants, many of whom are "unentitled" '.[82] In a response by the High Commission in Islamabad to the Runnymede Trust report, the Commission claimed that the 'balance of probabilities' was already the standard used, stating that '[n]o ECO expects to be fully satisfied, and no applicant is ever asked to prove his/her claim beyond reasonable doubt'.[83] A report on Evan Luard's visit to Pakistan in October 1976 complained that Lyon's directive on the 'balance of probabilities' had 'increased considerably' the rate at which applicants were being processed.[84]

By 1978, the Home Office, while affirming (in principle) that 'in immigration cases the standard of proof is the balance of probabilities', argued that '[t]he fact remains... that the burden of proof is on the applicant to satisfy the ECO of the genuineness of his [sic] claim'.[85] As many critics pointed out, including the CRE in its 1985 report, reliance on the discretion of the ECO or Immigration Officer to be 'satisfied' of an applicant's genuineness was fraught with problems caused by subjectivity. A submission to the CRE by the Haldane Society of Socialist Lawyers contended that 'many of the Immigration Rules are not in hard and fast terms but vest considerable discretion in an Immigration or Entry Clearance Officer', and thus the requirement that documents needed to 'produce satisfaction... is frequently a question of impression and subjective response'.[86]

As this chapter has shown, border control practices are predominantly grounded in the assumption that migrants from less desirable socio-cultural and economic backgrounds who seek to enter Britain are attempting to evade or deceive the system. Historically (and still in common occurrence today),[87] the default assumption underpinning the border control system was that certain migrant groups were not who they claimed to be when interacting with immigration officials. We have demonstrated that there has been a longstanding belief amongst immigration officials that South Asian migrants are unreliable in their entry clearance interviews and consequently the authorities have maintained a deep suspicion that documentary evidence provided by these migrants is likely to be fake. ECOs were supposed to weigh up their decisions 'on the balance of probabilities', but it was often the case that staff began from a point of total mistrust and shifted the burden of proof onto the person applying to enter the country. With this burden of proof placed upon the individual, it was frequently difficult to persuade the authorities that their reasons for seeking entry were genuine – a problem exacerbated by the presumption that testimony and documentary evidence provided by certain migrant groups was likely to be false. Under the intense scrutiny of the border control authorities, if testimony and documents were not considered to be adequately convincing, the focus of the authorities shifted to physical examination, with the body becoming the marker of 'truth'. As Didier Fassin and Estelle d'Hallunin wrote about refugees in the French border control system, 'their word is systematically doubted [and] it is their bodies that are questioned'.[88] Unlike Foucault's concept of torture, whereby the physical body is manipulated to extract the confession of 'truth' and the 'truth' is uttered or written by the tortured individual,[89] in the context under examination here the body becomes a text that is 'read' by the authorities, and the 'truth' is thus determined by those who 'read' it. In this process, the body reveals what the authorities want to see.

The medical examination of immigrants

The ways in which the physical body was to be examined within the British immigration system were codified in the various pieces of immigration control legislation and the internal instructions for immigration control staff and medical examiners circulated by the Home Office and the FCO. Officially, the primary purpose of the medical examinations to be conducted upon arriving migrants was to detect any health issues that might threaten the domestic population (and the migrant themselves), but this rationale was often used to disqualify 'undesirable' applicants and to extract further information from applicants (which could then be used to interrogate their claims if deemed unreliable). The ways in which this occurred are explored in more detail in chapters 3 and 4.

The requirement that Commonwealth migrants be subjected to a medical examination was enshrined in the Commonwealth

Immigrants Act 1962. The power to refuse entry on medical grounds after such an examination was outlined in the Act as follows:

> 2 (4) Nothing in subsection (3) of this section shall prevent an immigration officer from refusing admission into the United Kingdom in the case of any Commonwealth citizen to whom section one of this Act applies –
>
> (a) if it appears to the immigration officer on the advice of a medical inspector or, if no such inspector is available, of any other duly qualified medical practitioner, that he [sic] is a person suffering from mental disorder, or that it is otherwise undesirable for medical reasons that he [sic] should be admitted.

However, the full parameters of the medical examination and its purpose in the immigration control system were only outlined in internal documents. Instructions given to Medical Inspectors in 1967 detailed six categories of Commonwealth migrants that could be referred to a Medical Inspector:

> (a) holders of Ministry of Labour vouchers *and their dependants* (emphasis in the original text);
>
> (b) other Commonwealth citizens intending to make their home in this country or to remain for more than six months;
>
> (c) any immigrant appearing to ... be mentally or physically abnormal or both;
>
> (d) any immigrant appearing ... not to be in good health;
>
> (e) any immigrant appearing to be bodily dirty;
>
> (f) any immigrant in regard to whom there is any mention of health as a reason for his visit.[90]

The medical examination posed a bureaucratic hurdle for most Commonwealth migrants entering during the 1960s, as they entered on work vouchers that depended on a clean bill of health; but the fact that dependent wives and children were also subjected to these examinations demonstrates the 'desire for order' of the immigration control system. The Home Office acknowledged that the 'power to refuse on medical grounds does not apply to persons entitled

to admission as wives...or children under 16', but their referral to
Medical Inspectors reinforced notions that migrants from the former
colonies needed to be inspected to ascertain their physical 'worthiness' and that they needed to be screened as harbingers of disease.
The FCO's argument was that, although dependants could not be
refused entry for medical reasons:

> it is in their interests to be medically examined before leaving
> home, since if they require medical treatment, the medical report
> they bring with them will enable the British authorities to ensure
> that they receive such treatment as soon as possible after arriving
> in this country.[91]

We would argue that it was in the interests of the British state to
encourage those who did not technically require a medical examination to submit to one as this presented another administrative
obstacle for the applicant, and could be used as an impetus for the
authorities to find another official reason to deny them entry. FCO
advice released in 1969 reiterated that dependants could be refused
entry on medical grounds, but if an examination voluntarily submitted to 'reveals that the dependant will need treatment in the United
Kingdom', the FCO stated that 'a condition on admission may be
imposed'.[92]

The same advice called for pregnancy to be noted by Medical Referees and treatment recommended for the migrant in the UK, but
nowhere does the advice mention that Medical Referees needed to
examine migrant women for previous sexual activity or for children
already born. The purpose of the medical examinations was to identify those migrants who had a disease (such as tuberculosis) that
could threaten the health of the wider British community or a condition that would require significant medical treatment in the UK. But
as a letter from the Department of Employment and Productivity to
the Department of Health and Social Security, written in 1969, admitted, '[p]regnancy can hardly be described as an "undesirable medical
condition"'.

The powers of Immigration Officers to refer migrants to a Medical
Inspector and to refuse entry on medical grounds were made more
explicit in the Immigration Act 1971. Schedule 2 of the Act simply
stated:

(2) Any such person, if he [sic] is seeking to enter the United Kingdom, may be examined also by a medical inspector or by any qualified person carrying out a test or examination required by a medical inspector.

The Immigration Rules concerning medical examinations put forward that the 'general aim' of such examinations was 'to enable [the] Immigration Officer to refuse entry to persons having a serious illness which might endanger the health of others' or 'persons suffering from a mental disorder or some serious condition which would prevent them from supporting themselves and their dependants'.[93] However, as will become evident in the next two chapters, medical examinations were used to discredit the claims made by potential migrants and to intensify the scrutiny placed upon them. The scrutinising gaze of the immigration control system was thus cast upon the physical body as a marker of 'truth' when other forms of evidence (such as oral testimony and written documents offered by the applicants) were considered to be unsatisfactory.

Conclusion

In this chapter, we have argued that the British border control system has historically functioned as a tool to maintain the divide between 'white' British society and the colonial 'other' in the post-imperial era. The system is preoccupied with the concept of 'control' and is used to impose upon the potential migrant the dominance of the British nation-state over the rights of the individual, which represents a replication of the colonial relationships of the past between the coloniser and the colonised. As the immigration control system was strengthened in the 1960s and 1970s, the British authorities deemed that there were certain categories of migrant that could be considered potential violators of the system; and after the introduction of the Immigration Act in 1971, the most targeted group became dependants (primarily women and children) from the Indian subcontinent. As the largest group migrating to Britain in the 1970s, these people came under increasingly intense scrutiny and had to undergo a long process to verify their identity and worthiness of entry to Britain. This scrutiny was combined with the racist assumption that people from South Asia were more likely to be involved in acts of deception and attempts to evade the immigration control system. In particular, the ECOs who worked in the British High Commissions in India, Pakistan and Bangladesh claimed that the testimony and documentation of those applying for entry were often suspect and unverifiable. In practice, therefore, the burden of proof fell upon the applicant to demonstrate *beyond reasonable doubt* that they were indeed who they said they were and that their reason for entering the country was legitimate and real. As the testimony and documents of these potential migrants were not to be trusted, the authorities appeared to believe that the only way they could 'verify' an applicant's story was to inspect their physical body. Thus, in the 1970s, the medical examination became one of the preferred means of verifying the 'truth', with the most explicit examples of this being the practice of virginity testing on South Asian women between 1968 and 1979 and the use of X-rays for age assessment purposes conducted throughout the 1970s until 1982. These practices will be explored in depth in the next two chapters.

Notes

1. For example, see M. Bosworth, 'Border Control and the Limits of the Sovereign State', *Social and Legal Studies*, 17/2, 2008, pp. 199–215; A. Hall, ' "These People Could Be Anyone": Fear, Contempt (and Empathy) in a British Immigration Removal Centre', *Journal of Ethnic and Migration Studies*, 36/6, 2010, pp. 881–898.
2. See Commission for Racial Equality, *Immigration Control Procedures: Report of a Formal Investigation* (London: CRE, 1985); K. Woodfield, et al., *Exploring the Decision Making of Immigration Officers: A Research Study Examining Non-EEA Passenger Stops and Refusals at UK Ports* (London: National Centre for Social Research/Home Office, 2008).
3. S. Zimmermann, 'Reconsidering the Problem of "Bogus" Refugees with "Socio-economic Motivations" for Seeking Asylum', *Mobilities*, 6/3, 2011, pp. 335–352; D. Bögner, C. Brewin, and J. Herlihy, 'Refugees' Experiences of Home Office Interviews: A Qualitative Study on the Disclosure of Sensitive Personal Information', *Journal of Ethnic and Migration Studies*, 36/3, 2010, pp. 519–535.
4. John Solomos, *Black Youth, Racism and the State: The Politics of Ideology and Policy* (Cambridge: Cambridge University Press, 1988) p. 41.
5. Roxanne Lynn Doty, *Anti-Immigrantism in Western Democracies: Statecraft, Desire, and the Politics of Exclusion* (London: Routledge, 2003) p. 14.
6. Roxanne Lynn Doty, 'Racism, Desire, and the Politics of Immigration,' *Millennium: Journal of International Studies*, 28/3, 1999, p. 591.

7. Gilles Deleuze and Claire Parnet, *Dialogues* (New York: Continuum, 1987) p. 129.
8. Benjamin Fitz-Gibbon, *Imperial Endgame: Britain's Dirty Wars and the End of Empire* (Houndmills: Palgrave Macmillan, 2011) p. 1.
9. Fitz-Gibbon, *Imperial Endgame*, p. 3.
10. Ibid., p. 2.
11. Doty, *Anti-Immigrantism in Western Democracies*.
12. Gilles Deleuze and Felix Guattari, *Anti-Oedipus: Capitalism and Schizophrenia* (London: Continuum, 2004) pp. 242–260.
13. Teresa Hayter, 'Open Borders: The Case Against Immigration Controls,' *Capital & Class*, 75, 2001, p. 150.
14. See Paul Gilroy, *After Empire: Melancholia or Convivial Culture* (London: Routledge, 2004).
15. Ibid., p. 111.
16. E.J.B. Rose, et al., *Colour and Citizenship: A Report on British Race Relations* (Oxford: Oxford University Press, 1969) p. 229.
17. Melissa Autumn White, 'Transnational and Intimate Crossings: The "Threatening Body" of the Migrant Sex-Worker', *Reconstructions*, 7/1, 2007, http://reconstruction.eserver.org/071/white.shtml
18. See Giorgio Agamben, *State of Exception* (Chicago: University of Chicago Press, 2005).
19. Ibid., p. 50.
20. Ian Martin, *Entry Certificate Delays in Dacca: Report of a Visit to Bangladesh December 1974–January 1975* (London, 1975) 5, FCO 50/537, National Archives, London (hereafter NA).
21. Giorgio Agamben, *Homo Sacer: Sovereign Power and Bare Life* (Stanford, CA: Stanford University Press, 1998) p. 9.
22. See Joshi and Carter, 1984, 53–70; Sagger, 1995; Kathleen Paul, *Whitewashing Britain: Race and Citizenship in the Postwar Era* (Ithaca: Cornell University Press, 1997) pp. 131–169.
23. Frank Soskice corrected Fisher's claim that the rate of evasion was 5000 a year and that most of the offenders were students, stating that the actual numbers were '[b]etween 9,000 and 10,000 in 1964 and about 900 in 1963' and that '[t]hey were not all students'. (*Hansard*, 23 March 1965, col. 388).
24. *Hansard*, 23 March 1965 col. 388; col. 412.
25. See *Hansard*, 4 February 1965, col. 1284–1288; 9 March 1965, col. 248–258; 23 March 1965, col. 334–453; UK Government, 1965, Immigration from the Commonwealth, Cmnd. 2739, HMSO, London.
26. Immigration Act 1971, Part III, 26 [1].
27. K. Couper, and U. Santamaria, 1984, 'An Elusive Concept: The Changing Definition of Illegal Immigrant in the Practice of Immigration Control in the United Kingdom', *International Migration Review*, 18/3, Autumn, p. 441.
28. Select Committee on Race Relations and Immigration, 1978a, *Immigration, Vol. I: Report with Annexes and Minutes of Proceedings* (London: HMSO) p. xxvi.

29. See Miles and Phizacklea, 1984, pp. 79–117, 118–135; Hiro, 1992, pp. 246–260; Winder, 2006, pp. 400–419.
30. Stuart Hall et al., *Policing the Crisis: Mugging, the State and Law and Order* (London: Palgrave Macmillan, 1979) p. 333.
31. Numerous scholars, journalists and activists have detailed the tightly constructed and interconnected web of agencies employed by the British Government to prevent, detect and apprehend 'illegal immigrants'. Alongside Couper and Santamaria (1984) and Andrew Nicol, 1981, *Illegal Entrants*, Runnymede Trust/Joint Council for the Welfare of Immigrants, London, see Gideon Ben-Tovim and John Gabriel, 'The Politics of Race in Britain 1962–1979', in Charles Husband (ed.), *Race in Britain* (London: Hutchinson, 1982) p. 146; Gilroy, 1982, 'The Myth of Black Criminality', *Socialist Register,* 49 Sivanandan, 1982, pp. 29–30.
32. Gilroy, 'The Myth of Black Criminality', p. 47; Nicol, *Illegal Entrants*, p. 5; p. 42; Couper and Santamaria, 'An Elusive Concept', p. 442.
33. UK Parliament, 1973, *Hansard Parliamentary Debates (House of Commons),* 857, 12 June, col. 1212.
34. Brief for Evan Luard, 'No. 12: Race Relations in Britain,' 1976, FCO 37/1784, NA.
35. Nicol, *Illegal Entrants*, p. 5, cited in Couper and Santamaria, 'An Elusive Concept', p. 437.
36. Select Committee on Race Relations and Immigration, 1978b, *Immigration, Vol. II: Evidence and Appendices* (HMSO: London) p. 315.
37. Select Committee on Race Relations and Immigration, 1978a, *Immigration, Vol. I: Report with Annexes and Minutes of Proceedings* (HMSO, London) pp. xxvi–xxvii. Students, on the other hand, were amongst the most likely to overstay their visa. The focus of the present discussion is on the first two definitions of immigration evasion as defined by the Select Committee, namely, those immigrants who produced false or forged documents or entered under false pretences at border control stations. Students who overstay are not considered as they are not the primary focus of this chapter.
38. Migration and Visa Department, 'Immigration: Proposal for the Preparation of a Register of Dependants', 29 July 1976, 3, FCO 50/586, NA.
39. Communication from Merlyn Rees to the Prime Minister, 31 December 1976, FCO 50/586, NA.
40. H.C. Byatt and J.R.H. Evans, 'Report on British High Commission, New Delhi: Section 6 Consular and Immigration Work', March 1975, 6–7, FCO 50/130, NA; Letter from B.G. Smallman to D.F. Hawley, 2 September 1975, 2, FCO 50/524, NA; 'Visit to Bangladesh of Mr D F Hawley, Immigration', 19 November, 1975, 5, FCO 50/537, NA.
41. See Mohammed Akram and Jan Elliot, *Appeal Dismissed: The Final Report of the Investigation into Immigration Control Procedures in the Indian Sub-Continent* (London: Runnymede Trust, 1977).
42. Migration and Visa Department, 'Immigration,' p. 3.
43. Letter from Evan Luard to Shirley Summerskill, 23 June 1976, FCO 50/586, NA.

44. Ibid.
45. Communication from Merlyn Rees to the Prime Minister.
46. CRE, 'Proposal for a Formal Investigation of Immigration Control', 23 March 1979, pp. xvii–xviii, HO 418/29, NA.
47. Ibid., p. xviii.
48. Ibid.
49. Ibid., p. xviii.
50. Ibid., p. viii.
51. Ibid., p. ix.
52. Ibid., p. xxvi.
53. Ibid.
54. Ibid., pp. xviii–xix.
55. Ibid.
56. Ibid., p. xxviii.
57. Immigration Service, 1974a, 'A Review of the Charter Flight Procedure: Appendix H – Instructions to ECOs', p. 135, HO 418/40 338797, NA.
58. Immigration Service, 1974c, 'A Review of the Charter Flight Procedure: Appendix J – Instructions to IOs', p.6.3.7, HO 418/40, NA.
59. See Simon Holdaway, *The Racialisation of British Policing* (Houndmills: Macmillan, 1996) pp. 72–104; Ben Bowling, Alma Parmar and Coretta Phillips, 'Policing Ethnic Minority Communities', in Tim Newburn (ed.), *Handbook of Policing* (Devon, UK: Willan Publishing, 2003) pp. 528–555.
60. Immigration Service, 1974b, 'A Review of the Charter Flight Procedure: Appendix I – Instructions to IOs', p. 12.2.2, HO 418/40, NA.
61. B.A. Smith, 1982, 'Evasion of the Immigration Control', p. 2, HO 418/40, NA.
62. Smith, 'Evasion of the Immigration Control', p. 3.
63. Ibid.
64. Ibid., p. 7.
65. Ibid., p. 9.
66. Ibid., p. 3.
67. Imogen Tyler, 'Designed to Fail: A Biopolitics of British Citizenship', *Citizenship Studies*, 14/1, February 2010, p. 62; emphasis in original.
68. Tyler, 'Designed to Fail', pp. 61–62; emphasis in original.
69. Home Office, 1981, 'Discrimination in the Immigration Control', HO 418/40, p. 4, NA.
70. Home Office, 1983, 'Review of Immigration Control Procedures', HO 418/40, p. 10, NA.
71. Home Office, 'Review of Immigration Control Procedures', p. 6.
72. P. Woodfield, 1981, Letter to Miss Kippax & Mr. Boys Smith, 20 March, HO 418/40.
73. Smith, 'Evasion of the Immigration Control', p. 16.
74. Home Office, 'Discrimination in the Immigration Control', p. 7.
75. Ibid., p. 1.
76. P. Woodfield, 1981, Letter to Miss Kippax & Mr. Boys Smith.
77. Letter to Mr. Woodfield from D. Hilary, 9 March, 1981, HO 418/40.

78. Foreign and Commonwealth Office, 1978, Memorandum submitted to Select Committee on Race Relations and Immigration, 1978b, *Immigration, Vol. II*.
79. *Regina v Home Secretary ex parte Hussain* (Divisional Court 1972), cited in Mohammed Akram and Jan Elliot, *Appeal Dismissed: The Final Report of the Investigation into Immigration Control Procedures in the Indian Sub-Continent* (London: Runnymede Trust, 1977) p. 22.
80. Akram and Elliot, *Appeal Dismissed*, 23. Italics in original.
81. C.P. Scott, 'Immigration: Visit of Mr. Alexander Lyon MP, Minister of State at the Home Office, to Immigration Offices in Bangladesh, India and Pakistan, 27 December 1974 to 12 January 1975', 17 January 1975, p. 4, FCO 50/522, NA.
82. Scott, 'Immigration', p. 5.
83. Letter from B.D. Gately to F. Hensby, 21 February 1975, FCO 50/535, NA.
84. 'Visit of Mr Luard to Pakistan', n.d., p. 2, FCO 50/570, NA.
85. Letter from Brynmor John to Usha Prashar, 1 September 1978.
86. Haldane Society of Socialist Lawyers, 'Evidence Submitted by the Haldane Society of Socialist Lawyers to the Enquiry of the Commission of Racial Equality into Discrimination in the Immigration Service', n.d., pp. 6–7, RC/RF/1/01/B, Runnymede Trust archives, BCA.
87. Zimmermann, 'Reconsidering the Problem of "Bogus" Refugees'; D. Bögner, C. Brewin, and J. Herlihy, 'Refugees' Experiences of Home Office Interviews: A Qualitative Study on the Disclosure of Sensitive Personal Information', *Journal of Ethnic and Migration Studies*, 36/3, 2010, pp. 519–535.
88. D. Fassin and E. d'Halluin, 'The Truth from the Body: Medical Certificates as Ultimate Evidence for Asylum Seekers', *American Anthropologist*, 107/4, 2005, p. 598.
89. See Michel Foucault, *Discipline and Punish: The Birth of the Prison* (London: Penguin Books, 1991) pp. 35–42; Michel Foucault, *The History of Sexuality, Vol. 1* (London: Penguin Books, 2008) pp. 58–61.
90. 'Instructions to Medical Inspectors', n.d., FCO 50/132, NA.
91. 'Medical Examination Overseas of Commonwealth Citizens Coming to the United Kingdom', n.d., p. 2, FCO 50/132, NA.
92. 'Advice to Medical Referees', n.d., pp. 102, FCO 50/284, NA.
93. 'Instructions to Medical Inspectors', p. 1, RCRF/1/08, Runnymede trust archives, BCA.

3
Reorienting the South Asian Female Body: The Practice of Virginity Testing and the Treatment of Migrant Women

Through a February 1979 report in *The Guardian*, it became public knowledge that a number of women had been given gynaecological examinations by immigration control staff in the UK and at British High Commissions in South Asia, in a practice colloquially known as virginity testing. This chapter examines the culture of racism and sexism within the British immigration control system that allowed these 'virginity tests' to occur, and why South Asian women attempting to enter the country on temporary fiancée visas were subjected to these tests from the late 1960s and throughout the 1970s. This abusive practice must be seen in the context of the overall highly discriminatory treatment of migrant women coming from the Indian subcontinent evident from the late 1960s to the early 1980s.

It is our argument that the practice of virginity testing reflected deep-seated racist and sexist assumptions held by the British authorities, which replicated the attitudes that had been established in the colonial era. Pratibha Parmar argued in 1982 that the racist and sexist assumptions behind virginity testing were based on the 'stereotype of the submissive, meek and tradition-bound Asian woman'.[1] We propose that this stereotype was an ideological hangover from the Victorian era and that commonly held beliefs about South Asian women and sexuality were influenced by the attitudes of the British authorities formed in colonial India. Philippa Levine, who has written much on sexuality and the British Empire, made this link in a 2006 book chapter, writing:

> Women arriving as fiancées of South Asian men already in Britain were the targets of this [virginity testing] practice which rested on a slew of assumptions about gender and sexuality that we can trace back with little effort to colonial days.... [I]t points...and in vivid manner, to how ideas and assumptions about colonial sexuality found expression in Britain. Examples such as this not only demonstrate the effects of the colonial past within Britain, but also reveal just how central a role sexuality has played in shaping that complex legacy.[2]

The perception of the South Asian woman in the colonial era is the subject of a massive body of academic literature and it is not the purpose of this chapter to explore this literature in any depth. But the following section, which draws on the work of postcolonial feminist historians such as Antoinette Burton, Philippa Levine, Lata Mani and Angela Woollacott (amongst others), outlines the historiography to show how the idea of the submissive and meek South Asian woman was constructed.

Colonial use of the Indian subcontinent female body

Contact between the British and the people of the Indian subcontinent first occurred in the days of Queen Elizabeth I, when in 1599 the British East India Company was granted róyal permission to trade in the South Asian region. Until the Indian Mutiny of 1857, the East India Company remained the largest British presence in India – what K.N. Chaudhuri called 'a state within a state'[3] – although from the early 1800s, ever more administrative and legal powers were established by the British Crown. The convergence of trade and political interests in India, first initiated by the East India Company and then later by the British government, was not Britain's first foray into imperialism and engagement with indigenous populations (as the British had built a large trade in slavery and plantations between West Africa and the Americas by the 1700s), but contact with South Asia significantly reshaped British ideas of 'race' and European identity – what Edward Said called

'Orientalism'. This notion of 'Orientalism', Said wrote, fostered the idea that 'European identity [was] a superior one in comparison with all the non-European peoples and cultures' and established a 'flexible *positional* superiority, which [put] the Westerner in a whole series of possible relationships with the Orient without ever losing him [sic] the relative upper hand'.[4] As Said further explained, '[t]he scientist, the scholar, the missionary, the trader, or the soldier was in, or thought about, the Orient because he *could be there*, or could think about it, with very little resistance on the Orient's part'.[5] The presence of the British in India and the orientalist idea of European superiority produced a set of beliefs and assumptions about race and sex in the Indian subcontinent that were complex and pervasive, and developed from the 1600s until Indian independence in 1947, and, as Levine has put, continued to influence British thinking about South Asian men and women in the postcolonial era.

The idea of the submissive South Asian woman was widespread amongst the British in India. Antoinette Burton has written extensively about the concept of the 'Indian woman', who was seen by the British as 'a helpless, degraded victim of religious custom and uncivilized practices',[6] and this concept was used by various groups of British colonialists to justify their agendas for the local population. Missionaries, who came to the subcontinent in large numbers during the late 1700s, drew upon the idea of the downtrodden Indian woman to 'civilise' the local population through education and conversion to Christianity, whereby women were to be educated to a level (such as basic numeracy and literacy) that allowed them to manage the tasks of the household, based on British middle-class notions of domesticity. In the early 1800s, missionaries also implored the British authorities to prevent other abuses of women, such as widow burning (*sati*) and child marriage, which were cited by the British authorities as evidence of the barbaric and uncivilised nature of the Indian population. The 'seclusion of Indian women' was, argued Meredith Borthwick, used by the British to explain why they could not 'mix with Indians on equal terms' and to demonstrate the alleged inherent superiority of Western values over Eastern.[7] Lata Mani has described how the construction of the Indian woman as 'pure, weak and submissive' and the perceived status of women in Indian society were used to reinforce the moral necessity for colonial rule, and these women became objects of struggle between the British and indigenous male elites:

> In this process, women came to represent 'tradition' for all partici-
> pants: whether viewed as the weak, deluded creatures who must be
> reformed through legislation and education, or the valiant keepers
> of tradition who must be protected from statutory interventions
> and be permitted only certain kinds of instruction.... For all par-
> ticipants in nineteenth-century debates on social reform, women
> represent embarrassment or potential. And given the discursive
> construction of women as either abject victims or heroines, they
> frequently represent both shame *and* promise.[8]

Burton shows how this struggle was furthered by the imperial feminists who came to India in the late 1800s to 'save' the 'Indian
woman' as she was perceived by white, middle-class women in the
imperial metropole. The 'Indian Woman', Burton wrote, 'was "the
discourse terrain, the playing fields" on which Indian men and
British feminist women each imagined their own liberation'.[9] Within
these discourses, 'Indian women were rarely if ever featured as capa-
ble of self-representation' and were portrayed as either 'guarantors
of traditional values' or 'as security for the imperial status quo in
Western feminist rhetoric'.[10] Spivak has characterised this debate
as 'the dialectically interlocking sentences that are constructible as
"White men are saving brown women from brown men" and "The
woman wanted to die" ', but shows that the South Asian (or 'subal-
tern') woman was rendered silent in this debate.[11] Mani reiterates this
point by stating that 'the representation of women as victims discur-
sively positions women as objects to be saved – never as subjects who
act, even if within overdetermined and restricted conditions'.[12] The
'Indian woman' was thus perceived by all as an object to be used to
critique either traditional Indian society or the supposed superiority
of British colonialism, but within these critiques, both sides had 'constructed the Indian woman not as someone who acts, but as someone
to be acted upon'.[13]

The idea of the submissive South Asian woman was widespread
across most sections of the British colonial system in India. Under the
rule of the East India Company, the three main categories of British
persons in India were traders, soldiers and missionaries, with the

majority of the administrative work undertaken by the local Indian population. These three groups had somewhat differing, but over-lapping, ideas about the local Indian population, and a focus of this book is to identify how these groups influenced colonial ideas about South Asian women. In his work *Empire and Sexuality*, Ronald Hyam suggested that when the East India Company was more powerful, in the late 1700s and early 1800s, relationships (sometimes involv-ing marriage, but also de facto arrangements) between British men, such as traders, merchants and some soldiers, and Indian women were quite commonplace, calling such relationships an 'opportu-nity' to marry a docile wife. While a significant number of South Asian women entered into relationships with British men, Angela Woollacott has warned against viewing these relationships as neces-sarily voluntary and equal, stating that, as they were probably based on coercion at some level, these partnerships were not the 'idyllic and stable situation' that Hyam supposes.[14] South Asian women were desired in these relationships because they were deemed to be sub-missive and obedient to men in social terms, but, paradoxically, also less inhibited sexually.

However, Hyam notes that after the British Crown took full con-trol of the Indian colony in the early 1860s, 'it became increasingly shameful for an officer, civil or military, to live in a state which had been normal in previous generations' – a relationship between white British men and non-white South Asian women.[15] As more British women came to India to join their husbands, the authorities believed that the previous sexual relationships between British men and Indian women should cease (although in practice this was not the case). As Kenneth Ballhatchet wrote, '[t]he official elite ... were sup-posed to shun Indian mistresses and content themselves with British wives'.[16] Similar to the other European colonial societies in Asia at the time, relationships between white men and non-white women were disapproved of. As Anne McClintock has written, 'increasingly vigi-lant administrative measures were taken against open or ambiguous domestic relations, against concubinage, against mestizo customs' across the Asian colonies of the British, French and Dutch.[17] The British favoured white women coming out to the colonies to marry the British men who resided there and were of the view that the 'proper' relationship between men and women in the indigenous population was a heterosexual, monogamous marriage, based on the

Western notion of marriage. The only British men 'allowed' to have sexual relationships with South Asian women were soldiers, and these relationships were only to be carried out in the confines of regulated prostitution, through which the South Asian woman had a specific role to play and was of a particular use to the British male.

The migration of British wives to the Indian colony impacted upon ideas of race and sex, particularly in regard to South Asian men. Levine claims that while relationships between British men and indigenous women could be conveyed as a symbol of 'colonial conquest', '[r]elations between white women and men of colour were always regarded with greater unease', were 'signalled as deviant and disorderly', and seen by the authorities as a 'danger to the colonial state and to white men's supremacy'.[18] The colonisers portrayed the European woman's 'supposed vulnerability' in the colonial world, 'position[ing] white men as the guardians of their women who could and would contain non-white men with their primitive and lustful behaviour'.[19] British women in India were designated their own space away from the indigenous population, with their 'familiar white enclaves' preventing contact between white women and Indians, outside domestic servants and some limited charity work.[20] Hyam argues that the reason for this isolation was the 'sexual fear of the supposed lascivious Indian [man]'.[21] This view of the South Asian male as sexual deviant remained dominant throughout the 20th century, with myths in the 1950s and 1960s of South Asian men luring white women into sex, drugs and prostitution (similar myths were circulated in regard to African-Caribbean men). For example, a 1974 criminology paper argued that South Asian men in the UK were more likely to be involved in sexual offences than the white population[22] – a finding that was then cited by the Runnymede Trust as a reason to encourage South Asian women to join their male counterparts in the UK.[23]

The issue of sexual relations between British soldiers and Asian women was particularly fraught for the British authorities in India and has been the subject of much study. As several scholars, including Kenneth Ballhatchet, Ronald Hyam and Philippa Levine, have argued, the British authorities were very concerned about maintaining the masculinity of the soldiers and thwarting homosexual activities. At the same time, the authorities disapproved of soldiers forming relationships with the indigenous women of the Indian subcontinent. A Royal Commission on the Sanitary State of the Army in India, conducted in the early 1860s, proposed that the solution to this 'problem' was to encourage more British women to make their way out to India to marry soldiers, but asked 'where were wives to be found for successive relays of 70,000 men'.[24] In the short term, the British authorities, particularly those in the Army, condoned the use of prostitutes, predominantly Indian women from lower castes, by British soldiers to 'regulate' their sexual desires. In this context, miscegenation was allowed, but only for a particular purpose, such that the body of the South Asian woman was required to meet the needs of the British male, while other forms of sexual relations between the two groups were actively discouraged. These prostitutes were 'seen as playing a positive role' in 'satisfying the soldiers' masculine needs' and maintaining the 'manliness' of the Army.[25] But this was only if the prostitutes were considered 'healthy' and free of venereal disease, and Ballhatchet has argued that the prostitutes were also seen as 'threatening soldiers with diseases which might destroy their manhood'.[26] This concern about the spread of venereal disease led the British authorities to intervene physically with the South Asian woman's body in a manner that is reminiscent of the virginity testing carried out a 100 years later.

Motivated by a desire to 'protect' the Army against venereal disease but not wanting to subject enlisted men to compulsory examination, the British government introduced the Contagious Diseases Act 1864 to stop the spread of venereal disease in India. This Act focused predominantly on regulating the female body based on 'a set of moral and ideological assumptions' that prostitutes were responsible for these diseases and were so 'bereft of "self-respect"' that they could not protest against forcible examinations.[27] The Act applied to prostitutes (and sometimes other lower-class women) in the garrison port towns across southern England and Ireland, primarily Southampton and Portsmouth. It allowed for the authorities to request that a woman be examined for venereal disease, and if the woman did not 'submit herself voluntarily for Examination', she could be found guilty of a summary offence and detained for a month for a first offence, and up to two months for subsequent offences.[28] If it were 'ascertained that such [a] Woman has a Contagious Disease', the authorities could detain the woman in hospital for medical treatment for up to three months.[29] Amendments were made to the Act in 1866 and 1869, before it was abolished in 1886 due to its apparent ineffectiveness and in response to significant campaigning by Victorian feminists. Philippa Levine, along with other scholars, has demonstrated that this Act became the model for similar legislation across the British Empire.

Ballhatchet has written that, before the Indian version of the Act was introduced in 1868, 'weekly medical inspections [of prostitutes] were already held' in cantonments in India, but at the time technically 'women could not be "forcibly subjected to personal examination", nor did the military authorities have the power to expel them'.[30] It is important to insert the word 'technically' here because Ballhatchet does quote a surgeon in Secunderabad in 1855 as writing: 'Thus these poor creatures are, by a salutary amount of coercion, for their own benefit, as well as to prevent extension of disease to others, compelled to subject themselves to care and treatment.'[31] When the Act came into effect in the late 1860s, the authorities used it, through a forcible gynaecological examination, to identify women who were accessible and therefore 'desirable'. The Act crystallised the role the South Asian woman-cum-prostitute played within the cantonments, but also signalled that she had to be deserving, albeit free of venereal disease, to perform such role. Thus, it was seen that the only way to maintain what Anne McClintock has called 'the health and wealth of the male imperial body politic' was to ensure the 'sexual purity' of the South Asian woman.[32] Yet the speculum came to be seen by many oppositionists to the Act as an 'instrument of rape'[33] and these examinations as a totally unnecessary procedure forced upon women to reinstate the moral values of Victorian society. Nicole McManus has written that the prostitute's 'supposedly secure identity' was only determined by the 'male spectator's efforts to permeate, visualize, and classify... her vagina'.[34]

The Contagious Diseases Act regulated the geographical spaces that the South Asian woman could inhabit and what could occur within these spaces. The lock hospitals in which these women were detained and where these gynaecological examinations occurred can be seen as 'states of exception', the Victorian version of Agamben's 'camp', where these women's rights were suspended for the benefit of the colonial authorities, enabling the detained woman to be classified as 'useful' for the 'male imperial body politic' (to use McClintock's term). If the woman was considered to be 'diseased', and therefore 'undesirable', the abject woman was not permitted to inhabit the space within the cantonment that she once did, and could be expelled as her body no longer had any function in this realm, or else was detained until her body was regarded as 'fit' enough to resume her physical-cum-social duties.

After much protest, the Act was finally abolished in India in 1886, the same year that a similar Act was repealed in Britain. But as Burton wrote, '[d]espite the official declaration of repeal, several species of "cantonment Rules" continued to operate in India...that permitted brothels to operate within regimental lines and subjected Indian women to the now infamous compulsory examinations'.[35]

Elizabeth Kolsky has demonstrated that the racialised view of South Asian female sexuality and the colonial desire to examine South Asian women's bodies continued to exist within the colonial Indian legal system in various forms, such as in the criminal laws concerning rape and sexual assault. Kolsky has shown that South Asian women, particularly from the lower castes, were seen as untrustworthy and it was believed that their trustworthiness could only be determined by scientific and medical examinations. As she wrote, '[t]he notion that scientific facts were "infinitely more trustworthy" than oral evidence made the application of science to law especially meaningful in colonial India as it allowed administrators to locate truth in and on the body'.[36] This distrust of the oral testimony of South Asian women, and deferment to the body to locate 'the truth', is central to the administration of the criminal justice system in colonial India and is a recurrent theme in approaches adopted by the authorities to deal with South Asian women in the postcolonial era. Kolsky has also revealed a 'colonial preoccupation' with virginity, evident in the way the authorities viewed South Asian women, citing the 'search for physical "signs of defloration"' by medical personnel working in the criminal justice system[37] – in colonial India, the British believed that credibility was enhanced by virginity. She describes this supposed lack of credibility amongst sexually active South Asian women as the 'distrust of non-virgins'[38] that abounded in the late 19th century and throughout the 20th century. The image of the virginal (and thus 'good') South Asian woman constructed in colonial India influenced the post-imperial immigration control system, in that the British authorities came to form the belief that the credibility of a woman, worthy of marriage, was intrinsically bound to her virginity.

The historical legacy of the treatment of South Asian women by the British colonial authorities had a great deal of influence on how government agencies in the UK viewed South Asian women in the 20th century. This background may shed some historical light on a dark chapter of British history, namely the period in which South Asian women entering Britain were subjected to virginity testing. The racist and sexist attitudes formed in the Victorian era resulted in the harsh and discriminatory treatment of these women by the immigration control system in the 1960s and 1970s.

The construction of a mixed-race yet ghettoised society: The value and function of the female body

As explained in Chapter 1, labour migration to the UK was primarily composed of men – this had been a stable trend up until the introduction of the Immigration Act 1971. The exception was the recruitment of women from the Caribbean region as nurses by the National Health Service.[39] Over 23,400 Indian men migrated to Britain with work permits between 1962 and 1972, compared with just over 2600 Indian women. In the same period, over 22,600 Pakistani men migrated to Britain with work permits, compared to a mere 471 Pakistani women.[40] South Asian women were not injected into the labour market but were deemed, we argue, to have a wider socio-economic role to play that would benefit Britain. Their value was largely defined by the British government by their association with the male migrant, since they had no value in the labour market. Their role was thus seen to be directly connected to their utility within their community, mainly to act as a 'civilising' influence on South Asian men. This role came to be seen as paramount for the maintenance of a balanced, mixed-race society, in which the non-white migrant would be contained and ghettoised. The woman thus represents the pathway to achieving this aim within a society characterised by an artificially created gender imbalance. The government's concern grew as it formed an awareness that the migrant community was composed mostly of young and single (and thus potentially sexually active) men who had been allowed to enter the country in order to support Britain's economic needs during the 1960s and 1970s. Single men were viewed by the media and anti-immigrationist groups as particularly problematic.[41] In fact, and paradoxically, male migrants were threatening the ideal 'balanced', mixed-race society by potentially initiating interracial relationships that could culminate in 'mixed marriages'. A containment policy was therefore needed. Concern over this phenomenon was further exacerbated by the myth of the South Asian male as an uncontrollable sexual deviant, and the 'moral panic' caused by the potential involvement of South Asian men in promiscuous relations involving sex and drugs with young white women.[42]

The colonialist anxiety about the 'threat' of the South Asian male's sexual desire was, therefore, clearly still evident in post-war British society. Stories of South Asian men being drug pushers and pimps had filled the tabloid press and pulp fiction novels since the 1920s, when tales of illegal prostitution emerged from the multicultural port cities of Cardiff, Bristol and Liverpool. The South Asian male was seen as unable to control his sexual desire and it was believed that if a South Asian woman was unavailable to harness this, there would be a greater likelihood of interracial sex, which was viewed by many as undesirable. Even the pro-immigration activist groups sometimes bought into this rhetoric. A 1974 report by the Runnymede Trust, prepared to encourage the streamlining of South Asian women to join their spouses in Britain, wrote that a criminological study of the 'male-dominated demographic structure' of the Pakistani community had allegedly found that 'Pakistanis are disproportionately involved in sexual offences.'[43] This implied that too many single Pakistani men were a problem and that as there were insufficient numbers of Pakistani women to satisfy their sexual desires, these men resorted to sexual violence (implicitly assumed to be against white women). The study cited by the Trust also stated that 'another consequence' of more South Asian men travelling alone to the UK was 'the presence of a large number of half-coloured children...who are either illegitimate or the product of mixed marriages', claiming that these children were 'a high risk group for crime and deprivation'.[44] Along these lines, Lucy Bland and Ronit Visram have also referred to the fear of 'miscegenation' between South Asian men and white women expressed by the British authorities.[45]

The single female migrant of similar ethnic background was also considered problematic – a single woman was not necessarily connected to the male migrant and could be involved in sexual relations with a white British male, which was not seen as desirable. And this view of unattached South Asian women was reminiscent of colonial times; further, in postcolonial, mixed-race Britain, it was not a foregone conclusion that a single South Asian woman would enter into a relationship with a South Asian man to ensure monogamous and contained relationships within the migrant community. The woman needed to be *attached*, as either a 'genuine' wife or fiancée, to contribute to the formation of a stable and monogamous relationship. This would allow the state to accomplish its goal of containment which in turn would facilitate its economic targets. This point was summarised by the Conservative MP, Sir John Smyth, during a parliamentary debate on immigration in 1965:

> If we do not allow families to come into the country as units we shall have all sorts of trouble with women. The female element is absolutely essential, and the sooner the men here have their wives with them the better I shall be pleased.[46]

A moral panic surrounding 'containment policy' therefore underpinned the restriction of non-white male migration under the Commonwealth Immigrants Act 1962, which culminated in the virtual halt of such migration with the Immigration Act 1971. Here we see the border as once again facilitating the state's aims: a 'gate' to open and close according to the perceived needs of postcolonial British society. Further, legislative amendments were introduced to favour entrance for migrants classifiable as family members, such as child dependants and elderly relatives, and special attention was dedicated to 'genuine' wives and fiancées.[47]

With the introduction of the 1971 Act, which came into effect in 1973, came an increasing number of dependants entering Britain.[48] In 1978, the number of husbands of Commonwealth citizens accepted for settlement on arrival was 1152, with 4742 wives accepted upon arrival in the same year.[49] In addition to the 4039 husbands accepted for settlement on the removal of the time limit by reasons of marriage, 4187 wives were accepted on the same grounds.[50] The processing of dependants' visas occurred under the pretence of family reunification and socio-humanitarian concerns, but the underlying purpose was yet again to shelter the British community from unwanted outcomes while looking after economic and sociopolitical interests. Dolly Smith Wilson argues that the authorities had 'fears of interracial relationships' and a legislative plan was issued 'to encourage the arrival of women as dependants perhaps because they saw them as a force to control migrant men's sexuality'.[51] This is confirmed by evidence that the government aimed to regulate not only the economy but also the lives of migrants who it believed needed to be, as Chris Waters describes, 'well-adjusted', by adopting the 'western model of the egalitarian family and companionate marriage', and the government 'hoped to see such models adopted *within* the migrant community'.[52] Nuclear, monogamous, heterosexual marriages within migrant communities were desired by the British authorities, particularly as an alternative to the multiple marriages that existed within some Pakistani and Bangladeshi communities. The government thus encouraged migrant families from South Asia to construct themselves as *akin* to white British families to facilitate the assimilation process into what Margaret Thatcher called 'British values'. South Asian migrants were required to accept such values, as a mechanism enforced by the white British society to obscure the 'otherness' of the migrant family. This is what Homi Bhabha has described as the phenomenon of 'mimicry', whereby colonial subjects were taught to 'mimic' the behaviours and attitudes of their colonial rulers, but were at the same time required to recognise the colonial/racial hierarchy. In the words of Bhabha they were 'to be Anglicized' but '*emphatically* not to be English'.[53] South Asian women were therefore needed by the state to perform a specific function of ethnic containment, and were otherwise considered valueless.

The selection of South Asian women in postcolonial Britain: The special visa regime for fiancées

As Rachel A. Hall argues, the British authorities deemed the Indian subcontinent migrant woman to be 'downtrodden, housebound, and emotionally and materially dependent on her husband', and someone who would not enter the workforce or qualify for public assistance. Hall refers to the view held by the British immigration control administrators of the South Asian wife as a 'passive appendage': 'the South Asian wife [would] migrat[e] to the country in which her husband is settled'.[54] A woman who would not have agency, who would follow her man, who would not question her role in her society was, as Parita Trivedi put it when writing for *Feminist Review*, 'a figment of your [British] imaginings'.[55] And this imagining of the South Asian woman as 'submissive, meek and tradition-bound', which fuelled the British government's attempts to prevent arranged marriages through immigration control, also led to the practice of virginity testing.

Still, these assumptions were uncritically entrenched within a way of thinking that would allow the introduction of visa regimes because this female migrant was mostly regarded by the authorities as a 'legitimate applicant'.[56] Her entrance was facilitated by legislative norms that allowed this woman to fulfil her duties in Britain. The 1971 Act thus legitimised the entrance of wives, and fast-tracked the entrance of fiancées. Fiancées were given fast-tracked entry clearances to the UK and did not have to endure the long application process experienced by wives and children, but were only allowed into the country on short-term entry clearances that would be converted to a longer form of right of abode upon production of a legitimate UK marriage licence.

The legitimacy of the applicant had to be confirmed at the border; otherwise the usefulness of a fiancée would disappear and lead to rejection of her application to enter Britain. Legal and medical scrutiny was essential to form a judgement of the veracity of the applicant. And this scrutiny was based on traditional societal and medical stereotypes of moral and sexual expectations held by British society about Indian subcontinent fiancées. These women were seen by the immigration authorities as bodies to be 'consumed' by other men, for sex, marriage and domestic duties. This was confirmed by a report to the FCO from David Stephen, an FCO Special Advisor:

> There is a logic in the use of these procedures since the immigration rules require dependent girls [as children, not wives] to be unmarried, and fiancées do not need entry certificates while wives do. If immigration or entry certificate officers suspect that a girl claiming to be an unmarried dependent is in fact married, or if a woman arriving at London Airport and claiming to be a fiancée of a man resident here is in fact a wife seeking to join her husband and avoid the 'queue' for an entry certificate, they have on occasion sought a medical view on whether or not the woman concerned had borne children, it being a reasonable assumption that an unmarried woman in the sub continent would be a virgin.[57]

Therefore, their physical integrity, which would confirm their virginity status, was considered an objective element to be used to determine the outcome of the migrant's application, alongside other documents, in cases where the Immigration Officer would not otherwise be convinced that the applicant's claims were genuine.

In summary, this extremely intrusive test of the hymen, adopted as a practice at the border, can be seen as representing a culmination of cultural stereotypes. Worse, the normalisation of any single act of ascertaining the 'integrity' of the migrant woman's body confirmed the extent to which the British immigration authorities were willing to go to ensure that their migrant intake conformed to the desires of the nation-state. The virginity testing represented a rational, not accidental, 'choice' made by the state in seeking to achieve its socio-economic goals, while applying its 'whiteness' policy. The woman undergoing such an intrusive test could not refuse it, or her application would be rejected on the spot, and she would then be framed in terms of refusing to cooperate, which in turn would be seen as evidence of a fraudulent application insofar as she was not willing to let her body speak the 'truth'. Thus, she is seen as unable to communicate other than through the 'language' of her body. In such cases, the interview process is deemed to have failed, and so 'the evidence' is requested from the woman. The humiliation of this test speaks volumes of her lack of human rights and civil rights. She is a body to be used by the destination country; should she hope to achieve her aim of acceptance into the country, she must first fulfil the Immigration Officer's request. It was technically optional for the applicant to 'consent' to the physical examination requested by Immigration Officers if they wanted to reside in Britain, but refusal would probably lead to an unsuccessful application. The notion of 'consent' was thus induced by the threat of refusal to enter Britain, because a migrant's 'cooperation' was paramount to a successful application for admission. As Chief Medical Officer Sir Henry Yellowlees wrote to P.J. Woodfield, 'surely the sanction applied to any potential immigrant who refuses to submit to medical examination ... is simply to refuse him admission to the country?'[58]

The virginity test absolves the other task of signalling to the migrant woman what her purpose is once she is 'fortunate enough' to be allowed into the country. The humiliation removes any expectation on her part that her position in Britain is one of equal rights and opportunities. The test is a rite of passage to assert power over the female migrant body, to signify her position in the hierarchical order. Employing Doty's work on the 'schizophrenic' state, we argue that the 'desire for order' imposed at the border in this context created a regime that normalised the gross violation of human rights to assert the stratification of society based on colonialist–racist attitudes. This can be seen in the way that the immigration control system attempted to define the biopolitical space open to the South Asian female migrant, thus echoing the colonial past. While the British colonial administration sought to contain certain 'threatening' bodies, such as that of the South Asian prostitute, to certain designated spaces, as Kristeva and McClintock have described, the practical realities of the colonial project meant that these bodies often traversed the liminal boundaries that they usually inhabited. Ann Laura Stoler has described this phenomenon in relation to the colonial era:

> The cultivation of the European bourgeois self in the colonies, that 'body to be cared for, protected, cultivated, and preserved from the many dangers and contacts...' required other bodies that would perform those nurturing services, provide the leisure for such self-absorbed administerings and self-bolstering acts. It was a gendered body and a dependent one, on an intimate set of exploitative sexual and service relations between European men and native women,...shaped by the sexual politics of class and race. Those native women who served as concubines, servants, nursemaids and wives in European colonial households not only defined what distinguished bourgeois life: they threatened that 'differential value' of adult and children's bourgeois bodies that they were to protect and affirm...
>
> The self-affirmation of white, middle-class colonials thus embodied a set of fundamental tensions between a culture of whiteness that cordoned itself off from the native world and a set of domestic arrangements and class distinctions among Europeans that produced cultural hybridities and sympathies that repeatedly transgressed these distinctions.[59]

These transgressive bodies and the tensions created can also be seen in the era of postcolonial migration and within the British immigration control system. The system's desire for order tried to maintain a distinct barrier between domestic society and the colonial other – what Stoler calls above 'a culture of whiteness that cordoned itself off from the native world' – but the socio-political and economic requirements of the British state meant that these liminal spaces[60] could not be hermetically sealed and the colonial 'other' existed within the confines of domestic British society. If the physical liminal space could not be contained to prevent the threatening colonial body from being in contact with 'white' British society, the racial hierarchy of the colonial system had to be impressed upon the migrant in other ways. In the journey of the potential migrant from applicant to successful UK resident, the massive scrutiny, both physical and mental, placed upon them reinforced the dominance of the British state and required the migrant to acknowledge their powerless position when entering the country.

Exacerbating the situation facing the migrant seeking to enter the country, as discussed in the previous chapter, a common belief was shared by the British authorities that South Asian migrants were particularly untrustworthy, and this view was extended to women and children. The British High Commissioner in Dacca, F.S. Miles, wrote in an internal report that 'from bitter experience, Immigration Attachés find that the task far too often becomes one of sifting truth from lies'.[61] He further added that:

[t]he common case of dishonesty [was] that of a young wife who claims to be older than she looks, has several young children, and also two or three older boys, who often claim to be younger than they look.[62]

Miles also highlighted in the report that 'Bengalis, though friendly and likeable, are probably the most prone to invention and fabrication.'[63] An FCO circular presented to the Immigration Section of the British Embassy/High Commission in Islamabad in 1976 (later obtained by the Runnymede Trust) outlined the full list of documentary evidence required for wives attempting to join their husbands in the UK. The list included:

(a) A valid passport issued to the applicant;

(b) Evidence that the husband is settled in the United Kingdom in the form of a declaration of sponsorship giving the husband's full name, his address, details of his employment, passport details and the date of his entry into the United Kingdom;

(c) Evidence that a marriage has taken place. If the marriage was registered and took place after 1961, a certificate (*Nikah Nama*) issued pursuant to the Muslim Family Laws Ordinance should be produced; if the marriage was not registered an affidavit should be submitted. This should be sworn before a responsible official by a person who was present at the marriage ceremony but who is not related to the husband or wife;

(d) Any recent family correspondence relating to the applicant's proposed settlement in the United Kingdom;

(e) Two passport size photographs of the applicant;

(f) Attested photocopies of the sponsor's passport. If the sponsor holds a British Passport, photocopies of pages 1 to 6 inclusive and all other pages bearing frontier stamps should be produced. If the sponsor holds a Pakistani passport, complete photocopies of *all* passports in his possession should be produced. All copies should be attested on each page by a responsible person in the United Kingdom (a Notary Public, Commissioner of Oaths, or Solicitor) as being true copies of the original documents;

(g) Evidence that the husband is willing and able to support and accommodate his wife.

(Paragraph (g) does not apply to cases where the sponsor was, on 1 January 1973, a Commonwealth Citizen settled in the United Kingdom).[64]

The circular clearly instructed that:

> It lies with the applicant to satisfy the Entry Clearance Officer that she is the wife of her sponsor and she should produce at the time of her interview in support of her application...documentary evidence.[65]

This instruction places the burden of proof on the applicant, even though numerous official FCO documents technically gave applicants the benefit of the doubt applicant and the burden of proof supposedly lay with the agency to disprove any claims.

The schizophrenic state: Filtering numbers of dependants while honouring international agreements

The immigration of dependants was not only considered necessary in order to address Britain's internal needs. In an increasingly globalised world, in which Britain had more external watchdogs than ever before, it was also important to the government to be seen by external parties to be fulfilling its international obligations, in particular the European Convention on Human Rights. The Migration and Visa Department for the Ministerial Group of Immigration Policy in early 1977 briefed its staff by claiming:

> The obligation to receive dependent wives and children of persons already settled in the UK is established in the Immigration Act and in the Rules made under the Act. The total withdrawal of these commitments would be extremely difficult to defend on general humanitarian and legal grounds. It would arouse strong and understandable objections by immigrant communities, the countries of origin and international organisations such as the European Human Rights Commission.[66]

This diplomatic exercise had to be balanced against internal strategies to regain control over the flow of migrants into Britain. This point was considered pressing for two reasons. First, feedback from the immigration agency at the time suggested that 'bogus' dependent migrants from the Indian subcontinent were abusing the system of family reunification. And, second, the system itself had to be conceived of as having a natural end. The Minister for Immigration, Alex Lyon, reiterated this point in a 1975 address to entry clearance staff at the British Embassy in Islamabad, stating the government's commitment:

> in respect of the dependants of heads of families who were settled in the U.K. on 1st January 1973. These dependants have a statutory right of admission, and while it is possible to hold differing views about the number of these dependants, it is clear that this is a finite commitment.[67]

At the same time, the suspicion that the family reconciliation programme was being abused by its users can be seen in the statement

by the Home Secretary Merlyn Rees that 'the Government is determined to honour its commitment to the close dependants of those
settled here... [However] the Government's aim is to prevent evasion
and abuse of the immigration control'.[68]

The government and immigration authorities therefore sought to
be seen as honouring their legal commitments, and yet the goal was
to limit and eventually stop the family reconciliation programme.
Soon after the Immigration Act 1971 came into effect in 1973, traces
of this line of thought became evident. As the extract below reveals,
the South Asian Department, on suggestions from the British High
Commissions in Delhi and the Chairman of the Select Committee
on Race Relations and Immigration, considered the option of closing
down the system:

> as long as it was clear that it was not racially discriminatory (e.g.
> white dependants as well as brown dependants were excluded):
> indeed if it carried with it a reaffirmation that we were prepared to
> meet our responsibilities to United Kingdom Passport Holders and
> not try to swing them on India, there would be a lot to be said for
> it here.[69]

The battle of numbers was always a top priority for the government in determining its policy strategies, with the Home Office
estimating that 'stop[ping] the entry of dependants of heads of
households coming here in the future might... reduce arrivals by
some 10,000 a year'.[70] Alternatively, the introduction of quota was
seen as another possible means of limiting numbers, as the British
High Commissioner in Dacca proposed in 1975:

> It is... worth pointing out that if in these circumstances it were
> decided by HMG [Her Majesty's Government] to move to a quota
> system, this would save a great deal of public money in Bangladesh
> by speedier handling of applications and saving of staff.[71]

We see here emerging a further factor that led to the normalisation
of virginity testing, which was highlighted in the previous chapter –
a pressure on Immigration Officers to select entrants according to
the needs dictated by statistical data. This meant that discriminatory
elements were injected into the system, which should otherwise have

involved the simple policy of family reunification. As FCO officials advised the Home Secretary in 1973:

> to achieve the desired result [to limit the number of dependants], it would have to be accepted that they [amendments to our legislation] would in practice be discriminatory, not so much on colour as on education and cultural grounds. The object would be to avoid the entry of any families whose assimilation in this country would be at all difficult because of race, religion, cultural background or language.[72]

And yet, statistical data do not prove the point that the fiancée visa regime was being abused. The *Labour Party Campaign Handbook* published in 1978 stated that in the previous year only 4930 women, or 11 per cent of all migration from the 'New Commonwealth and Pakistan', were fiancées accepted to settlement upon marriage.[73] Out of the overall figure of 8510 non-patrial women who were accepted for settlement on marriage in 1977, 21 per cent were from India, 14 per cent were from Pakistan and 5 per cent were from the USA.[74] These numbers suggest that a little over half of all women from India, Pakistan or elsewhere within the 'New Commonwealth' had been accepted for settlement on marriage grounds. Yet it was mainly women from these countries who were intimately scrutinised by immigration officials. Labour also acknowledged that 'the number of people attempting to enter this country illegally is not large'.[75] During the Conservative government's review of the Immigration Rules in 1980 for the incoming British Nationality Bill 1981, the FCO admitted that '[t]he 1979 immigration statistics indicate that not many foreign fiancées enter the UK', with 1900 of a 2130 total coming from Pakistan, 70 from the USA and another 30 from South Africa.[76]

Nevertheless, the perception that 'bogus marriages' were a prime example of systematic deception was reinforced continuously, as a draft Home Office document reveals.[77] In a 1982 document, the Chief Immigration Officer B.A. Smith suggested that 'bogus' dependants, primarily 'bogus' wives, from the Indian subcontinent were a major problem for ECOs, stating, '[i]n the field of importing bogus dependants Asians have always figured most prominently'.[78] This was in contrast to reports by organisations, such as the

Runnymede Trust, who stated that 'refusal rates may be considerably higher than the true number of fraudulent or ineligible applications', citing the example that only two of 58 cases investigated were 'clearly fraudulent'.[79]

Conclusion

Virginity testing was essentially reserved for female migrants from the Indian subcontinent, coming to the country predominantly on fiancée entry clearances, while African-Caribbean or other female migrants were not subjected to such a procedure. Therefore, its imposition was determined not only by gender, but also by race, nationality, marital status, age and socio-economic status. The practice of virginity testing was based on three assumptions. The first was the perception that the fast-tracked fiancée visa regime was being abused by South Asian female migrants – a claim that is not supported by the numbers we found in official documents. The second assumption was that these women, since they had not married in an official bonding ceremony, must be virgins, based on a stereotypical and narrow view of the South Asian woman which has deep historical roots. And third, it was assumed that the test would provide conclusive medical evidence of sexual activity – a wrong assumption about how the female body works.[80] And none of these assumptions were critically analysed since they were seen to offer a 'solution' to an alleged problem in Britain, by maintaining the balance of a mixed-race society while ghettoising the non-white citizens within it.

This chapter has explored the culture within the British immigration control system that allowed these racist and sexist assumptions to manifest. The next chapter will detail how the British government responded, in both public and private, to the publication of details of the practice of virginity testing. It will also demonstrate how revelations about virginity testing led to further revelations about immigration control practices that violated the physical body, primarily the use of X-rays for age assessment purposes.

Notes

1. Pratihba Parmar, 'Gender, Race and Class: Asian Women in Resistance', in Centre for Contemporary Cultural Studies (ed.), *The Empire Strikes Back: Race and Racism in 70s Britain* (London: Hutchinson, 1986) p. 245.

2. Philippa Levine, 'Sexuality and Empire', in Catherine Hall and Sonya O. Rose (eds), *At Home with the Empire: Metropolitan Culture and the Imperial World* (Cambridge: Cambridge University Press, 2006) p. 122.

3. K.N. Chaudhuri, *The Trading World of Asia and the English East India Company 1660–1760* (Cambridge: Cambridge University Press, 1978) p. 20.

4. Edward W. Said, *Orientalism* (London: Penguin Books, 2003) p. 7.

5. Said, *Orientalism*, p. 7.

6. Antoinette Burton, *Burdens of History: British Feminists, Indian Women and Imperial Culture, 1865–1915* (Chapel Hill & London: University of North Carolina Press, 1994) p. 8.

7. Meredith Borthwick, *The Changing Role of Women in the Bengal 1849–1905* (New Jersey: Princeton University Press, 1984) p. 122.

8. Lata Mani, *Contentious Traditions: The Debate on Sati in Colonial India* (Berkeley: University of California Press, 1998) pp. 79–80.

9. Burton, *Burdens of History*, p. 31.

10. Ibid.

11. Gayatri C. Spivak, *A Critique of Postcolonial Reason: Toward a History of Vanishing Present* (Cambridge, MA & London: Harvard University Press, 1999) p. 287.

12. Mani, *Contentious Traditions*, p. 162.

13. Ibid.

14. Angela Woollacott, *Gender and Empire* (Houndmills: Palgrave Macmillan, 2006) p. 91.

15. Ronald Hyam, *Empire and Sexuality: The British Experience* (Manchester: Manchester University Press, 1990) p. 118.

16. Kenneth Ballhatchet, *Race, Sex and Class under the Raj: Imperial Attitudes and Policies and Their Critics, 1793–1905* (London: Weidenfeld & Nicholson, 1980) p. 2.

17. Anne McClintock, *Imperial Leather: Race, Gender and Sexuality in the Colonial Conquest* (New York & London: Routledge, 1995) p. 48.

18. Levine, 'Sexuality and Empire', pp. 134–135.

19. Woollacott, *Gender and Empire*, p. 54.

20. Hyam, *Empire and Sexuality*, p. 120.

21. Ibid.

22. J.W. McCulloch, N.J. Smith and I.D. Batta, 'A Comparative Study of Adult Crime amongst Asians and Their Host Population', *Probation Journal*, 24/1, 1974, pp. 16–22.

23. Runnymede Trust, 'The Crisis of the Pakistani Dependants', Briefing Paper 2/74, April 1974, pp. 8–9, RC/RF/1/06, Runnymede Trust archives, BCA.

24. Ibid., p. 40.

25. Ibid., p. 20.

26. Ibid., p. 20.

27. Judith R. Walkowitz, *Prostitution and Victorian Society: Women, Class, and the State* (Cambridge: Cambridge University Press, 1980) p. 3.

28. Contagious Diseases Act 1864, Cap. 85., ss15, 17.

29. Ibid., s16.
30. Ballhatchet, *Race, Sex and Class under the Raj*, p. 24.
31. Cited in Ballhatchet, *Race, Sex and Class under the Raj*, pp. 28–29.
32. McClintock, *Imperial Leather*, p. 47.
33. Walkowitz, *Prostitution and Victorian Society*, p. 109.
34. Nicole McManus, 'Purging the Self: Entering the Abject in Victorian Texts of Vaginal Exploration', *Australasian Journal of Victorian Studies*, 13/1, 2008, p. 3.
35. Burton, *Burdens of History*, p. 135.
36. Elizabeth Kolsky, ' "The Body Evidencing the Crime": Rape on Trial in Colonial India, 1860–1947', *Gender & History*, 22/1, April 2010, p. 112.
37. Ibid., p. 114.
38. Ibid., p. 119.
39. See Jacqueline Bhabha and Sue Shutter, *Women's Movement: Women under Immigration, Nationality and Refugee Law* (Oakhill: Trentham Books, 1994) pp. 164–166.
40. Figures calculated from Home Office, *Control of Immigration Statistics* (London: HMSO, 1963–1973).
41. See Chris Waters, ' "Dark Strangers" in Our Midst: Discourses of Race and Nation in Britain, 1947–1963', *Journal of British Studies*, 36/2, April 1997, pp. 207–238; Paul Gilroy, *There Ain't No Black in the Union Jack: The Cultural Politics of Race and Nation* (London: Routledge, 2002) pp. 95–104; Louise A. Jackson, ' "The Coffee Club Menace": Policing Youth, Leisure and Sexuality in Post-war Manchester', *Cultural & Social History*, 5/3, September 2008, pp. 296–301.
42. See note 30.
43. Runnymede Trust, 'The Crisis of the Pakistani Dependants', p. 8.
44. Cited in Runnymede Trust, 'The Crisis of the Pakistani Dependants', p. 9.
45. L. Bland (2005) 'White Women and Men of Colour: Miscegenation Fears in Britain after the Great War', *Gender & History*, 17/1, pp. 29–61; R. Visram (2002) *Asians in Britain: 400 Years of History* (London: Pluto Press).
46. *Hansard*, 23 March 1965, col. 371.
47. Parita Trivedi, 'To Deny Our Fullness: Asian Women in the Making of History', *Feminist Review*, 17, Autumn 1984, p. 45.
48. Ian R.G. Spencer, *British Immigration Policy Since 1939: The Making of a Multi-racial Britain* (London: Routledge, 1997) p. 143. According to Home Office figures given in Parliament in 1978, approximately 93,800 wives and children from the New Commonwealth were accepted for settlement in Britain between 1973 and 1977, compared to approximately only 14,900 people who entered under annual work vouchers. *Hansard*, 3 February 1978, col. 339w.
49. Home Office Statistical Department, *Home Office Statistical Bulletin*, IV.
50. Ibid.
51. D. Smith Wilson (2008) 'Gender, Race and the Ideal Labour Force', in L. Ryan, and W. Webster (eds), *Gendering Migration: Masculinity, Femininity and Ethnicity in Post-war Britain* (London: Ashgate) p. 99.

52. Waters, ' "Dark Strangers" in Our Midst' p. 228; italics are in the original text.
53. Homi Bhabha, *The Location of Culture* (London and New York: Routledge, 2008) p. 125.
54. Hall, 'The Interaction of Gender and Ethnicity', pp. 189, 13.
55. Trivedi, 'To Deny Our Fullness', p. 38.
56. Hall, 'The Interaction of Gender and Ethnicity', pp. 189, 13.
57. David Stephen, 'Immigration Control Procedures at Delhi and Dacca: Report on My Visit', 9 March 1979, 9, FCO 50/662, NA. It is interesting, for contemporary reasons, to see also the reference to the concept of 'queue'. The term 'queue-jumper' was used in official Home Office and FCO documents, discussing Asian migrants from East Africa.
58. Letter from Henry Yellowlees to P.J. Woodfield, 15 March 1979, HO 418/29, NA.
59. Ann Laura Stoler, *Race and the Education of Desire: Foucault's* History of Sexuality *and the Colonial Order of Things* (Durham & London: Duke University Press, 1995) pp. 111–112.
60. The term 'liminal space' comes from the work of Homi Bhabha which describes the concept of being 'in-between the designations of identity', such as between 'black and 'white or the 'colonizer' and the 'colonized', for example. As Bhabha wrote in *The Location of Culture*, the 'liminal space' is an 'interstitial passage between fixed identifications [which] opens up the possibility of a cultural hybridity that entertains difference without an assumed or imposed hierarchy'. Bhabha, *The Location of Culture*, p. 5.
61. F.S. Miles, 'Immigration from Bangladesh: Will It Ever End?', 29 June 1979, p. 5, FCO 50/660, NA.
62. Ibid., p. 5.
63. Ibid., p. 5.
64. 'Wives Wishing to Join or Accompany Husbands for Settlement in the United Kingdom', May 1976 RC/RF/1/06, Runnymede Trust archive, BCA.
65. 'Wives Wishing to Join or Accompany Husbands for Settlement in the United Kingdom'.
66. Brief for Meeting of the Ministerial Group on Immigration Policy (GEN 24) 21 February 1977, FCO 37/1842, NA.
67. 'Summary of Address by Mr. Alexander Lyon, M.P., Minister of State, Home Office, to Entry Clearance Officers on the Staff of the British Embassy at Islamabad on 10th January 1975,' FCO 50/522, NA.
68. 'Immigration and the Swamping Controversy,' n.d., attached to letter from A.J. Butler to N.J. Saunders, 27 March 1979, PREM 16/2100, NA.
69. Memorandum by I.J.M. Sutherland, n.d., FCO 50/460, NA.
70. Home Office, 'Future Commonwealth Immigration (Excluding UKPH): Entry of Dependants of Commonwealth Already Settled Here,' n.d., FCO 50/360, NA.
71. 'Visit to Bangladesh of Mr D F Hawley, Immigration,' 19 November 1975, FCO 50/533, NA.

72. 'Immigration: Admission of Dependants,' 28 March 1973, 2, FCO 50/460, NA.
73. Labour Party, *Race, Immigration and the Racialists* (London: Labour Party Campaign Handbook, 1978) p. 19.
74. Ibid., p. 15.
75. Ibid., p. 17.
76. P.A. Marshall, 'Review of Immigration Rules', 29 October 1980, FCO 50/688, NA.
77. 'Distinctions between Nationalities in the Immigration Field', pp. 3–4, HO 418/40 338797, NA.
78. B.A. Smith, 'Evasion of the Immigration Control', July 1982, p. 11, HO 418/40 338797, NA.
79. CRE, 'Proposal for a Formal Investigation of Immigration Control', 23 March 1979, p. 9, HO 418/29 338797, NA.
80. 'Hymen', in Vern L. Bullough and Bonnie Bullough (eds), *Human Sexuality: An Encyclopaedia* (New York: Garland Publishing, 1994) p. 293.

4
Deny, Normalise and Obfuscate: The Government Response to the Virginity Testing Practice and Other Physical Abuses

On 1 February 1979, journalist Melanie Phillips broke the story about the practice of virginity testing on the front page of *The Guardian*. The Labour Party, coming out of the 'winter of discontent' and facing a slump in the polls in the lead-up to the May general election, sought to lessen the harm this claim could do the government of James Callaghan. Home Secretary Merlyn Rees made a public statement that this was essentially an isolated incident, claiming that it had only happened twice before in the previous decade and that it was a regrettable outcome of a 'normal' medical examination. However, over the next month, further details emerged that seemed to contradict Rees's account, suggesting that more cases had occurred in British High Commissions in South Asia and that various government officials had prior knowledge of this practice happening. Questions about the frequency of these gynaecological examinations were raised in the media, by migrant groups and by MPs, such as Jo Richardson, in Parliament. Documents uncovered by the authors from the FCO files at the National Archives show that the government became aware in March 1979 that the number of 'tests' that had occurred up until that time were likely to be more than 80, and that by 1980, when Willie Whitelaw had taken over as the new Conservative Home Secretary, it was suspected that more than 120 such tests had been carried out on the Indian subcontinent.

This chapter will reveal that both Labour and the Conservatives, as well as the staff in the Home Office and the FCO, sought to minimise public knowledge of the extent of the virginity testing practice and explain away the cases of its use as unfortunate, yet exceptional, events that occurred as part of the 'normal' medical examinations carried out on immigrants, as set out by the Immigration Act 1971. The chapter will also demonstrate how the Home Office and the FCO attempted to thwart an investigation into abuses within the immigration control system conducted by the CRE, the government's peak anti-racial discrimination body. This effort to hinder the CRE's investigation was characterised by attempts to normalise racial (and sexual) discrimination as inherent to the immigration control system, to minimise any outright abuses that were alleged to have occurred and to challenge the authority of the CRE to investigate the system.

Finally, this chapter will outline other human rights abuses (predominantly physical) to which potential migrants from South Asia were subjected in the 1970s and early 1980s, as details appeared in the press (particularly of X-rays for age assessment purposes) in the wake of the virginity testing controversy. Once again, the actions of the government were to deny, normalise and obfuscate the allegations made against it, with the full extent of the X-rays controversy being deflected by the promise of an internal investigation by the Chief Medical Officer Sir Henry Yellowlees. Based on the internal FCO and Home Office files we uncovered at Kew, the role of the government in seeking to cover up the story is clear.

The government response to the breaking of the controversy

Writing on the history of the struggles of South Asian women in Britain, Pratibha Parmar has stated that the practice of virginity testing was grounded in a cultural belief informed by an 'absurd generalisation' and a clear 'racist and sexist assumption that Asian women from the subcontinent are always virgins before they get married'.[1] The government's desire to shield itself from criticism such as this prompted its initial reaction of denial. In response to *The Guardian*'s first report on a test performed on an Indian woman at Heathrow Airport, Home Secretary Rees denied in Parliament that the virginity tests were 'normal practice', although he admitted that they were occurring on 'rare occasions'.[2] He followed this minor admission with a legal justification for the tests, citing paragraph 2 of schedule 2 to the Immigration Act 1971.[3] As mentioned in Chapter 2, this paragraph states that medical examinations were in place to guard against migrants who:

(a) endanger the health of other persons in this country;
(b) [are] unable for medical reasons to support himself or his dependants in the United Kingdom or
(c) require major medical treatment.[4]

Evident from this passage are the priorities of the British government: first, the need to avoid contagious diseases; and second, the consideration given to the seriousness of illnesses, and the individual's ability to self-finance a possible cure. Yet it is clear that being a virgin does not fall within these criteria, so the Home Secretary's explanation of virginity testing with reference to this paragraph does not offer sufficient grounds to justify its application under the 1971 Act. Further, not even a broader interpretation of this section of the Act would justify virginity testing.

The Home Secretary's intervention was the result of internal communications exchanged on the day on which the story broke. In these memorandums, we can trace an attempt to normalise the virginity testing practice as a routine aspect of the medical examinations falling within the legal regime introduced by the 1971 Act. One letter, for example, states that those immigrants who intended to stay in Britain for more than six months were '*normally* referred to the medical inspector for examination' (emphasis added).[5] The same letter also stated that the decision to request all sorts of medical examinations rested within the discretionary powers afforded to Immigration Officers, powers 'which they are required to exercise sparingly'.[6] This latter point reflects both a denial of the pressure placed on Immigration Officers to produce results, and an attempt to avoid any discussion regarding whether such discretionary powers were limited by official instructions. The decision to make use of discretionary powers in the case cited of the Indian woman at Heathrow was dictated by a spurious conclusion arrived at by the officials in charge which obscured the veracity of the woman's story. First, the woman was 35 years old, which was taken as proof that she must have been a 'consumed woman'. And second, she was accompanied by her fiancé, whom the Home Office alleged she 'had met only 2 days previously'.[7] This so-called evidence was seen to support a version of the truth that departed significantly from that offered by the woman, because the Immigration Officer suspected 'that she might be already married'.[8]

The day following this exchange of internal communications on the matter, the Home Office issued a media release in which it confirmed that '[a]n Immigration Officer may refer any passenger for examination by a medical inspector at any point',[9] thus expanding the discretionary powers given to Immigration Officers. The Home Office's statement highlighted, in a matter-of-fact tone, that 'this fact [of a woman not being a virgin] could be relevant to [the] decision [over] whether a passenger should be admitted', because it would provide the evidence as to whether 'a passenger seeking admission [is] the dependant of a person settled in the United Kingdom'.[10] This point essentially justified the behaviour of the Immigration Officer in this case as a normal procedure aimed at protecting the internal community from non-genuine dependants. Together with the legal justification presented to the Parliament by Rees, this response reveals the government's wariness in handling the situation, particularly considering that its knowledge of virginity testing was far greater than was revealed at that point in time. Reading between the lines, we can see the Home Office seeking to determine the best strategy. From an examination of both sides of the story – the internal communications and official statements – emerges therefore a richer picture than the official account offered up to this point in time. The government was thus caught between attempts to minimise the incident involving the woman at Heathrow Airport and an increasing pressure arising in response to its admission that virginity testing and other harmful practices were taking place at the border, and sought to justify its actions.

How many cases?

We will never know how many women underwent virginity tests, in part because the government pursued a policy of denial and minimisation. Its reconstruction of the facts – and the shielding of evidence –

suited its strategy of maintaining 'good race relations'. For example, on 19 February 1979, Home Office Secretary Rees asserted in Parliament that 'a vaginal examination ... may have been made only once or twice during the past eight years, according to records which have been looked at'.[11] Yet in contrast to this assertion, we know from Amrit Wilson's visits to immigration detention centres in 1977 that ' "virginity tests" were routine',[12] suggesting a completely different picture of what was taking place on British soil. From official and internal documents, we could only establish that the practice was mainly recorded offshore, at the High Commissions on the Indian subcontinent.

In mid-March 1979, more information emerged at the official level about offshore cases. In the House of Commons, Labour MP Jo Richardson, citing the Indian Minister for External Affairs, revealed that 'at least 34 cases of virginity testing' had occurred at the British High Commission in New Delhi.[13] Behind closed doors, stories of these cases and others were already emerging and being shared amongst certain parties at the Home Office. In a letter in early March 1979 from the FCO to 10 Downing Street staff, Private Secretary J. S. Wall stated that '[t]he facts, as far as India is concerned, are that since October 1975 ... there appear to have been nine cases in Bombay and 73 in New Delhi'.[14] By January 1980, the FCO had a much clearer picture of the figures, but was reluctant to make them, or the extent of their impact, known. This was evident in a handwritten note to D. W. Partridge from the Migration and Visa Department of the FCO that we identified, which noted that those 73 cases that had occurred at the British High Commission in Delhi since October 1975 were examinations that 'formed part of the normal medical examination' and 'all examinations [of the genitals] had been visual only'.[15] The same note said there had been 10 cases in Bombay, three of which involved internal vaginal examinations, with it unclear whether the other seven examinations were internal or external examinations of the genitals.[16]

The note to D. W. Partridge also stated that in Islamabad there had been 'no requests specifically for vaginal examinations made since 1975', but acknowledged that 'in some cases ECOs had asked [the] doctor to report "signs of marriage" ', which was a euphemism amongst High Commission staff for scrutiny to be placed upon the applicant's genitals, breasts and stomach.[17] It further stated that 'no record of the number of such cases' existed but that 'they may account to a total of under 20 a year in the past two years'.[18] The note emphasised that in Dacca, where Alex Lyon knew of previous cases of virginity testing occurring in the mid-1970s, '[n]o women were ever referred for vaginal examination', but admitted that '*one* virginity test' (emphasis in original) was performed in 1978 'by purely external examination, not involving examination of [the] vagina'.[19]

The same note also referred to the Dacca High Commission, where it was much more common for women to be examined for physical evidence that they had borne children, upon the request of an ECO, which involved doctors examining the breasts and stomach for stretch marks. These cases numbered 20–30 per year.[20] The note mentioned that on 'rare occasions' women were examined 'to establish whether they were pregnant when they claimed not to be but obviously were', and 'whether the applicants had borne children if conflicting evidence from other family members' was available.[21] The note concluded that 'it is not possible for us to quote a precise and accurate figure', but gave the approximate figures for the number of women given some form of physical examination to determine whether they had borne children or had ever had sexual relations, as requested by ECOs in South Asia:

Delhi	73
Bombay	10
Dacca	40–60 (over two years)
Islamabad	[unknown]
Karachi	[unknown]
Total	123–143[22]

There is no evidence in the file that this note was ever typed up and distributed within the FCO other than to Mr Partridge. We also do not know whether and, if so, how Mr Partridge communicated with others on this matter. However, this is the most detailed document that we have identified in our research that records the number of victims of virginity testing and other forms of physical examination imposed upon South Asian women by the British immigration control system. Even though we have captured these figures, there remains a sense that the total picture is difficult to access. Yet these numbers do help us appreciate that virginity testing was far from an isolated practice. This handwritten note to D. W. Partridge also attempted to draw a distinction between the examinations that occurred at Heathrow and those that occurred in South Asia. Discussing the examinations carried out in Delhi, the note stated that these 'formed part of a normal medical examination', but acknowledged that the gynaecologist 'had been asked to advise on the marital status of the female applicants'.[23] However, even though the gynaecologist later stated that 'all examinations had been visual only and that she had not carried out any internal examinations',[24] the examination of the genitals for administrative immigration control purposes, rather than for a medical purpose, was a violation of the human rights of the women involved. The note confirmed that the 10 cases in Bombay involved examinations of daughter dependants (all over the age of 18), with three definitely involving a vaginal examination, as mentioned previously.[25] While the FCO claimed that these cases were 'part of a normal medical examination', a telegram from the High Commission in Delhi stated that it was 'the practice at all posts in India not . . . to refer or encourage wives and children under 18 for settlement to have a routine medical examination'.[26] The telegram claimed that in the second half of 1979 no women or children under 18 had been referred for medical examination in India, in contrast to 281 husbands.[27] This suggests that the physical examination of women at British High Commissions in India was carried out but was not officially recorded, as were medical examinations for men seeking to migrate to Britain.

Obfuscation and hindrance: The internal response by the government

Under both Labour and later under the Conservatives when Margaret Thatcher won the May 1979 election, the Home Office (under Merlyn Rees and then Willie Whitelaw), as well as the FCO, acted to downplay any wrongdoing by immigration officials and to hinder any scrutiny of the alleged practices. We know that by March 1979, the Home Office had confidentially received and commented, either in public or in private, on enough information to prove that it had knowledge of the existence of such examinations. However, each public admission was followed by a recontextualisation of what occurred by the Home Office. We provide two examples of this. The first relates to the public admission offered by the former Labour Minister of State for the Home Office Alex Lyon. He was reported by *The Guardian* as admitting his knowledge of the fact that, between 1974 and 1976, many 'such gynaecological examinations had been performed in Dacca', a place where many potential migrants to Britain sought entry certificates at the time.[28] Lyon declared, '[t]hey did it fairly frequently in Dacca to discover whether a woman was or was not a virgin when she was claiming to be a wife',[29] although we believe that Lyon meant that tests were conducted when a woman claimed to be a fiancée. In making this official statement, Lyon sought to deny his direct involvement by suggesting that he had previously given instructions for this practice to cease in September 1976: 'I told them they had to stop it and instructions went out to *all* immigration and entry certificate officers' (emphasis added).[30] Lyon's admission of the widespread use of the practice was the target of a strategy of minimisation then adopted by the Home Office, as evident in an internal draft briefing document written for the Sub-Committee of the Select Committee on Home Affairs in 1980. In this brief the Home Office suggested that Lyon had intervened only in reference to one specific case:

> Mr Lyon's instructions arose from a single case in Islamabad where in the course of the general medical examination of a fiancée the doctor noted in her report that she detected signs of marriage although the applicant claimed to be unmarried.[31]

However, the Home Office did not elaborate upon the nature of such 'signs of marriage', which we can assume is coded language for the absence of a hymen. Nor did the Home Office explain how this could be noted in a 'general medical examination' under the guidelines for medical inspectors stipulated by the Immigration Act 1971.

A 1977 letter from R. S. Weekes of the Home Office to the FCO's Migration and Visa Department discusses a similar instruction given by Shirley Summerskill, Under-Secretary of State for Home Affairs, in 1975, referring to an 'embargo on the use of evidence of sexual intercourse' in fiancée cases.[32] The 1977 letter states that 'Dr. Summerskill has decided, *following a recent case*, that the embargo . . . should extend to cases involving female dependents' (emphasis added).[33] The full instruction attached to the letter read:

> Posts have already been advised that where a fiancée agrees to be medically examined and the examination reveals that she has experienced sexual relations this information must not be used against her as evidence that she is already married. This note is to make it clear that the restriction applies to any evidence, however acquired, that the applicant may have experienced sexual relations and includes cases where the evidence reveals that the applicant is or has been pregnant. The restriction also applies where a woman seeks admission under paragraph 44 HC 79 or 39 HC 81 as an unmarried daughter under 21.[34]

It should be noted that these instructions do not direct the staff at British High Commissions to stop conducting examinations that may reveal 'signs' of sexual intercourse, but that such examinations could not be used, at least not explicitly, to deny someone entry to Britain. The aforementioned letter from Weekes to the Migration and Visa Department indicates that the results of such examinations might be useful as background information, advising, 'where refusal of an entry clearance is contemplated in these circumstances other proof of the applicant's marital status must be adduced to support the decision'.[35]

A telegram from the British High Commission in Islamabad to the High Commission in Dacca, sent in February 1979, offered a conflicting opinion on the purpose of these tests. The telegram pointed out that 'Mr Lyon's instruction of 9 September 1975 did not specifically ban marriage medical examinations but instructed that the results of any such tests made should not be used for immigration purposes'.[36] On the one hand, the telegram admitted that '[l]ogically, therefore, the tests have since been pointless', while on the other, it disclosed that '[o]ccasionally, our panel doctors have offered information gratuitously' and '[w]hen this happens it could influence a decision on whether or not a field trip might be productive'.[37]

While this may have been the case in Islamabad, the British High Commission in Dacca claimed that it had received no instruction from Alex Lyon in 1975. As the controversy spread in February 1979, the High Commission in Dacca telegrammed the FCO (as well as the Commissions in Delhi and Islamabad) declaring that 'there is no record on our files to show that Mr Lyon instructed ECOs not to ask for medical examinations to determine whether women had had sexual relations or had borne children'.[38] Figures of any such examinations occurring in Dacca have not been recorded, but the same telegram acknowledged that such a gynaecological examination 'had been done on one occasion involving a fiancée in the past and that occasionally other ladies had had similar medical examinations'.[39]

Although Alex Lyon stated in 1979 that he had ordered the practice to stop, an interview he gave to journalist Amrit Wilson in 1978 revealed the logic that left open the possibility for vaginal examinations of migrant women to continue, under the spurious grounds of checking for communicable diseases:

> Q. *Do you approve of a woman having to have a vaginal examination as part of a routine medical examination to enter Britain?*
>
> A. The fact of the matter is that any medical examination is carried out to see if they have any communicable disease. If they do, it is thought unwise to allow them to come and settle in this country by and large. If they had a communicable disease and it entailed investigating the vagina to find out, then I suppose the doctor is entitled to do that.[40]

The second example of the Home Office rationalising the practice of virginity testing involved Willie Whitelaw, who took over as Home Secretary after the 1979 election. Whitelaw issued a statement about the virginity testing incident at Heathrow Airport, which furthered the minimisation strategy adopted by the previous government. He admitted that the Home Office was aware that 'in Delhi in the past some adult daughters applying for settlement were referred to a medical adviser (an Indian lady gynaecologist) with questions as to their marital status', but claimed that '[t]hese cases were very different from the circumstances of the Heathrow incident'.[41] No further explanation was offered to elaborate on the differences between the Heathrow case and the cases that had occurred outside Britain, although both involved a physical examination to determine whether a woman was married or not. Whitelaw further qualified that the incident at Heathrow was 'not a "virginity test"', but claimed that the Immigration Officer in this case simply asked the medical inspector during a 'normal examination' to 'give his opinion [on] whether she had borne children'.[42] However, as previously discussed, medical examinations usually did not occur at ports of entry, unless an Immigration Officer suspected that the person entering the country had a disease that would endanger the health of others or would require major medical treatment in the UK. Yet we know from various Home Office and FCO documents that the medical examination conducted on the woman at Heathrow was specifically requested by the Immigration Officer, and that the woman was informed of the request and that she had to sign a consent form to be subjected to a gynaecological examination to check for any physical indicators that she had previously borne children.

Alongside its minimisation strategy to limit the negative impact of such revelations, the government desired to be seen as taking immediate action to put a halt to the virginity testing practice altogether. This is evident in an official statement issued by the Home Secretary in February 1979 that claimed that the practice had been officially terminated.[43] Evan Luard's announcement in Parliament attests to this, when he declared on 2 February 1979 that 'all our missions in the Indian sub-continent were instructed that they too should not ask for examinations of applicants for entry clearance to establish whether they had borne children or had had sexual relations'.[44] From another source of evidence (the drafting of the Yellowlees Report, discussed below), we identified that this matter concerning the Home Secretary's instructions to stop the practice of virginity testing had been investigated by the Indian press. The FCO's guided response on this question was that evidence was not really required 'because pages of documentation are not needed to show that something is *not* happening' (our emphasis). It further stated that Dr Evans, who carried out the investigation in South Asia for the Yellowlees Report, 'has given his firm assurance that the instructions are being obeyed'.[45]

Nevertheless, there was an apprehension amongst critics to accept this claim on face value, as it seemed that the Home Secretary had twice before, in 1968 and 1976, been aware that the practice was occurring but had failed to stop it, as claimed by Mary Dines from the JCWI.[46] In early March 1979, the CRE sought evidence that the government was truly taking action to end the practice. The CRE requested that the Home Secretary publish instructions to Immigration Officers to terminate the practice.[47] It also pushed for 'an independent public inquiry into the application of the Immigration Act and Rules to individuals, especially members of the non-white ethnic minorities'.[48]

The CRE assumed the role of watchdog regarding this matter and claimed that its duty was to conduct an investigation into immigration control procedures due to the potentially racially discriminatory nature of the practice of virginity testing.[49] The Commission identified the strategic role played by immigration control in building and maintaining good race relations in Britain. It argued that the failure to appreciate the nexus between what takes place in the internal community and at the border would lead to the opposite results:

> any discriminatory practices in the immigration procedures and services are not conductive *but* detrimental to good race relations.[50]

However, the CRE's approach to this matter was not supported by the government. Indeed, the Home Office embraced a defensive strategy in relation to the immigration control procedures. It claimed that the immigration system was inherently discriminatory on the grounds of 'nationality' and that there was no valid alternative to it. Geoffrey de Deney, an Under-Secretary of State in the Home Office, wrote to Deputy Under-Secretary of State P. J. Woodfield in 1980 stating that the CRE was 'doing race relations in this country no service' by giving the impression that 'immigration control is a race relations issue'.[51] Another internal communication from Home Office staffer D. H. J. Hillary to Woodfield in 1981 highlighted as 'a well-known fact' that immigration laws 'discriminate on their face between nationalities' and that 'a greater proportion of citizens of some countries fall foul of the control'.[52]

This point was echoed in a letter from J. D. Semken in the Home Office to the department's legal representative James Nursaw:

> Migration is essentially a racial matter, and the only basis upon which the periodic migrations to which all peoples are subject can be regulated, is by numbers according to race. How else can

one regulate a flood, whether of East African Asians or Vietnamese Chinese?[53]

The Home Office went to extreme measures to prevent the CRE from initiating an investigation, taking the case before the courts. Its strategy was to argue, as we see several Home Office staffers did, that discrimination was a necessary part of immigration control. The following extract from a statement by the Home Office's legal representation, published in *Race & Class* journal, shows this way of thinking:

> The whole system of immigration control is based upon discrimination. It is the essence of the Immigration Act that people will be discriminated against on the grounds of race or nationality and it is the function of certain officials to ensure that that discrimination is effective.[54]

A telegram from the FCO to the British High Commissions in South Asia tried to disassociate the British government from the words of its legal counsel, stating that 'Mr Peter Scott QC is not a Home Office spokesman but council [sic] employed by the Home Office in their dispute with the CRE'.[55] But Scott made further remarks that affirmed for many that discrimination based upon national group was part of the immigration control process, which were quoted by the FCO:

> It has been drawn to my attention that in certain newspapers great play has been made of the fact that I said that immigration is based on discrimination. I thought I had made myself plain. Under the Race Relations Act 1976, discrimination is defined in a way which includes nationality. Immigration control, whether in this or any other country, is inevitably based on some form of discrimination of that nature. I drew a distinction between discrimination in that sense and the way an Immigration Officer carries out his [sic] duties. I mentioned the Immigration Rules which expressly require that Immigration Officers carry out their duties without regard to race, colour or religion.[56]

The Labour government was seeking to manage this matter very carefully since it did not wish to foster a view that it was acting in a discriminatory manner. This had been a concern throughout Labour's term in office. Evan Luard had previously argued that treating incoming dependants too harshly might jeopardise Labour's relationship with the migrant communities in Britain. In a letter to the FCO, Luard stated that any restrictions upon dependants:

> would certainly be strongly denounced by the representatives of the minority groups in this country and would badly damage the Labour Party's respectability amongst these minorities (who, as has frequently been pointed out, could determine the result in a number of marginal constituencies at the next election).[57]

This reflects a concern that the immigration control system had to be perceived as balanced – to be seen as sufficiently restrictive to placate the anti-immigration lobby and as sufficiently fair by Britain's migrant communities and progressives, while also maintaining Britain's role as a protector of human rights and democracy. However, when the CRE sought to investigate racial discrimination within the immigration control system under the remit of the Race Relations Act 1976, Labour (and later the Conservatives) argued that the laws against racial discrimination did not apply to government institutions, especially the immigration control system.

The CRE obtains permission to investigate

It was the Race Relations Act 1976, however, that gave the CRE more space to manoeuvre. The Commission held that under sections 43 and 48 of the Act, it was able to hold an inquiry into immigration control procedures on the basis of seeking to promote good race relations in Britain. The wording of these sections in the 1976 Act became very important in enabling the government's non-compliance with the Commission's proposed investigation. Section 43 of the Act established the CRE and bestowed upon it the following duties:

(a) to work towards the elimination of discrimination;
(b) to promote equality of opportunity, and good relations, between persons of different racial groups generally;[58]

Alongside this, Section 48 stated that 'the Commission may if they think fit... conduct a formal investigation *for any purpose* connected with the carrying out of those duties' (emphasis added).[59] Thus, the CRE believed that it was duty bound to conduct an investigation into immigration control procedures because the possibility of discrimination occurring within the immigration control system hindered the promotion of good race relations. However, both the outgoing Labour government and the incoming Conservative government attempted to dissuade and obstruct the CRE from conducting an investigation for a number of differing, and possibly contradictory, reasons.

The government argued, unsuccessfully, that the Race Relations Act was not applicable to its own institutions, including the immigration control system. The Home Office claimed that the CRE could not investigate the activities of the state as this would be outside the scope of its duties as defined under the Act. It also claimed that the duties bestowed upon the CRE in Section 43 of the Act were limited to the fields of employment; housing; the provision of goods, facilities and services to the public; and clubs, which are covered by earlier parts of the Act, and that the functions of the government fell outside these designated categories, stating, '[i]t is important to note that the Act is in no way concerned with Crown functions (i.e. the functions of government)'.[60] This argument formed the basis of the Home Office's legal challenge to the CRE's investigation launched in late 1979 under the Conservatives. The *All England Law Reports* cited that the CRE had 'believed that the Immigration Act 1971 was being applied more harshly to coloured immigrants than to white immigrants' and 'wished to examine Home Office documents, to interview immigration officers and to conduct sample surveys of refusals of entry into the United Kingdom or refusals to vary leave to enter or remain'.[61] The Home Office sought a court order to establish whether it was actually in the Commission's power under the Race Relations Act 'to investigate the manner of discharging government functions'.[62] Justice Woolf, who presided over the case, found that an investigation into the control of immigration was within the parameters of the CRE's duty under the 1976 Act, and declared, 'I cannot accept that Parliament must be assumed to have intended, as the Home Office contends, that the field of immigration should be a no-go area for the Commission.'[63] The CRE was thus allowed to proceed with the investigation, but the Home Office was not obliged to cooperate with the investigation.

Alongside this challenge to the legality of applying the Race Relations Act 1976 to the functions of the state, the Home Office ran other arguments concurrently with the aim of hindering the CRE's investigation. One argument cited the apparent bias of the Commission, which some claimed would not allow an objective inquiry to take place, and was first raised by Labour and later reiterated by the Conservatives. In March 1979, Brynmor John criticised the CRE's call for an independent inquiry as 'symptomatic of an increasing tendency on the part of the CRE to become diverted from its essential tasks'.[64] Throughout 1980, the Home Office reported the CRE's widespread 'credibility problem' amongst immigration control staff.[65] The Immigration Service Branch of the Society of Civil and Public Servants (SCPS) was cited by Home Office officials as expressing that 'the CRE would be incapable of conducting an impartial inquiry'.[66] This suspicion of the CRE was, as Woodfield explained to Stephen Boys-Smith in an internal Home Office document, directed at the Commission's rank-and-file staff, who shared the same union, the SCPS, with immigration staff and who had used the union to criticise immigration officials over the virginity testing incident at Heathrow.[67] This hostility had a serious impact upon the progress of the investigation. By 1982, the Immigration and Nationality Department had reported that '[t]he main obstacle to the Commission's enquiries remain their inability to visit ports and interview staff because of union problems'.[68]

Despite all of the arguments put forward by the government, the CRE was permitted to proceed with its investigation. However, this did not mean that the government was willing to cooperate, and there was a slight element of obstruction in the actions of the Home Office in relation to the investigation. Internal Home Office documents reveal that the government feared the 'potential embarrassment' that might result from having to hand over documents and files to Parliament, such as 'the General Instructions to the Immigration Service', and believed that it could not provide 'files containing officials' advice to Ministers'.[69] The Home Office expressed to the CRE that it hoped that 'the Commission will confine its requests to the Home Office to the minimum', stating that there was a 'particular problem with regard to material that is classified in the security sense', which the Home Office was reluctant to release.[70] The Home Office informed its employees that 'for presentational reasons' they had to 'be seen to co-operate as fully as possible with the CRE', but demanded that the CRE agree to restrictions upon the dissemination of any information it obtained from the Home Office.[71] This investigation took place between 1981 and 1982 and the results were eventually published in 1985. These results are discussed in Chapter 6.

X-rays and the Yellowlees Report

Alongside virginity testing and other scrutinising practices at the border, *The Guardian* also revealed that X-rays were being taken of women and children from the Indian subcontinent for the purpose of ascertaining the age of suspected 'bogus' migrants. With the significant number of migrants applying to enter the UK under the guise of family reconciliation, particularly as children aged under 18, the UK authorities were of the opinion that this category presented a loophole that could be exploited, particularly as documentation regarding children was frequently less substantial than that available for an adult (for example, children often did not have their own passports and were simply listed on an adult's passport). The UK border control staff were especially concerned about teenage male migrants, who, if they were over the age of 18, would not be allowed to enter the UK and who were the least 'desirable' category of migrant (due to their potential labour capacity) in 1970s Britain. Therefore, to determine whether teenagers were falsely claiming to be under 18 for migration purposes, the UK border control system, particularly at the British High Commissions in South Asia where applications for entry clearance certificates were first assessed, used X-rays of the wrists of individuals to estimate the skeletal age of the applicant.

Although X-rays had been used throughout most of the 1970s, it was not until *The Guardian* published details of gynaecological examinations being conducted on migrating South Asian women in early 1979 that the practice became widely known. At the height of the virginity testing controversy in February 1979,[72] details also emerged that X-rays were being taken of women and children to ascertain the age of suspected 'bogus' migrants, alongside tests purportedly aimed at checking for communicable diseases. It was claimed in *The Guardian* that these X-rays were being conducted by Immigration

Officers at Heathrow who were not qualified to use X-ray machines, as well as at High Commissions abroad, which 'expose[d] both the passengers and clerks to considerable radiation hazards'.[73] *The Guardian* also reported that at the British High Commission in Dacca, a pregnant woman had her skull X-rayed (for reasons not divulged), 'despite the fact that Department of Health regulations would prevent such a test on pregnant British women'.[74] A possible indication that the British government held strict immigration control as a major priority, over and above the need to adopt a humanitarian approach to the treatment of potential migrants, was evident in the response to these allegations by Eric Deakins, a junior Department of Health Minister, who said that 'immigration screening cannot be measured against [domestic] NHS [National Health Service] standards'.[75] As in the case of virginity tests, the veracity and usefulness of these examinations were questioned, with Labour MP Jo Richardson stating, 'medical opinion...is beginning to query the practice. It is beginning to say that it is an unreliable method of determining age'.[76] In response to the questions surrounding the use of X-rays in immigration control, the Labour government acquiesced somewhat in the face of mounting criticism and Rees announced that the Chief Medical Officer Sir Henry Yellowlees would 'carry out a review of the objects and nature of all medical examinations in the immigration control context'.[77]

Various critics, including Jo Richardson and the editors of *The Guardian* in particular, condemned the lack of transparency in the government's immigration control procedures. Ms Richardson declared in Parliament that it was 'high time that the secret instructions given by the Home Secretary to immigration officers under the immigration legislation were made public'.[78] The treatment of legitimate migrants and the scrutiny placed upon applications to enter Britain were shaped in large part by the discretion of individual ECOs, but the manner in which these discretionary powers manifested was not open to any kind of evaluation by anyone outside the border control system. A *Guardian* editorial criticised the extent of the discretionary powers of ECOs and the lack of transparency in the application of such powers:

> The central issue thrown up by the variety of medical tests remains that of discretion and its monitoring....When the virginity tests

first came to light, we said that investigation of a particular case was not enough and that a full debate on immigration procedures was needed.... But it cannot begin until the full codes of guidance for immigration officers and their medical colleagues as well, are published and the scope of their practices is clearly and publicly disclosed.[79]

Frustration amongst sections of the media and migrants' groups with the internal inquiry being conducted by Henry Yellowlees led in part to the CRE's independent investigation into discrimination within the immigration control system. The inquiry performed by Yellowlees and his assistant Dr N. J. B. Evans was undertaken over the years 1979 to 1980, with the final report released to Parliament in April 1980.

Evans travelled to South Asia in 1980 to investigate the broad topic of medical examination within the immigration control system and, based on his fieldwork, much of the final report was written by him. A draft version of the Yellowlees Report stated that, according to 'orthodox radiological opinion in the UK and overseas', it was 'acceptable to use such bone X-rays to assist in estimating the age of children',[80] while the final report concluded that X-rays were 'a potentially more accurate method of estimating the age of children' than other examinations of the body, such as 'skin texture, wrinkling or firmness of tissues, and of noting indications of puberty'.[81] Drawing on the findings of North American studies, the report claimed that '[t]he accuracy attainable is in the order of plus or minus six months and the radiation exposure negligible'. And while it noted that tables of skeletal maturity were based on North American children and that there is 'very little firm data' on how these tables compared with the skeletons of children from South Asia, the report argued that it was assumed that skeletons matured earlier in South Asian children and so such data were thus still useful.[82]

In several instances, High Commission staff complained that the use of X-rays for age assessment was a practice initiated by applying migrants, rather than implemented by ECOs, and affirmed that the results were indeed helpful in making decisions on immigration cases. A telegram from the High Commission in Islamabad to the FCO headquarters in London stated that 'in practice, like Dacca, we find [X-rays] a useful instrument of control in the circumstances of immigration from Pakistan', and claimed that 'our immigration panel doctors are unanimous that x-rays are the only means at their disposal for assessing age'.[83] The telegram added, 'unsuccessful applicants often call for their own x-rays to be made where age is in question or ask us [for] the x-rays we have done for use at appeals'.[84]

F. S. Miles, the High Commissioner in Dacca, wrote in a mid-1979 detailed report to the FCO, titled *Immigration from Bangladesh: Will It Ever End?*, that the 'X-ray is the one scientific tool we have' against bogus applications, after asserting that 'Bengalis...are probably the most prone to invention and fabrication.'[85] Miles claimed that criticism of the use of X-rays came from 'the pro-immigrant lobby' and that 'there has been no criticism in Bangladesh of the use of x-rays', arguing that the Bangladeshi government used X-rays for the same purpose.[86] Even if there were risks, Miles contended, the fault lay with the Bangladeshi applicants (whom he considered to be untrustworthy):

> my Immigration Section did not start the system. It began some years ago when Bangladeshi applicants began to produce X-rays of themselves to prove their age, and our staff decided we would have to have our own X-rays to discover whether those which had been produced were in fact the X-rays of the applicant and not of someone else.[87]

While the Yellowlees Report was being finalised, some in the FCO queried whether there was a problem with it focusing on the use of X-rays in South Asia and the fact that the fieldwork was only conducted in the Indian subcontinent. A telegram from John Thomson, the British High Commissioner in Delhi, to John Graham, Deputy Under-Secretary to the FCO, in December 1979 suggested that some 'passages seem directed only to Commonwealth or even Asian immigrants', and that instead the report needed to state 'explicitly that there is no discrimination against immigrants from the subcontinent'.[88] A day earlier, Thomson had sent another telegram to the FCO headquarters in London stating that, while realistically the report only needed to focus on the X-raying of South Asian migrants as 'there is little continuing immigration to the UK elsewhere than from the sub-continent', the report, to stave off criticism, needed to enquire as to 'whether at any time in the past other posts...ever used (in however limited a way) x-rays for age assessment purposes'.[89]

Thomson recommended the need to identify whether the High Commissions in Nairobi or Dar es Salaam used X-rays for these purposes during the exoduses of African Asians from Kenya, Uganda and Malawi, and put forward Nicosia, Valletta and Lagos as other places where it would be worth making such enquiries.[90] Records indicate that Thomson's suggestion to enquire into practices at other High Commissions was not adopted, but clarification was to be inserted into the draft report as to why there was a focus on South Asia:

> The Indian sub-continent was chosen as the location for viewing procedures on the ground because it is in that region that our entry clearance issuing posts are under greatest pressure and where our procedures have met most criticism. The recommendations are, of course, intended to have general application (except to the extent that EEC obligations may supervene).[91]

Documents from the National Archives opened in 2010 show that, before the use of X-rays was publicised in *The Guardian* in 1979, the JCWI and the Labour Party's Human Rights Sub-Committee raised questions about the use of X-rays for age assessment purposes. The JCWI and the Sub-Committee questioned the validity of such procedures, and in June 1978, W. Jones of the FCO's Migration and Visa Department sent a letter to the High Commissions in South Asia to enquire about their use and whether there was consensus on the subcontinent that 'medical estimates, X-rays and visual impressions are valueless in making age estimates'.[92] In another letter to the High Commission in Islamabad, Jones noted that the Human Rights Sub-Committee had stated that:

> Estimates of age from doctors or the use of x-rays should not be considered since the DHSS [Department of Health and Social Security] consider they are unreliable within certain limits.[93]

In the same letter to Islamabad, Jones also cited the reply to the Sub-Committee by Shirley Summerskill:

> We are well aware of the limitations on estimates by age by doctors and the use of X-rays in this context. Nevertheless when other evidence suggests that the applicant is not the age stated then any

reports from a doctor which reinforce this belief must be taken into account.[94]

The correspondence between Jones and the High Commissions referred to an Immigration Appeals Tribunal case from 1973 in which an ECO in Dacca used X-rays to dispute the age of a child seeking to join his parents in the UK, on the belief that the child who presented for examination in Dacca was not the age they claimed to be on their application documents (and in the view of the ECO, was possibly not the same child). This estimate was challenged, and a medical report solicited by the applicant's family from Dr James at the London School of Hygiene and Tropical Medicine stated:

> I do not think that one can rely on the medical evidence as excluding the possibility that this child was 12 years old. The serious effects of environmental factors on bone growth [in Bangladesh] are sufficient to make me hesitate to put an age to this child on the basis of medical and some X-Ray evidence alone.[95]

The Appeals Tribunal agreed with the findings of this report and allowed for precedent to be set in disregarding X-rays as evidence in age disputes concerning children from the Indian subcontinent. However, this was not to be the case as X-rays were routinely used throughout the late 1970s and early 1980s.

The purpose of Jones's letter to the High Commissions was to attempt to source information that could 'rebut the inference that, there being no standard table for assessing age from bone characteristics in the sub-continent, estimating the age of people in Pakistan, India and Bangladesh is largely a waste of time'.[96] The High Commission in New Delhi replied that it was 'entirely in agreement' with Summerskill's statement and said that there was little use of X-rays for age assessment purposes at its post.[97] John Perris in New Delhi wrote to the Migration and Visa Department of the FCO in London that 'age estimates have little value over the age of about 25' and that the ECOs 'do not send the very young or very old for examination', clarifying that it was 'normally in the range of 11–22 years that we seek evidence of age (always by an x-ray)'.[98] Perris's letter indicated that 12 people had been X-rayed for age assessment purposes in the first half of 1978, with four age estimates being higher than the stated age. Perris wrote that, of this 12, 'ECs [Entry Clearances] were issued in 3 cases and the remainder were either referred or deferred', adding that '[i]n no case was a decision taken to refuse'.[99]

Other National Archives documents reveal that there were doubts expressed by staff in Pakistan about age estimates conducted by X-ray as early as 1969. T. R. Peters from the British High Commission in Lahore wrote to the FCO in London in April of that year informing it that one of the doctors used by the High Commission was not basing his age estimates on X-rays and explained that 'after puberty an X-ray was of no help when attempting to distinguish between a 13 or 14 year old and a 17 year old'.[100] R. C. Trant, from an unspecified High Commission in South Asia, wrote to the FCO headquarters in response to Peters's letter, agreeing that X-rays were 'of no real value in cases approaching the borderline [ages]' before stating, 'we feel that since the use is so limited, it is probably better not to use this method at all for age determination'.[101]

The Yellowlees Report, drafted by Dr Evans, appeared in late 1980, although it was only released to Members of Parliament and not published by Her Majesty's Stationery Office. The major finding of the report regarding the use of X-rays for age assessment purposes was:

5. I conclude that the use of X-rays of the bony skeleton provides a useful, fairly accurate and acceptable safe way of estimating the age of children when it is important to do so. (Children in this context means up to about 21 years ...) Only one or two X-ray pictures need be taken, of the upper limb or the lower limb excluding the hips. Provided proper shielding is used in accordance with normal radiological practice, the radiation dose to the parts X-rayed is minimal and the scattered gonadal dose is insignificant. These views accord with informed radiological opinion in the UK and overseas.[102]

The report also concluded that 'United Kingdom radiological opinion holds that X-rays are not particularly useful for estimating the age of adults', stating that the FCO had instructed ECOs in October 1979 that X-rays should not be administered on anyone thought to be over 21 years of age.[103]

Despite the Yellowlees Report recommending that the border control system continue to use X-rays to assess the age of migrants thought to be under 21 years of age, several other people and organisations criticised this viewpoint. At the Annual General Meeting of the British Medical Association (BMA) in 1979, a resolution was passed that stated that 'radiological examinations, carried out solely for administrative and political purposes, are unethical', and proposed that the BMA 'make the strongest possible representation to the Government to ban these practices'. A report prepared by Edward White for Lord Avebury, a Liberal member of the House of Lords, cited the past chair of the National Council of Radiation Protection as warning against unnecessary X-rays and claiming that 'there is no safe level of exposure'. White also questioned the accuracy of age assessment through the use of X-rays, particularly in relation to the use of generalised data on the age-bone ratio based on North American children to assess South Asian children, and concluded:

> After a thorough and objective examination of the practice, one must conclude that radiological examinations are a highly inaccurate method of determining chronological age.[104]

As mentioned previously, the Yellowlees Report evaded the issue of data on the skeletal maturity of South Asian children and recommended that further research in this area be conducted. The JCWI stated that the report, in relation to its findings on X-rays, 'managed to contradict itself and most accepted medical opinion regarding the reliability of such assessment'.[105] However, FCO briefing notes on responses to press questions on the report stated that the Home Secretary was 'not aware that the balance of informed medical opinion is against such tests',[106] and the government persisted with the claim that X-rays for age assessment purposes were both useful and relatively safe.[107]

Confidential correspondence between the FCO and the British High Commission in Delhi showed that, despite the high level of use of X-rays for age assessment purposes in Pakistan and Bangladesh, High Commissioner John Thomson recommended that the practice be ceased in India. Thomson argued in a telegram to the FCO's London headquarters that 'they are ... very little used here and do not therefore make a significant contribution to the control of immigration'.[108] The FCO ministers had secretly debated 'whether political considerations make it desirable to stop the practice', and while publicly standing by the stance taken by Whitelaw, they allowed the British High Commission in Delhi to stop the practice as 'a matter of local discretion'.[109] While allowing Thomson to order his staff to discontinue using X-rays for age assessment purposes, the FCO warned that this should not be made publicly known as 'it could embarrass Sir Henry and the Home Secretary, who have both gone on record as saying that there are no grounds of medical practice or ethics why such examinations should not continue'.[110] Thomson instructed his staff in Bombay and Calcutta according to the following:

> I have sought and obtained FCO confirmation that the use of x-rays for age assessment is a matter for local discretion. In the circumstances I have decided...our interests here would best be served by discontinuing, at any rate for the time being, the practice of using x-rays of the limb joints of a young person to help assess his or her age. I should be grateful if you would ensure that this instruction is complied with forthwith.[111]

In a later telegram, Thomson, in an effort to keep this decision from becoming public knowledge, directed to the High Commissions in Bombay and Calcutta as follows:

> you should not...issue the instruction to your medical referees but should instead instruct your ECOs if they wish to refer an applicant to a medical referee for age assessment, to specify that the examination should be clinical only and not include an x-ray.[112]

Citing that the Dacca High Commission staff found X-rays to be 'a valuable instrument of immigration control', the FCO decided that the decision taken by Thomson would not extend to Pakistan and Bangladesh.[113] So the X-raying of children continued in Pakistan and Bangladesh throughout 1980 and 1981. In January 1981, the Foreign Minister, Lord Carrington, stated in the House of Lords that in the last nine months of 1980, around 360 children under 21 had been X-rayed in Dacca and around another 300 in Islamabad.[114] The following January, Parliamentary Under-Secretary for the FCO, David Trefgarne, announced in the House of Lords that, during 1981, approximately 420 children had been X-rayed in Islamabad and 262 children in Dacca.[115]

In February 1982, Home Secretary Whitelaw announced that the FCO would no longer be carrying out X-rays on children for these purposes. He stated in Parliament that Yellowlees had revised his opinion since his report was released in 1980, and advised the Home Secretary that X-rays were now 'unlikely to provide more accurate evidence of age than the assessment of other physical characteristics of an individual, and therefore can add little to the general clinical examination'.[116] The Runnymede Trust archive at the Black Cultural Archives in London contains a copy of the letter that Yellowlees wrote to Whitelaw, which concluded that 'the usefulness of the X-ray method of estimating age must be limited in the immigration context'. Yellowlees maintained that X-rays were relatively safe, but chiefly found that using the template of the skeletal maturity of North American or European children to assess the age of South Asian children was inadequate to make an accurate assessment of age among the latter. He stated, 'the scientific foundation for this when applied – for example – to Asian children must be open to doubt'.[117] An internal Home Office memo outlined that advice from the DHSS had informally recommended that 'to achieve a 95 per cent [sic] degree of accuracy from X-ray assessments the minimum tolerance that should be applied to adolescents in the Sub-continent . . . is three years either way, and a tolerance of four years would not be unrealistic'.[118] This meant that:

> when an ECO is confronted with an applicant who has a bone age of 14 years, he could at the most say that his age falls between 11 and 17 years and, if challenged, would have to admit that it might well fall in the range of 10 to 18 years.[119]

Whitelaw said in Parliament that Yellowlees had 'concluded that such X-ray examinations are of limited value and their continued use in the immigration context can no longer be justified'.[120]

A letter from Whitelaw to Carrington in January 1982 indicates that Yellowlees's change of opinion might not have been the only deciding factor in abandoning X-rays for age assessment purposes. We have documented that the High Commission in India had banned the use of X-rays for these purposes in 1980 and a letter from the Home Secretary to the Foreign Secretary states that the use of X-rays had been recently suspended in Dacca, leaving 'Islamabad alone of the posts on the sub-continent...continuing this practice'.[121] With the weight of medical opinion on one side and the eventual decision of High Commissions in South Asia to scrap the use of X-rays on the other, it would have been easier for Whitelaw to call for an end to the practice in early 1982 than to maintain the line established a year or so earlier.

In its report on the investigation into discrimination in the immigration control system, the CRE argued that since the government had acknowledged that X-rays were not reliable for estimating age, 'it should attempt to review previous cases where such evidence was a substantial factor leading to refusal', but this recommendation was not pursued by the government.[122] A document outlining the government's response to the CRE report, held in the Runnymede Trust archive, stated that it was 'not feasible' to review all of these cases 'given the immense amount of work it would involve'.[123]

Since Whitelaw's decision to end the use of X-rays for the assessment of age in migrant children, from time to time parliamentarians have referred to the topic. For example, in the House of Lords debate on the Asylum and Immigration Bill 1996, Lord Avebury sought to insert an amendment which would effectively ban the use of X-rays for the assessment of age, but was rebuffed by Lord David Renton who said that, '[i]t is difficult for the immigration officers, medical people, or anyone to say what those people's ages really are. If the X-ray can decide the matter, we should keep an open mind on the issue'.[124] Aynsley-Green et al. have identified that the matter was brought up again in 2006 and 2009, and most recently was revived by the UK Border Agency in early 2012.[125]

Conclusion

This chapter has outlined how the British government, under both Callaghan's Labour and Thatcher's Conservatives, responded to the revelation of the virginity testing practice by *The Guardian* in early 1979. The initial reaction of the government, led by Home Secretary Rees, was to question whether the tests on South Asian women had taken place in the manner alleged and to claim that any such test was part of a 'routine' medical examination to which most migrants were subjected. However, these claims were contested as details emerged that the practice was much more common than first thought, with numerous cases alleged to have occurred in British High Commissions across the Indian subcontinent. The strategy of the Home Office and the FCO was thus to deny publicly the number of examinations conducted (even though internal correspondence reveals that by March 1979 the Prime Minister's Office knew of at least 80 cases), and to hope that public criticism would be stemmed by the announcement of an investigation into the process of medical examinations of immigrants by Sir Henry Yellowlees.

Soon after the practice of virginity testing was revealed in the mainstream press, the CRE announced that the Home Secretary should allow an independent investigation to pursue allegations of racist (and sexist) discrimination within the immigration control system. However, the Home Office was keen to resist this and challenged the questions raised by the CRE, claiming that discrimination was necessary to ensure the effective control of immigration, as well as launching legal action against the CRE, disputing whether it had the necessary powers to investigate another government institution. The CRE's investigation eventually led to the publication of a report in 1985, which is explored in detail in Chapter 6.

The same strategies of denial, justification and obfuscation were adopted by the Home Office and the FCO when similar questions were asked about the use of C-rays within the immigration control system, with criticisms that X-rays were being performed upon minors not for medical reasons, but to verify their entry clearance applications. The Yellowlees investigation was used by the incoming Conservative government to deflect enquiries about the administrative and non-medical use of X-rays. Although the Yellowlees Report, released to MPs in April 1980, sanctioned the use of X-rays for age assessment purposes, the documents we have uncovered show that the Home Office and the FCO, internally, were in doubt over the usefulness of X-rays and quietly abandoned using them in all overseas posts except the High Commission in Bangladesh. But eventually Yellowlees, for reasons unknown, reassessed his position, and in 1982, Willie Whitelaw announced in the House of Commons that X-rays would no longer be used to determine the age of potential migrants. Since this 1982 embargo, there have occasionally been calls to reintroduce X-rays to verify the claims of potential migrants (and more recently, asylum seekers). While we have shown that, by the early 1980s, both the practice of virginity testing and the use of X-rays for age assessment were officially ended by the government, other examinations of migrants' bodies were used to scrutinise those trying to enter the country. Using the case of British-Pakistani woman Anwar Ditta, the next chapter will demonstrate how, while some practices were discontinued, other forms of physical inspection continued to be used to interrogate migrants' applications for entry.

Notes

1. Pratibha Parmar, 'Gender, Race and Class', p. 245.
2. *Hansard*, 5 February 1979, col. 1w.
3. *Hansard*, 5 February 1979, col. 1w.
4. 'Instructions to Medical Inspectors', p. 2, HO 418/33, NA.
5. Letter from Mr Hillary to Mr Flesher, 1 February 1979, HO 418/29, NA.
6. Ibid.
7. Ibid.
8. Ibid.
9. 'Medical Examinations at Ports: Statement by the Home Office', 2 February 1979, HO 418/29 338797, NA.
10. Ibid.
11. *Hansard*, 19 February 1979, col. 221.
12. Wilson, *Dreams, Questions, Struggles*, p. 78.
13. *Hansard*, 21 March 1979, col. 672w.
14. Letter from J.S. Wall to N. Stephens, 5 March 1979, PREM 16/2000, NA.
15. '[Mrs K]: Claim for Compensation', 9 January 1980, p. 1, FCO 50/675, NA.
16. Ibid.
17. Ibid., p. 2.
18. Ibid.
19. Ibid.
20. Ibid.
21. Ibid., p. 3.
22. Ibid.
23. '[Mrs K]: Claim for Compensation', 9 January 1980, p. 1, FCO 50/675, NA.
24. Ibid.
25. Ibid., pp. 1–2.
26. Telegram from British High Commission in Delhi to FCO, no. 35, 9 January 1980, FCO 50/676, NA.
27. Ibid.
28. *The Guardian*, 2 February 1979, pp. 24, 1.
29. Ibid., p. 1.

30. Ibid.
31. 'Briefing for the Sub-Committee of the Select Committee on Home Affairs', 18 December 1980, p. 2, HO 418/33, NA.
32. Letter from R.S. Weekes to G. Brownlee, 8 September 1977, FCO 50/612, NA.
33. Ibid.
34. 'General Guidance: Fiancées and Female Dependants', attached to Letter from R.S. Weekes to G. Brownlee, 8 September 1977, FCO 50/612, NA.
35. Ibid.
36. Telegram from Islamabad British High Commission to Dacca British High Commission, 'Mr Luard's Visit: Immigration Medical Examinations', 20 February 1979, FCO 50/661.
37. Ibid. A field trip refers to a visit by FCO officials to the village or town where the applicant resides. These were conducted if a significant problem arose in the processing of entry clearance certificates, such as a visit by FCO officials to the Syhlet region of Bangladesh to examine how people from the region were claiming kinship for tax and migration purposes.
38. 'Mr Luard's Visit: Immigration Medical Examinations', Telegram from Dacca British High Commission to FCO, 19 February 1979, FCO 50/661.
39. Ibid.
40. Amrit Wilson, *Finding a Voice*, p. 76.
41. 'Statement on Yellowlees Report – Notes for Supplementaries', n.d., p. 2, FCO 50/679, NA.
42. Ibid., pp. 2–3.
43. *Hansard*, 5 February 1979, col. 2w.
44. Ibid.
45. Telegram from FCO headquarters to certain missions and dependent territories, Telno. 128, 16 December, 1980, FCO 50/680, NA.
46. *The Guardian*, 1 February 1979, p. 28.
47. 'Text of resolution passed by the Commission for Racial Equality on 7 March 1979', 8 March 1979, HO 418/30 338797, NA.
48. Ibid.
49. Ibid.
50. Letter from David Lane to Merlyn Rees, 12 February 1979, HO 418/29, NA.
51. Letter from G.I. de Deney to P.J. Woodfield, 4 June 1980, HO 418/30, NA.
52. Letter from Mr Hillary to Mr Woodfield, 9 March 1981, HO 418/40, NA. Although in other documents, the Home Office tried to argue the opposite.
53. Letter from Mr Semken to Mr Nursaw, 18 June 1979, HO 418/30, NA.
54. Cited in 'Background: British Racism', *Race & Class*, 23/2–3, 1981, p. 242.
55. Telegram from FCO to British High Commission in Islamabad, Telno. 868, 16 October 1980, FCO 50/688, NA.

56. Ibid.
57. Letter from Evan Luard to Ted Rowlands, 1 February 1977, FCO 37/1832, NA.
58. Race Relations Act 1976, Part VII, Section 43–(1).
59. Ibid., Section 48–(I).
60. CRE, 'Formal Investigation: Immigration Control Procedures', 29 August 1979, HO 418/30, NA; 'Extent of the Power of the Commission for Racial Equality to Undertake Formal Investigations', n.d., p. 1, HO 418/30, NA.
61. *Home Office v Commission for Racial Equality*, 1981, All England Law Reports, p. 1042; See: Ann Dummett and Andrew Nicol, *Subjects, Citizens, Aliens and Others: Nationality and Immigration Control* (London: Weidenfeld & Nicolson, 1990) p. 252.
62. *Home Office v Commission for Racial Equality*, p. 1042.
63. Ibid., p. 1050.
64. Letter from Mr Flesher to Mr Chilcot, 8 March 1979, HO 418/29, NA.
65. N.A. Nagler, 'CRE Investigation of Immigration Control', 3 December 1980, HO 418/40, NA.
66. 'Meeting with the Commission for Racial Equality', n.d., HO 418/29, NA.
67. Letter from Mr Woodfield to Mr Boys-Smith, 19 December 1980, HO 418/40, NA.
68. Immigration and Nationality Department, 'CRE Investigation into Immigration Control: Progress Report', September 1982, HO 418/40, NA.
69. Letter from Mr Woodfield to Mr Halliday, 14 April 1981, HO 418/40, NA.
70. 'Draft Letter for Mr Woodfield to send to Mr David Lane', n.d., HO 418/40, NA.
71. Note from Elizabeth Moody to Neville Nagler, 6 April 1981, HO 418/40, NA.
72. See Smith and Marmo, 'Uncovering the "Virginity Testing" Controversy'.
73. *The Guardian*, 9 February 1979, 1.
74. Ibid.
75. Ibid.
76. House of Commons, *Hansard*, 19 February 1979, col. 216.
77. Cited in S. Juss, *Discretion and Deviation in the Administration of Immigration Control* (London: Sweet & Maxwell, 1997) 109.
78. House of Commons, *Hansard*, 19 February 1979, col. 217.
79. *The Guardian*, 10 February, 1979, 8.
80. Henry Yellowlees, Draft of *The Medical Examination of Immigrants: Report by the Chief Medical Officer*, 1980, appendix 1, 2, FCO 50/676, National Archives, London (hereafter NA).
81. Henry Yellowlees, *The Medical Examination of Immigrants: Report by the Chief Medical Officer*, 1980, appendix 1, 1–2, FCO 50/677, NA.
82. Ibid., appendix 1, 2.
83. Telegram from High Commission in Islamabad to FCO headquarters, Telno. 1413, 29 December 1980, FCO 50/688, NA.
84. Ibid.

85. Miles, 'Immigration from Bangladesh', pp. 5–6, FCO 50/660, NA.
86. Ibid., p. 6.
87. Ibid.
88. Telegram from John Thomson to John Graham, Telno. 960, 11 December 1979, p. 2, FCO 50/679, NA.
89. Telegram from John Thomson to FCO, Telno. 844, 10 December 1979, FCO 50/679, NA.
90. Ibid.
91. Draft memorandum from Lord Privy Seal to the Home Secretary, n.d., FCO 50/679, NA.
92. Letter from W. Jones to T. Condor, 19 June 1978, FCO 50/637, NA.
93. Cited in letter from W. Jones to D. Harrison, 19 June 1978, FCO 50/637, NA.
94. Ibid.
95. *Iqbal Haque v Entry Certificate Officer, Dacca*, 19 October 1973, TH/612/73(204), *Immigration Appeals Review*, 3, 1974, p. 53.
96. Letter from W. Jones to D. Harrison, 19 June 1978.
97. Letter from John Perris to Wilfred Jones, 4 July 1978, FCO 50/637, NA.
98. Ibid.
99. Ibid.
100. Letter from T.R. Peters, 18 April 1969, FCO 50/284, NA.
101. Letter from R.C. Trant to R. Slinger, 28 May 1969, FCO 50/284, NA.
102. Yellowlees, *The Medical Examination of Immigrants*, appendix 1, 3. The draft version of this finding adds that as well as X-rays of the limbs, 'sometimes a pelvic X-ray will be taken to look for ossification of the iliac crests' (Yellowlees, Draft of *The Medical Examination of Immigrants*, appendix 1, 3.)
103. Yellowlees, *The Medical Examination of Immigrants*, appendix 1, 3–4.
104. Cited in P. Gordon, 'Medicine, Racism and Immigration Control', *Critical Social Policy*, 3/7, 1983, pp. 15–16.
105. JCWI, *JCWI Annual Report 1980/81* (London: JCWI, 1981) p. 13.
106. FCO, 'X-Ray Examinations', 1980, FCO 50/679, NA.
107. For example, see FCO, 'Notes for Press Enquiries: Yellowlees Review', 1980, FCO 50/679, NA.
108. Telegram from British High Commission in New Delhi to FCO headquarters, Telno. 1005, 30 December 1980, FCO 50/680, NA.
109. Telegram from FCO headquarters to British High Commission in New Delhi, Telno. 890, 23 December 1980, FCO 50/680, NA.
110. Ibid.
111. Telegram from British High Commission in Delhi to Bombay, Telno. 356, 31 December 1980, FCO 50/680, NA.
112. Telegram from British High Commission in Delhi to FCO headquarters, Telno. m1008, 31 December 1980, FCO 50/680, NA.
113. Telegram from FCO headquarters to British High Commission in New Delhi, Telno. 890, 23 December 1980.
114. House of Lords, *Hansard*, 19 January 1981, col. 336w.

115. Ibid., 28 January 1982, col. 1114w.
116. Ibid., 22 February 1982, col. 279–280w.
117. H. Yellowlees, Letter to Willie Whitelaw, 14 January 1982, RC/RF/1/08, Runnymede Trust archive, BCA.
118. S. Littler, 'X-Rays for Age Assessment', 20 January 1982, HO 418/33, NA.
119. Ibid.
120. House of Commons, *Hansard*, 22 February 1982, col. 279–280w.
121. Letter from Willie Whitelaw to Peter Carrington, 22 January 1982, HO 418/33, NA.
122. CRE, *Immigration Control Procedures*, 40.
123. Home Office, 'Commission for Racial Equality (CRE) Report into Immigration Control Procedures: Government Comments', 1985, 12, RC/RF/1/01/B, Runnymede Trust archive, Black Cultural Archives, London.
124. House of Lords, *Hansard*, 20 June 1996, col. 562–563.
125. Aynsley-Green et al., 'Medical, Statistical, Ethical and Human Rights Considerations in the Assessment of Age in Children and Young People Subject to Immigration Control', *British Medical Bulletin*, 102, May 2012, pp. 17–42.

5
The Postcolonial World Stage: Immigration and Britain's International Reputation

The British government felt exposed to public and international scrutiny when details of the virginity testing of the Indian woman at Heathrow Airport emerged in the press in February 1979. Strategies were considered on how to limit the potential damage to its reputation. As the controversy unfolded, the government was receiving reassurance from the South Asian Department of the FCO that the Indian government was 'generally unconcerned' with Britain's immigration control policies.[1] Nevertheless, the Indian government was described as being 'very concerned' that immigration control practice 'is (and is seen to be) racially discriminatory'.[2] An April 1979 brief for the incoming (Thatcher) government also highlighted that, 'though Indian Ministers and officials are usually responsible and restrained, the same cannot be said of the media or parliamentarians who are ever ready to believe the worst of us'.[3] A similar warning was made in a Steering Brief for the July 1979 visit by the new Foreign Secretary, Lord Carrington, to India. This brief stated that 'Indians have from time to time expressed concern at alleged harassment by Immigration Officers of Indians coming to the UK for visits'. Another brief advised Lord Carrington 'not to say anything on this subject unless the Indians raise it with him'.[4] As is evident from these briefs, the British government was anxious to minimise the impact of its immigration policy not only within its internal constituencies but also amongst a wider audience. As mentioned earlier, even if accurate data existed on how many cases of virginity testing were taking place, evidence indicates that these tests were primarily carried out offshore. The government's 'othering' strategy served the purpose of keeping the practice – and its disclosure – far from Britain, in an attempt to replicate the dominant, colonial control over information flow and over former colonies' governments reminiscent of British colonial rule. Unfortunately for Britain, in the postcolonial and more globalised age, information flow had proven to be too difficult to constrain. Further, it clearly underestimated the reaction of the Indian government to the revelations of the virginity testing practice. This chapter explores these points more closely, focusing first on the role of the FCO in managing relations with the Indian government. Second, the chapter examines a potential compensation scheme for women that was considered by the British government, in order to shed light on the defensive strategies adopted by the government in seeking to close the Heathrow case as soon as practical. And third, the chapter will look at the case of virginity testing raised at the UNCHR, (a committee replaced by the UN Human Rights Council in 2006).

Initial reaction of the Indian government and attempts to manage the fallout

When the virginity testing practice was revealed in the British media in February 1979, the Indian High Commission complained to the British government about this procedure being conducted on one of its citizens (although she was now seeking to become a British national). The Indian media reported widely on the controversy as it developed, and on 21 February 1979 it was debated in the Indian Parliament (*Lok Sabha*). The controversy came at a critical point for the centre-right cabinet of the Indian Prime Minister Morarji Desai, which by early 1979 was on the verge of collapse, and while raising the point in Parliament, the Desai government was criticised for not taking greater action against Britain. Minister for External Affairs, Atal Bihari Vajpayee, raised the issue, declaring:

> deep feelings of indignation and concern have been aroused all over India by the grave indignity recently inflicted on an Indian lady at Heathrow Airport in Britain.[5]

He then commended the Indian woman who suffered the test at Heathrow for coming forward about her experience, stating:

> We share these feelings and convey our sympathies to the victim for the humiliation she was subjected to. We applaud her

courage in bringing the painful experience to our notice and thank the British paper which first called public attention to it. The only consolation is that her case has put a stop to certain obnoxious practices which were resorted to by the British officials in the name of controlling migration from the subcontinent.[6]

Vajpayee confirmed that there were 'at least 34 cases last year in New Delhi alone where the British High Commission requested medical opinion on the marital status of women applicants from a lady doctor',[7] which was cited a few days later in the House of Commons by Labour MP Jo Richardson (see the previous chapter). Vajpayee stated that the Indian government recognised Britain's right to restrict immigration into the country, but said that 'if its rules or the manner of applying them are patently discriminatory on a racial basis to our detriment, it cannot but cast a shadow on our thriving friendship as equal nations and peoples'.[8] This notion of India and Britain being equal nations and peoples in the postcolonial era was raised again at the UNCHR session held in the following month, although Britain seemed to desire that a colonial relationship should be maintained, with Britain as the dominant power, as will be discussed below.

Opposition member A.R. Badri Nayan claimed that 'it is part of the policy of the British government to have the immigrants examined gynaecologically' and questioned whether the Indian High Commission in London was 'not aware that this practice has been resorted to for six or seven years', asking:

Why did they sleep over the matter all these years? The External Affairs Minister should explain why they did not protest against this abominable crime all these years.[9]

Vajpayee replied that the Indian High Commission was not aware of this until *The Guardian* printed its revelations but did lodge a protest once the revelations were made public. However, another opposition member, M.V. Chandrasekhara Murthy, proposed that 'eight Hindu women in 1968 were subjected to the virginity test at the same Heathrow Airport' and asked whether the Indian government had responded to this.[10] Vajpayee claimed that the government had no knowledge of the test occurring in 1968,[11] but as we mentioned in the previous chapter, Mary Dines, former chair of the JCWI, did suggest to *The Guardian* that tests at Heathrow had begun in 1968. Vajpayee stated that the Indian government would raise the issue at the UN the following month, which, as we will show, further raised tensions between the two countries.

Despite reassurances sought from Desai by Prime Minister James Callaghan in relation to potential actions against Britain for the discriminatory nature of its virginity testing practice,[12] through archival documents we can trace a rising tension between the British High Commission in Delhi and the FCO in London over further repercussions. For example, a telegram from the British High Commissioner in Delhi John Thomson to the FCO at the end of February 1979 revealed that British officials thought 'that the subject was closed but now it was apparently being reopened'.[13] It underlined that the Indian Prime Minister was aware that High Commissioner Thomson 'had been distressed' at the government of India's decision 'to make a reference at the UN Human Rights Commission' to the case of the woman tested at Heathrow.[14] As a possible way to prevent the Indian government from registering a complaint with the UN, Thomson advised the British government that 'from the Indian point of view it would still not be too late to make an apology to the lady in question'.[15] Thomson expressed that he believed that an apology to the woman who was examined at Heathrow would have 'a significant effect on public opinion here [in India]'.[16] Nevertheless, the Indian government did file a complaint before the UN at the end of February 1979, yet the British government did not fully expect India's complaint to be seriously considered by the UN, adopting a dismissive attitude towards any serious attempt to repair the relationship with India. Revealing in this regard is the brief to the Secretary of State Lord Carrington on the occasion of his visit to India in July 1979, in which he was advised to redirect questions on the matter by stating that the Home Secretary was waiting for Sir Henry Yellowlees's investigation into the use of medical examinations of migrants to finish, 'without committing...to a formal approach to the Indian government'.[17]

The British government saw this as an opportunity to return responsibility for the matter to the Indian government, on the view that blame-sharing would persuade the Indian Prime Minister to reconsider his government's approach. This is evident from a letter dated early March 1979 from British Prime Minister Callaghan to Indian Prime Minister Desai about the 'problems' faced by British immigration control caused by the many 'bogus' immigrants from India:

> I well understand that this incident has caused feelings to run high in India. Especially, as you know the fact that a significant number of would-be immigrants to Britain seek to evade our laws causes emotion here.[18]

Conservative Home Secretary Willie Whitelaw wrote to Lord Carrington in September 1979, arguing along similar lines:

> The fact is that the deception which is known to be practised by a proportion of those seeking entry, in order to establish a foothold here in the hope of avoiding detection and removal, leads to numbers of *bona-fide* travellers having to be questioned to establish their intentions and credentials.[19]

Whitelaw complained that 'some Indians are particularly sensitive about questioning at the ports', lamenting, 'I am afraid that the so-called "virginity test" did much to undo the attempts that had been made to allay their anxieties.'[20]

Potential purposes of compensatory payment

The FCO also explored whether it would be politically, and legally, beneficial to offer a compensatory payment to the woman (referred to here as Mrs K) who had been examined at Heathrow Airport in January 1979 and reported the incident to *The Guardian*. In offering the woman an ex gratia payment, the FCO sought certain outcomes: that the payment would ward off criticism from the Indian government at the next meeting of the UNCHR and that any payment would be tied to an agreement that the woman would not seek redress through the European Court of Human Rights. A letter to the FCO's Migration and Visa Department from its legal advisers outlined that any payment would require authority to proceed 'before the beginning of the upcoming UN Human Rights sessions or else we will receive no advantage from making the payment and much unnecessary criticism'.[21] The same letter also warned that in the payment agreement 'any form of words used in the undertaking not to institute proceedings should cover an application to Strasbourg'.[22] The legal adviser wrote a few days later that it would be in the interest of the FCO to find out the intentions of the Indian government for the forthcoming UNCHR meeting and that if it were to raise the virginity testing matter, '[i]t might be in our interests to make a small payment to [Mrs K]...to stop the Indians raising the matter'.[23] In the same letter, it was noted that Mrs K could possibly make a claim under the European Convention on Human Rights that she had 'suffered degrading treatment' which was a violation of Article 3, but the legal adviser stated that it was 'difficult to say in the light of recent decisions by the Commission how they would decide such applications'.[24]

Further correspondence from the FCO's legal adviser highlighted 'the fact that [Mrs K]...signed a consent form' as 'proof that she underwent the examination freely and that there was no assault'.[25] Although others had noted and criticised the catch-22 situation confronting the woman in choosing between consenting to an examination or facing the possibility of being refused entry, the legal adviser wrote that Mrs K 'would need to prove that she was forced to sign the document under duress to bring a successful claim for assault'.[26] Refusing to consider that the intense scrutiny placed upon the woman at the port of entry into the country could be defined as 'under duress', the FCO was advised by its lawyers that it would be 'in effect considering paying her a sum for moral damages because of the indignity which she suffered' and complained that this sum 'would have been reduced if the event had not been publicised'.[27] Another of the FCO's legal advisers wrote that the Treasury Solicitor 'was of the opinion...that there was no liability in respect to [Mrs K]' and explained her position as follows:

> the consent she gave was a valid and effective consent. While it would no doubt be argued that in all the circumstances there was little option for her but to agree to the examination, nevertheless there is a clear consent and one apparently understood by her. There is not recognised by the law an independent tort in respect of mental distress.[28]

Despite this legal advice, the FCO and Home Office decided to continue to pursue their inquiries into how to proceed with offering an ex gratia payment to Mrs K. The next discussion was over the amount to be offered. The Treasury wrote to John Halliday at the Home Office, noting the difficulty of arriving at a figure because Mrs K had not 'suffered damages or costs of a kind which can be readily evaluated' and there was no 'body of precedent to consult'.[29] Therefore, the Treasury suggested, '[a]ny payment should be large enough to settle the business' and added, '[w]hile it is desirable not to be seen as niggardly, equally one should not over react'.[30] The Treasury then proposed an amount of £500. Graham Archer from the FCO's South Asian Department advised Mr Partridge that this amount would 'in the context of the Sub Continent appear to be a very generous offer', and that the FCO's Migration and Visa Department should 'agree with the Treasury view that this sum is adequate'.[31]

However, a number of issues made the FCO and Home Office reluctant to follow through with the offer of £500. First, it emerged that Mrs K's marriage had broken down and she had returned to India within a year of the examination. The agencies were of the view that her return to India meant that she was looking to leave the incident in the past and that there was no jurisdiction in India that would allow her to pursue legal action against the British government. When Mrs K's estranged husband contacted the Home Office seeking payment, D.W. Partridge from the FCO's Migration and Visa Department wrote a confidential internal memorandum stating that Mrs K was 'not herself asking for compensation and to make payment would mean seeking her out in India'.[32] However, another letter from Partridge to J.F. Halliday in the Home Office warned that, while this might be difficult, 'there is a mounting practical case for doing this on the grounds that parliamentary opinion in this country and also official and public opinion in India will not be satisfied unless this is done'.[33] A Treasury representative also suggested that while the Treasury was willing to pay the £500 to Mrs K, it disputed whether Mrs K had experienced 'hardship', stating that '[h]ardship is a difficult ground and this is one of the problems, incidentally, in making any ex gratia payment' to her, particularly as 'the decision for [Mrs K] to return to India is their [was her] own', and in the Treasury's opinion, 'any "hardship" is self-imposed'.[34]

Second, the FCO and Home Office were reluctant to offer a payment because they feared that other Indian women would seek similar compensation, especially with Mrs K returning to India. An internal FCO memorandum claimed that 'the risk of women in India jumping on the band-wagon would presumably be greater if payment were made to [Mrs K] in India',[35] although Graham Archer of the FCO's South Asian Department stated that this was 'a slight risk'.[36] In a letter from Partridge to Halliday, he expressed concern that if the purpose of offering the payment to Mrs K was to achieve positive publicity in India to stave off criticism at the UN, this 'could lead to other women in the sub-continent making a claim against us', but noted that, at that time, 'no woman has identified herself as having been so examined'.[37] Partridge suggested that even if some women did come forward in the future, the cases of virginity testing in India were, in the eyes of the FCO, not the same as the 'affront...suffered by [Mrs K]'.[38] Drawing on the distinctions made by the FCO earlier that year, Partridge claimed that since the form used by medical officers overseas contained a section on the urogenital system, an 'intimate examination' in this context was 'normal' and 'there [was] no reason to believe that any doctor...told an applicant that he [sic] was carrying out an examination for marital status'.[39] Partridge made this statement, even though he had admitted earlier in the same letter that '[i]t is known that ECOs in the Indian sub-continent, when referring applicants for the routine medical examination, have on occasion asked the doctor for an opinion on a woman's marital status' – by examining her genitals – and acknowledged that this had occurred 'in at least 34 cases'.[40] Partridge suggested that in these cases 'we can argue...that any internal examination was made as part of a general medical examination and not specifically to answer the question put by the ECO',[41] although he admitted that gynaecological examinations for the purpose of satisfying the curiosity of the British immigration control system did occur, even if as part of a wider medical examination. A draft version of the letter from Partridge to Halliday pointed out that the 'distinctive feature of [Mrs K's] examination' was that 'by asking her to sign a form of consent the doctor provided her with clear and irrefutable evidence of what he was doing' (looking for signs of sexual activity or childbirth), but that amongst those examined at British High Commissions in South Asia, 'no woman examined...could produce such evidence'.[42] This would mean that the doctors who performed examinations in South Asia, if ever questioned, could claim that these women were only subjected to a routine examination, with no specific mention of looking for signs of sexual activity of childbirth. Insofar as such women had not consented to an invasive practice, which was carried out regardless, the legal position taken by the FCO and Home Office was that these women could not claim that they were examined without their full and informed consent, because consent was not requested and thus not verbally denied. Handwritten in the margins of the letter, someone had highlighted this as quite a pedantic position, writing, '[n]evertheless, we must accept that there is a real risk of a rush of claims from the subcontinent, and we cannot expect such claimants to accept the subtle distinction between their cases and the Heathrow incident', adding that '[w]e could find ourselves in difficulties'.[43]

Britain at the UNCHR

The Indian government's lodgement of a complaint before the UNCHR occurred within three weeks of *The Guardian*'s exposé of the practice of virginity testing. On 23 February 1979, the Indian representative for the UNCHR declared that 'United Kingdom authorities systematically discouraged immigrants from the Indian subcontinent', by employing practices that 'reflect prejudices dating back to the dark ages'.[44] That such harsh words reached the UN in such a short period of time suggests that a level of uneasiness had been felt for more than three weeks. The tactic of allowing access to Britain while at the same time discouraging it through humiliating practices would have been the subject of many discussions in the Indian subcontinent. Following the Indian representative's speech at the UN, the representative from the Syrian Arab Republic supported India's condemnation, stating that the practices employed by British Immigration Officers 'reflected the persistence of racism and colonialism in a disguised form'.[45] Both representatives highlighted not only a number of racial and neo-colonial dimensions to the issue, but also made explicit reference to the effect of the practice on women. The Indian representative described the test as a 'humiliating treatment' and an 'affront' to migrant women. The Syrian Arab Republic representative said that the practice was 'an insult to the dignity of women in general and Asian women in particular'. According to the UN documents, no 'white' nation stood up to declare its position on the matter.

The British government responded at the following UNCHR meeting, by minimising the episode and its occurrence. 'Deep regret' for the incident at Heathrow was expressed to the Indian government by the British representative, who insisted that '[n]o element of racial discrimination was involved'. The British representative could afford at that point in time to say that the incident at Heathrow was an isolated one and 'should not have taken place', suggesting that it was more an oddity when he added that 'it did not constitute a systematic abuse of human rights by the United Kingdom government'.[46] We now know that, while this was taking place before the UN, the Home Office knew much more about the prevalence of this practice, both onshore and offshore, than was revealed at this meeting.

At the end of his speech, the British representative called for a greater focus on the impact of tragic worldwide events of the time, such as the apartheid regime in South Africa and the killing fields of Cambodia.[47] This helped the British government to highlight its commitment to world justice and human rights, as much as it served the purpose of deflecting attention away from what it described as a random, isolated incident.

Even if the speech given by the British representative did not resemble an apology, with the exception of the expression of 'deep regret', in late 1980 the Home Office defined such expression as an apology on behalf of the British government, when more details of the practice had emerged in the public domain.[48] Yet there is no trace of a proper apology that openly acknowledged the practice of virginity testing.

During the same UNCHR meeting in early March 1979, the Indian representative had an opportunity to rebut, arguing that virginity testing was more than an isolated incident: 'it was symptomatic of a more profound malaise and a reflection of the arrogance which the former colonial power still showed from time to time'.[49] He also spoke of the origins of this practice as closely linked to the origins of British colonialism in India, which 'lay in the doctrine of racial superiority' – a point the Indian government believed to be still dictating the relationship between Britain and India.[50] Moreover, it was far too evident that the Indian representative received no support from any white delegations at the meeting: 'only non-white delegations had expressed concern' he said,[51] suggesting a wider problem within the Commission itself. The Indian representative also invited, but without success, the matter to be dealt with by the UN's Sub-Commission on Prevention of Discrimination and Protection of Minorities, to 'study the "racially discriminatory treatment" by immigration authorities of the United Kingdom', and argued that this study could be widened to include 'other countries who receive immigrants'.[52]

The UN meetings held subsequently kept Britain and its new government in a state of tension. The Conservative government was apprehensive about the possibility of a repeat of what happened in 1979 at the 1980 session of the UNCHR. While the government tried to distance itself from the criticisms directed towards the previous government and was of the view that the virginity testing issue had been dealt with, the Conservatives were wary that the controversy could be reignited by the Indian representative and used to launch opposition to the new immigration rules proposed by the Conservative Party. Sir Peter Marshall, the Deputy Secretary to the UK's representative at the UNCHR, Lord Colville, sent a telegram to Foreign Secretary Lord Carrington, stating:

> The atmosphere here is unusually highly charged politically. The Indians could well spark off discussion[s] which [could] get out of control. This might spill over into discussion of the issue at home as well. The combination of resurrecting last year's row about medical examinations for immigration purposes and revised immigration rules could put us in a very awkward and isolated position.[53]

Carrington had earlier expressed to the UK Mission in Geneva that 'it would be better to avoid saying anything to the Commission' about British immigration practices and the forthcoming rule changes, but anticipated that the Indians would raise the issue of virginity testing and 'refer to the general question of immigration policy...in particular the revised immigration rules'.[54] Carrington further stated that 'we would like to ride them off this', but was 'not optimistic' and suggested the government seek to issue, with the Indian government, a 'joint statement on quote virginity tests unquote because it could help keep the subject out of any controversy which might follow on the Immigration Rules'.[55] He warned that, without an agreement with the Indian government, 'there is a danger that the quote virginity tests unquote issue might be dragged willy-nilly into a wider debate'.[56] In the days leading up to the 1980 UNCHR session, the FCO approached the Indian government to make a joint statement to the Commission 'acknowledging the steps we have taken to ensure that such an incident [the virginity tests] does not recur', which would 'bury the matter' for the British government, although Carrington had to admit that the British government did not know 'what the outcome of this approach [would] be'.[57] A letter from the FCO's Migration and Visa Department shows that other FCO and Home Office staff were pessimistic about the possibility of reaching an understanding with the Indian government, particularly if news of the revised Immigration Rules became public:

> Whatever we are able to agree with them on 'virginity testing' it seems likely that the Indians will raise the revised Immigration Rules in Geneva. They could do so either in the context of last year's complaint or independently.[58]

Another letter from the FCO indicated that it hoped to 'firm up' the possibility of a joint statement with the Indian government but realised that 'the Indians will almost certainly renege if they want to make an issue out of the new Immigration Rules'.[59] The FCO was also critical of the Home Secretary's decision to announce the Immigration Rules in Parliament while the UNCHR session was simultaneously occurring in Geneva, therefore providing the Indian government with further ammunition to condemn British immigration control practices. The FCO, including Carrington, suggested that Whitelaw wait until March to announce the new rules, but the Home Secretary stated that he was 'under strong pressure from the Prime Minister and does not want to delay matters'.[60] Based on our examination of the National Archive files, we could find no evidence of whether an agreement was reached on the virginity testing issue between Britain and India.

Conclusion

In only a few days of *The Guardian*'s revelations, the practice of virginity testing shifted from being a purely internal concern to a bilateral (Britain–India) and international issue. From the documents we retrieved, a sense of uneasiness is identifiable on both sides throughout this period. The British government did not dismiss its immigration policy; in fact it sought to justify and reinforce its approach further. Yet the Home Office became caught up in having to account for its actions to numerous parties. In the midst of these events, on the international scene the government sought to minimise the incident at Heathrow, while also seeking not to undermine its purported role as a champion of human rights. The agenda-dictating role usually played by Britain in its bilateral and international relationships had to be compromised, albeit temporarily and relatively, with the British government suggesting that the upper echelons of the Home Office and FCO had no awareness of the practice of virginity testing occurring. This contradictory behaviour, in fact, is represented well in the portrayal of the 'schizophrenic' state, with its multiple and contrasting aims. Britain was accused on the international stage of replicating the colonial relationships of the British Empire with its now independent former colonies and indulging in racially discriminatory behaviours towards its former colonial subjects, which did not align with any of the humanitarian obligations that Britain was supposed to be upholding at the same time. However, in both areas a desire is evident on the part of the British government to dominate using different, even contradictory, instruments.

Notes

1. H.J.S. Pearce, 'Briefs for the Incoming Government: India,' 17 April 1979, FCO 37/2155, NA.
2. Ibid.
3. Ibid.
4. 'Secretary of State's Visit to Delhi: Brief No. 4 – Race Relations and Immigration (Including New Nationality and Immigration Legislation),' 3, July 1979, FCO 37/2169, NA; 'Brief on Race Relations and Immigration for Lord Carrington's Visit to India,' June 1979, FCO 37/2167, NA.
5. *Lok Sabha*, 21 February 1979, col. 222.
6. Ibid., col. 222.
7. Ibid., col. 224.
8. Ibid., col. 225.
9. Ibid., col. 228.
10. Ibid., col. 230.

11. Ibid., col. 231.
12. See Letter from James Callaghan to Morarji Desai, 8 March 1979, PREM 16/2100, NA.
13. John Thomson, Telegram 200 from Delhi to FCO, 28 February 1979, PREM 16/2100, NA.
14. Ibid.
15. Ibid.
16. Ibid.
17. 'Secretary of State's Visit to Delhi: Brief No. 4,' 4.
18. Letter from James Callaghan to Morarji Desai, 8 March 1979.
19. Letter from Willie Whitelaw to Lord Carrington, 8 September 1979, FCO 50/663, NA.
20. Ibid.
21. Letter from Mrs A. Glover to Mr Partridge, 11 January 1980, FCO 50/675, NA.
22. Ibid.
23. Letter from Mrs A. Glover to Mr Partridge, 16 January 1980, FCO 50/675, NA.
24. Ibid.
25. Letter from Mrs A. Glover to Mr Partridge, 5 February 1980, FCO 50/675, NA.
26. Ibid.
27. Ibid.
28. Letter from Sally Evans to Mr Scoble, 25 July 1980, FCO 50/675, NA.
29. Letter from L. Watts to J. Halliday, 5 March 1980, FCO 50/675, NA.
30. Ibid.
31. Letter from G.R. Archer to Mr. Partridge, 31 March 1980, FCO 50/675, NA.
32. D.W. Partridge, 'Heathrow "Virginity Testing" Incident: Claim for Compensation', FCO 60/675, NA.
33. Letter from D.W. Partridge to J.F. Halliday, 8 February 1980, FCO 50/675, NA.
34. Letter from L. Watts to J. Halliday, 5 March 1980.
35. Partridge, 'Heathrow "Virginity Testing" Incident: Claim for Compensation'.
36. Letter from G.R. Archer to Mr. Partridge, 31 March 1980, FCO 60/675, NA.
37. Letter from D.W. Partridge to J.F. Halliday, 8 February 1980.
38. Ibid.
39. Ibid.
40. Ibid.
41. Ibid.
42. Draft letter from D.W. Partridge to J.F. Halliday, n.d., FCO 50/675, NA.
43. Ibid.
44. UN Commission on Human Rights, 35th Session, 23 February 1979, para. 26, E/CN.4/SR.1494.
45. UNCHR, 35th Session, 23 February 1979, para. 27.
46. UNCHR, 35th Session, 5 March 1979, para. 3; para. 2, E/CN.4/SR.1506.

47. Ibid., para. 4.
48. 'Briefing for the Sub-Committee of the Select Committee on Home Affairs', 18 December 1980.
49. UNCHR, 35th Session, 5 March 1979, para. 15.
50. Ibid., para. 17.
51. Ibid., para. 319.
52. UN press release, 'India Proposes Study of Alleged Discrimination in British Immigration Practices', 26 February 1979, Press Release HR/710, RC/RF/1/08, Runnymede Trust archives, BCA.
53. Telegram from UK Mission in Geneva to FCO headquarters, Telno. 93, 12 February 1980, FCO 50/681, NA.
54. Telegram from FCO headquarters to UK Mission in Geneva, Telno. 16, 22 January 1980, FCO 50/681, NA.
55. Ibid.
56. Ibid.
57. Letter from the Foreign Secretary to the Home Secretary, 1 February 1980, FCO 50/681, NA.
58. Letter from Mr Shepherd to Mr Murray, 24 January 1980, FCO 50/681, NA.
59. Letter from D.F. Murray to A. Shepherd, 6 February 1980, FCO 50/681, NA.
60. Letter from D.F. Murray to Mr Luce, 5 February 1980, FCO 50/681, NA.

6
Discrimination by Other Means: Further Restrictions on Migrant Women and Children Under the Conservatives

As demonstrated in earlier chapters, the issues of race and immigration were contentious in the 1979 general election, with the tone of the election essentially set by Margaret Thatcher's interview with *World in Action* in early 1978, in which she claimed that 'white' British people were feeling 'rather swamped' by non-white migrants (see Chapter 2). Labour was rocked by the virginity testing controversy and the subsequent revelations about the X-rays conducted on South Asian children but was also very concerned about the publicity given to the National Front and its racist agenda. The Conservatives were able to capitalise on Labour's problems, and Thatcher's tough stance allowed her party to siphon off some of the less committed National Front vote, while the Tories campaigned that under a Conservative government non-EEC migration would be further restricted.

When elected to office in May 1979, the Conservatives inherited the virginity testing controversy from Labour and, as revealed in Chapter 4, tried to close down any substantial investigation into the immigration control system. As the new Home Secretary, Willie Whitelaw allowed the Yellowlees review of the medical examination of immigrants to continue, but he wanted things to return to normal as quickly as possible in order to maintain Britain's 'decent' image abroad (particularly in South Asia). So while the practice of virginity testing was officially discontinued after Whitelaw's predecessor Merlyn Rees ordered it so in February 1979, the X-raying of

South Asian children for administrative purposes continued until 1982. Furthermore, other forms of scrutiny, both mental and physical, were imposed upon South Asian women and allowed to continue throughout the 1980s.

First, this chapter explores in detail the case of Anwar Ditta, a British-Pakistani woman who sought to bring her three children from Pakistan to join her in Britain in the late 1970s. The authorities initially believed that she was bringing the children of another woman into Britain, and only after several years campaigning and blood tests paid for by Granada Television did they relent and accept that Ditta's children were legitimately hers (and thus were allowed into the country). Several commentators have retrospectively lamented that, had DNA testing been available in the early 1980s, Ditta may have been able to prove kinship much earlier. However, as the second section of this chapter shows, while DNA testing for kinship purposes has been available since the mid-1980s, the immigration control system was slow to adopt it, and in most cases it has been used to disprove kinship, rather than allowing families to unite. Third, this chapter demonstrates that the use of intrusive processes (such as blood and DNA tests) and the continued scrutiny placed upon the South Asian female body must be understood against a background of the Conservatives' enduring desire for restrictive immigration control measures, even in the face of criticism from the CRE and the European Court of Human Rights (ECtHR). The ECtHR decided in a 1985 case in Strasbourg that changes made to Britain's Immigration Rules in 1980 and the introduction of further restrictions under the British Nationality Act 1981 were racially and sexually discriminatory, but this judgement only led the Thatcher government to institute further restrictions, instead of removing the discriminatory policies. At the same time, the CRE released its long-awaited report which recommended significant changes to the British immigration control system. However, like their response to the ECtHR ruling, the Conservatives ignored these criticisms and rebutted by asserting that a strict immigration control system was necessary for Britain's economic and social stability. This chapter evinces that, despite the revelations of abuses and discriminatory practices in the late 1970s and early 1980s, the immigration control system continued to function much as it had previously – with substantial discriminatory and coercive powers, tempered by limited accountability.

Deferring to the body again: The Anwar Ditta case and other anti-deportation campaigns

The story of Anwar Ditta and her husband, Shuja Ud Din, is long and complicated (with the most concise narrative found in Paul Gordon's 1984 book chapter, 'Outlawing Immigrants').[1] But the crux of the matter was that, in 1979, the British High Commission in Islamabad refused to give entry clearances to Anwar Ditta's three children who were residing in Pakistan at the time, on the grounds that the authorities had doubts that Ditta was the biological mother of these children. Ditta, who was born in Birmingham but had lived in Pakistan since adolescence, and Ud Din, a Pakistani national, had both travelled separately to the UK in the 1970s and, after finding a place to live in Rochdale, requested that their three children join them. This began what *The Guardian* called a 'Kafkaesque' journey through the immigration control system that lasted over three years.

After settling in Rochdale and marrying in 1975, Ditta and Ud Din requested of the immigration authorities that their three children, who were living with their grandparents in Pakistan, be permitted to join them in the UK. In 1977, the children applied to the High Commission in Pakistan and were 'interviewed' by ECOs in 1978, along with Ud Din's mother and sister since, as Gordon wrote, 'the children were too young to be interviewed'.[2] In early 1979, the Home Office refused to provide entry clearances for the children, stating that it was 'not satisfied that Kamran, Imran and Saima were related to Anwar Sultana Ditta and Shuja Ud Din as claimed'.[3] The reasons given by the Home Office did not relate specifically to the children, but were based on a 'premise of suspicion' of Ditta and Ud Din's application.[4] As Gordon wrote, 'the entry clearance officer at Islamabad did not argue directly that the three children were not those of Anwar Ditta', but from the position that 'the application was fraudulent' and thus proceeded to 'build up a case of apparent discrepancies in statements supplied *on behalf* of the children' (our emphasis).[5] Gordon further explained that for the immigration control authorities these discrepancies were 'sufficient to argue that the children were not those of Anwar Ditta and Shuja Ud Din'.[6]

The Friends of Anwar Ditta, a campaign organisation, reproduced the reasons given initially by the Home Office in a pamphlet it produced to publicise her campaign, arguing that the 'Home Office arguments clearly do not stand up' and were 'not based on positive evidence'.[7] As the pamphlet showed, the reasons for the refusal all related to the details of the (admittedly complicated) backgrounds of Ditta and Ud Din, including discrepancies in the ages of Ditta when she married in Pakistan and when she later remarried in Britain, the fact that Ditta and Ud Din remarried in Britain in 1975 despite having a Muslim marriage in 1968 in Pakistan, discrepancies in the account of the marriage ceremony in Lahore (which by then had occurred over a decade prior), the fact that Ud Din admitted to over-staying his visitors entry clearance and the fact that Ditta applied for a UK passport under her maiden name although she was married under Muslim law. The pamphlet categorically addressed all of these supposed discrepancies raised by the Home Office, stating that the reasons were 'all irrelevant' and that 'none of them disprove the fact that [Kamran, Imran and Saima] are Anwar and Shuja's children'.[8]

Probably the most serious argument that the Home Office had was that Ud Din had entered the country on a tourist visa and stayed in the country after this visa expired. The pamphlet said that, although Ud Din's residency was not regularised until 1976, 'the Home Office admit that he was anyway entitled to remain here as the husband of a British woman', and added that '[e]ven if Shuja had come in illegally it would not show anything about the parentage of his children'.[9] A report by feminist magazine *Spare Rib* on the case revealed that the 'Home Office had never previously raised the issue of their [Ditta and Ud Din's] entry and does not dispute their right to stay', but used it to deny entry to her children.[10] Indeed, Ditta and Ud Din, along with a fourth child born in Britain in 1976, despite the purported 'discrepancies' in their stories, were allowed to reside in Britain, even though the 'Home Office us[ed] these issues to throw doubts on [Ud Din's] credibility and that of Anwar Ditta.'[11]

The Home Office further argued that there were two women by the name of Anwar Sultana Ditta, with a pamphlet by the Anwar Ditta Defence Committee (ADDC) citing this 'extra-ordinary suggestion' from the statement provided by the ECO handling their case:

It appeared that there might be two Anwar Sultana Dittas, i.e. One who married Shuja Ud Din in Pakistan in 1968 and the other whom Shuja Ud Din married in the United Kingdom in 1975.[12]

Gordon also identified that the 'official line was that the children were those of her sister-in-law'.[13] The Home Office did not have to substantiate these claims as the burden of proof rested on Ditta and Ud Din to prove that the children were actually hers. Ditta's course of redress was to appeal the Home Office's decision and her case was sent to the Immigration Appeal Tribunal, where it was heard by the Adjudicator C. P. Rushton in April 1980 and a decision was handed down the following month.

Leading up to the date of the appeal, a campaign around the Ditta case began to emerge, first under the Friends of Anwar Ditta, then led by the ADDC. This committee, which included people from the Asian communities in the North of England and the legal fraternity in Manchester, as well as from the labour movement and the anti-racist movement, mobilised quickly and began a campaign of letter writing to politicians, the media and potential supporters of Ditta, alongside the publication of several pamphlets and flyers and arranging public speaking engagements by Ditta.

Even before the Tribunal meeting with the Adjudicator, Ditta's case came to be focused on an appeal to the body as the facilitator of 'the truth' because her testimony and documents were not believed by the authorities. A leaflet published in late 1979 said that Ditta had suggested that 'a blood test would establish that she was the mother of the children', but reported that 'the Home Office replied: "There is no need to go that far"'.[14] The leaflet argued that there was a need to go this far, as the Home Office had used blood tests in another case, when trying to deport Abdul Azad.[15] An article in the newspaper of radical leftist group the Revolutionary Communist Group at the time also highlighted another case in which the Home Office employed blood tests – that of Afzal and Shemin Mohammed – writing:

> The Home Office used blood tests to try and prove Afzal Mohammed was not the father of his two children, that he had engaged in a marriage of convenience and that he should be deported. Because of the large amount of public support Afzal Mohammed received, the Home Office has so far failed to deport him, but the case shows quite clearly the lengths the British state will go to deport someone who is black.[16]

The ADDC leaflet also compared Ditta's case to that of South African Shirley Webb, who had been abandoned by her husband, but, after appealing to the Prime Minister, was allowed to enter the UK with her four children.[17] The leaflet alleged that the difference in the response of the British government to the Ditta and Webb cases was based on their ethnicity, noting that 'Mrs. Webb is white, and Anwar is black.'[18]

Momentum built behind the campaign, with a large march held in Rochdale in March 1980, before the meeting with the Adjudicator in April of the same year. At times the campaign organisers seemed confident that enough evidence had been gathered to make a successful case. The ADDC leaflet claimed that '[s]olicitors say that the evidence is so conclusive that it need only be presented at the appeal to prove the case'.[19] But this was not so. After the Tribunal met in April to hear Ditta's case, the Adjudicator presented his decision in July 1980 (this was delayed from May), which upheld the original rejection by the Home Office.

In accounting for his decision (reprinted by the ADDC in numerous pamphlets and leaflets), the Adjudicator stated that the 'oral testimony *could be* sufficient to tip the balance in the appelants [sic] favour' (our emphasis), but that he deemed the witnesses in the case to not be credible, stating, '[t]he parents of the appelants [sic] have on their own admission on several occasions lied to, or deceived, persons in official positions both in the UK and Pakistan'.[20] The Adjudicator thus based his decision on the 'credibility' of the adult witnesses in the case, as well as on the long and complex history of Ditta and Ud Din's marriage and immigration status; however, the decision was supposed to ascertain whether the children could enter the UK as Ditta's children. As an ADDC bulletin from February 1981 stated, '[t]he only issue relevant to the case was whether Anwar was the parent of the three children'.[21] In an article for the *New Statesman*, David Holmes cited the Adjudicator as saying that the documents outlining the relationship between Ditta and her children were 'too few in number to outweigh the deficiencies in the oral evidence', but pointed out that 'in a rather careless sentence', the Adjudicator actually referred to Ditta and Ud Din as 'the *parents* of the appellants' (our emphasis).[22]

A letter sent by the ADDC to potential supporters stated:

> The adjudicator not only disregarded the available evidence, but also launched a most scandalous racist attack on the

parents and their witnesses. He repeatedly questioned their 'credibility' on matters which had no bearing whatsoever on the case in hand. His racist slurs and abuse were intended to subject the family to a personal trial for nothing more than the fact that they have stood up and fought for their rights.[23]

The Adjudicator's questioning of the credibility of the family and their witnesses was evident in his statement that he 'could not accept that Anwar Ditta and Hamida Rafique [Ditta's sister] were simple Asian village women' and his 'finding' that '[a]lthough they left the UK in mid-childhood' and were 'lacking in education', the sisters had 'an excellent command of English and were far more westernised and sophisticated in their demeanour than the average member of the immigrant community'.[24] This statement could be taken to suggest that Ditta and her family could not be believed because they were educated immigrants and were therefore presumed to be more devious and calculating than the 'average' South Asian migrant. The British view of the South Asian woman was, as defined by the colonial 'experience', that she would be meek and duly observant of the (colonial) authority. Yet the authorities concurrently expected the South Asian woman to assimilate into Western society. Once again, Bhabha's idea of 'mimicry' can be seen here. Ditta had assimilated into British life, in line with the desired behaviour of immigrants promoted by the authorities, but at the same time she was too 'Westernised' and 'sophisticated' to prostrate herself before the British state, and was thus seen as 'undesirable'. However, as a British citizen, she could not be deported and she fulfilled a use for the British authorities by being married to Shuja Ud Din. Yet in the eyes of the British state, there was no socio-economic benefit for her children to enter the country too. Despite its formal adherence to the rights of family reconciliation for migrants, the British government had no desire for families to be together unless they served a purpose for the host society.

The Adjudicator concluded that he '[could] not find that the appelants [sic] have on the balance of probabilities discharged the burden of proof upon them',[25] and thus dismissed the appeal. However, as we have shown earlier, the burden of proof did not technically lie with the applicant and the balance of probabilities was supposed to weigh in favour of the migrant, unless the authorities had overwhelming proof that the applicant was being dishonest. The Adjudicator explicitly referred to what the CRE had long suspected, and sought to investigate – that the burden of proof lay squarely upon the potential migrant and that it was up to the applicant to prove their desirability to the authorities.

After the Adjudicator handed down his decision, the next course of action available to Ditta was to appeal this decision, but leave to appeal was denied by the Tribunal in September 1980. This meant the only avenue left open to Ditta was to appeal to the Minister for Immigration, Timothy Raison, for his consent to allow her children to enter Britain. The ADDC argued that a strong public campaign would be necessary to convince Raison of such. In a letter to potential supporters, the ADDC stated: 'The adjudicator's decision demonstrated that there can be no justice or democracy by appeals to the British state. These can be won only with the support of the black community, the working class and the socialist movement.'[26]

With her testimony disbelieved, Ditta once again turned to the physical body in the hope that it would reveal 'the truth' and that the authorities would accept this, rather than Ditta's words, as convincing evidence. In an ADDC pamphlet, she pleaded:

> I am willing to give a medical test. I am willing to give a skin test. I am willing to go onto a lie detector to prove that they are my children. I'm not telling them any lies, why should I tell them lies? Why should I claim other peoples [sic] children?[27]

By December 1980, the ADDC had collected further evidence to submit to the Home Office, with the help of Labour MP Joel Barnett which included 'a report of a medical examination of Anwar Sultana Ditta, [and] evidence relating to the authenticity of fingerprints on identity cards obtained by Anwar whilst in Pakistan', amongst other items.[28] However, the ADDC announced in a January 1981 press statement that 'the Home Office wrote back to say that this was not enough'.[29] In a letter from Timothy Raison to Joel Barnett (written after Ditta's children were finally allowed to join her), Raison stated that regarding the evidence presented in December 1980, he acknowledged that there was 'fresh relevant material', but 'was not convinced that it was sufficient to justify overturning the decision confirmed by the appellate authorities' and that the case would be reconsidered after blood tests were conducted (to which the Home Office had refused to agree in 1979).[30]

In early 1981, Granada Television's *World in Action* paid for blood tests to be conducted on Ditta and her three children in Pakistan. The press statement by the ADDC described this as 'a final effort to prove beyond all doubt that they are related as parent to child'.[31] On the same day on which this press statement was released, the reports of the blood tests were received by Raison, who publicly stated:

> I now believe that there is the substantial new evidence which I invited you [Joel Barnett] to submit to justify reversing the original decision. The entry clearance officer will be instructed to issue entry clearances to Kamran, Umran, and Saima to join Anwar Ditta and Shuja Ud Din.[32]

Raison cynically added, 'I regret that it has taken so long to bring this case to a conclusion and hope that the children will have happy lives here',[33] as if it were not the fault of the Home Office that the case took so long to conclude.

Ditta's children joined her in Britain a few months later, but this was a special case where the appellant had claimed victory over the British state. There were a significant number of other cases in which families had been separated by the immigration control system who did not have the fortunate outcome that Ditta had. With Ditta's case finally reaching a positive conclusion, migrant rights campaigners hoped that the decision in this case would increase pressure on the government to alleviate the strict nature of the controls system and believed that Ditta's case would highlight the difficulties that immigrants faced when trying to enter the country. As *The Times* wrote, '[t]he case has raised serious doubts about the fairness of procedures being used to screen would-be entrants to Britain'.[34] In the House of Lords, Lord Avebury, who had campaigned against the introduction of X-rays for immigration control purposes, asked whether the Home Office would conduct blood tests on Riaz Ahmed 'whose application to join his father made originally on 15th February 1972 was refused on the grounds that the entry clearance officer did not believe that the relationship was as claimed'.[35] The Conservative leader of the

House of Lords Lord Belstead replied that '[i]t is not our practice to conduct blood tests to establish relationship for the purposes of the immigration rules'. He added, however, that it was 'open to an applicant for entry clearance to submit whatever evidence he [sic] wishes in support of his [sic] case',[36] even though Belstead would have been aware that these tests were too expensive and too difficult to conduct for many migrants from South Asia. Lord Avebury further asked whether the Home Office or the British High Commissions in South Asia would 'arrange for blood tests to be carried out by a doctor nominated by the High Commission for this purpose', in cases in which the ECO had doubts about the relationship of a dependant applying to join a parent in the UK.[37] In response to Lord Avebury's question, Lord Belstead stated that the government had 'no plans to arrange for blood tests to be carried out'.[38]

In his letter to Willie Whitelaw in January 1982, in which he expressed a change of opinion on the acceptable use of X-rays to determine an applicant's age (see Chapter 4), Sir Henry Yellowlees also warned against the use of blood-typing to test blood relationships. Yellowlees advised that there 'would be considerable practical difficulties in undertaking such tests as routine' and further pointed out that 'a definite risk of hepatitis exists'.[39] He concluded that he 'could not recommend the adoption of blood-typing in the present circumstances without a review of the staff and facilities which would be used'.[40] In 1985, the report by the CRE also warned against blood tests to establish kinship becoming a common practice, arguing that, '[w]hile tests of a very sophisticated kind can sometimes show a high level of probability that a claimed relationship exists...they will often leave considerable room for doubt'.[41] The CRE was concerned that if these tests were to become common practice, they would 'add to the costs and difficulties of the procedures and only rarely be of positive benefit either to applicants or ECOs'.[42] One of the possible outcomes of such a scenario would be that the Home Office might come to rely solely on evidence gathered from the physical body of the applicant, and thus deem all testimony and documentary evidence to be irrelevant. An article in *The Guardian* in 1999 claimed that the 'advent of DNA testing means [that Ditta's] case won't happen again',[43] but it is likely that in the current climate DNA testing is relied upon by the authorities in lieu of other evidence presented by potential migrants.

What the Anwar Ditta case reveals are the extreme lengths to which the British immigration control system has gone in the past to deny the credibility of a migrant's testimony and the authenticity of documentation provided by applicants from the developing world. It thus appears that only the physical body is to be believed by the authorities.

The advent of DNA testing

Advances in the testing of blood to establish familial links were made in the 1980s, before the advent of DNA testing in the year 1985–1986. But while blood tests were more frequently used in British immigration control cases during the first half of the 1980s, they could not provide the conclusive results desired in most cases. These tests could demonstrate a familial link between two people, but could not conclusively show a parent–child relationship. As Janet M. Ihenacho has written:

> Evidence expressed in terms of the probability of people being related as claimed rather than being completely unrelated is inappropriate in immigration cases where the sponsor–applicant relationship is close, but may not necessarily be that of parent and child.[44]

As immigration law only allowed dependent children into the UK and not other close familial relatives, the fact that blood tests could not differentiate between the two meant that these tests were not helpful to applying migrants – there was still room to manoeuvre for the authorities to decide that the evidence was inconclusive.

For example, in the case of *R v Immigration Appeals Tribunal ex parte Ashiq Ali* (1985), a blood test was conducted to determine whether Ashiq Ali was the son of Rohinum Nessa Khatun and Mohammed Siddik Ali, but the report of the test stated only that 'the blood groups of Ashiq Ali fit well with his being a son of Rohinum Nessa Khatun and Mohammed Siddik Ali'. Justice Mann found that this report did 'not express itself in terms of balance of probabilities' and only 'demonstrates ... the exclusion of the possibility that the applicant was not the son', adding, '[m]ore than that it did not do'. Thus,

Justice Mann denied the appeal, ruling that the evidence was still inconclusive.

DNA testing was trialled in the immigration control system in 1986 by the Home Office and since the late 1980s has been used in determinations of kinship between applicants in developing countries. However, rather than being used to prove kinship and thus to unite families in Britain, DNA testing predominantly became used to disprove kinship and as a further measure to keep people out of the country. It has also proved to be a costly measure that more often than not must be paid for by the applicant, rather than the Home Office. This makes the process of applying to enter Britain more difficult and more costly for the applicant, which is particularly burdensome for those from the developing world.

Against a background of further restrictions

These measures used to scrutinise the migrant body and to ascertain the 'truth' from undesirable migrants must be understood against a background of ever-increasing restrictions placed upon migrants seeking to enter and reside in Britain. The Conservatives implemented two changes to the immigration control system in the early 1980s that had a drastic effect upon migrants, particularly South Asian and/or female migrants: the introduction of the British Nationality Act 1981 and the 1980 changes to the Immigration Rules.

First, the British Nationality Act 1981 brought the British Nationality Act 1948 into line with the Immigration Act 1971 and the concept of 'patrial' was transformed into the concept of the 'British citizen'. As set out in the 1971 Act, to enter, reside and work in the UK, one had to prove an ancestral link to the country through someone who had been resident there for more than five years prior to 1 January 1973. Such persons were predominantly white British nationals, while non-white migrants from the former colonies were mainly excluded. But a much wider group of Commonwealth and Irish nationals enjoyed other civic rights not defined by the Immigration Act 1971 (such as voting, standing for public office and some access to the NHS, the DHSS and the legal system).[45] These civic rights were removed by the British Nationality Act 1981, and since 1983, only 'British citizens' have had access to them, as well as the right to enter, reside and work unrestricted in the UK. Imogen Tyler has written that the 1981 Act was essentially:

> an immigration Act designed to define, limit and remove the entitlements to citizenship from British nationals in the Commonwealth... thereby restricting immigration to the territorial space of the British Isles and creating 'aliens' within and at the borders of a newly circumscribed nation-state... while race and ethnicity were never directly named in the wording of the Act, it redesigned British citizenship so as to exclude black and Asian populations in the Commonwealth while leaving 'routes home' for white nationals born within the territorial boundaries of the British Empire.[46]

Second, in 1980, the Conservatives changed the Immigration Rules (which did not require a change in legislation so this was merely an administrative shift) to remove the automatic right of women to sponsor their spouse for entry and residency, which was then reinforced in 1983 by the enactment of the British Nationality Act 1981. As mentioned in Chapter 3, the number of wives and fiancées from Commonwealth countries allowed into Britain per year in the 1970s was much higher than the number of husbands and fiancés, but Willie Whitelaw focused on the 5000–6000 men being sponsored by British women to enter the country each year, describing their ability to gain entry via marriage as 'a loophole' that needed to be closed.[47] A Cabinet document from October 1979 revealed the concern that Whitelaw and other Conservative ministers had about this loophole, as '[h]usbands and fiancés were now virtually the only source of male primary immigration', predominantly from the Indian subcontinent.[48] To prevent the migration of men from the Indian subcontinent, the Conservatives would have to crack down on the right of all British women to sponsor a spouse or potential spouse to enter the UK. The Cabinet meeting documents show that the Conservatives acknowledged that this policy 'would be criticized on the grounds that they discriminated between the sexes' and ran the 'risk of an adverse judgment in the European Court',[49] but Whitelaw proceeded anyway.

In the White Paper that followed, the prevention of husbands and fiancés from gaining entry clearance was proposed as a way to stop 'sham marriages' from occurring (a 'concern' that had been raised since the mid-1970s), with the paper stating:

> 50. The husband of a woman who is settled in the United King-dom...is to be admitted if he holds a current entry clearance granted to him for that purpose. An entry clearance will be refused if the *entry clearance officer* has reason to believe:
>
> (a) that the marriage was one entered into primarily to obtain admission to the United Kingdom; or
>
> (b) that one of the parties no longer has any intention of living permanently with the other as his or her spouse; or
>
> (c) *that the parties to the marriage have not met.*[50] (Italics in the original text)

Similar wording was provided in the section on fiancés, although it added that entry clearance would not be issued unless the ECO was 'satisfied that adequate maintenance and accommodation will be available for the fiancé until the date of his marriage without the need to have recourse to public funds', with a further ban on employment during this time.[51] However, the White Paper warned that:

> *A marriage to which none of (a) to (c) above applies gives a man no claim to enter but an entry clearance may be issued provided that the wife is a citizen of the United Kingdom and Colonies born in the United Kingdom.*[52] (Italics in original text)

In the memorandum accompanying the White Paper presented to Cabinet by Whitelaw, he stated that these restrictions on husbands and fiancés pose the 'very real risk' of being 'found to contravene the European Convention on Human Rights', as well as the Sex Discrimination Act 1975. But he believed that the government's position 'could be made more defensible if the Rules applied equally to wives and fiancées'.[53]

This change came in 1985. After the 1980 change to the Immigration Rules and their solidification as part of the British Nationality Act 1981, the British government was challenged in the ECHR in 1985 following a long campaign by various migrant and women's groups, such as the Runnymede Trust, the JCWI and the Women, Immigration and Nationality Group.[54]

As the UK had been one of the founding members of the Council of Europe and the European Court of Human Rights, the British government, under both Labour and the Conservatives, had been unwilling to challenge the ECtHR on matters of immigration. For example, in 1973 Conservative Home Secretary Robert Carr wrote to the Foreign Secretary Alec Douglas-Home advising against a language test for dependants as suggested by the British High Commissioner in Dacca because it 'would be open to attack on human rights grounds'.[55] Similarly, in 1976, FCO Legal Adviser I. K. Mathers warned Anthony Shepherd from the Migration and Visa Department that a register of dependants, such as that proposed by the Franks Group, could possibly violate Articles 8 ('the right to respect for...family life') and 14 ('the enjoyment of rights and freedoms...without discrimination').[56] While Labour was in power between 1974 and 1979, immigration policymakers were wary about potential challenges from the ECtHR, yet the Conservative government under Thatcher took a different position and was more willing to challenge the Court.

In May 1985, the case of *Abdulaziz, Cabales and Balkandali v the United Kingdom* was decided by the ECtHR in Strasbourg. The three women complained of 'being deprived...or threatened with deprivation...of the society of their spouses', which violated Article 8 of the European Convention on Human Rights. They also claimed that they had experienced 'unjustified differences of treatment...based on sex, race and also...birth', which violated Article 14, and that they 'had no effective remedy for their complaints' at the national level, which violated Article 13.[57] The government argued that discrimination on the grounds of sex was 'justified by the need to protect the domestic labour market at a time of high unemployment', which the complainants claimed 'ignored the modern role of women and the fact that men may be self-employed' (which was a likely scenario for many men from South Asia).[58] The government also claimed that 'firm and fair control secured good relations between the different communities living in the United Kingdom', but the complainants responded to this by arguing that 'the racial prejudice of the United Kingdom population could not be advanced as a justification for the measures'.[59] The ECtHR found against the UK government for violations of a combination of Articles 14 and 8, stating that:

> the Court is not convinced that the difference that may neverthe-less exist between the respective impact of men and women on the domestic labour market is sufficiently important to justify the difference of treatment, complained of by the applicants, as to the possibility for a person settled in the United Kingdom to be joined by, as the case may be, his wife or her husband.[60]

The Court also stated that, while the 1980 Rules may have had the aim of 'advancing public tranquillity', 'it is not persuaded that this aim was served by the distinction drawn in those rules between husbands and wives'.[61]

This finding meant that the Immigration Rules needed to be changed, and on 10 July 1985, Willie Whitelaw's successor as Home Secretary, Leon Brittan, announced in Parliament that the 'provisions for the admission of husbands and wives for settlement are brought into line with each other'.[62] But rather than removing the restric-tions placed upon husbands, these restrictions were also applied to wives, 'including the requirement to satisfy the entry clearance officer that the marriage was not entered into primarily for immigration pur-poses, which at present appl[ies] only to husbands'.[63] The 1985 rule changes also instigated that fiancées and fiancés both needed entry clearances to come to the UK for the purpose of marriage, which had been the 'loophole' that the practice of virginity testing had been implemented to close more than a decade earlier. Jacqueline Bhabha and Sue Shutter have argued that these rule changes 'foreshadow[ed] the main plank of government policy on immigration control for the next 10 years – the investigation of motives for marriage and the refusal of people who could not prove that their marriage was not entered into primarily for immigration reasons'.[64]

Burying the investigations: The government's response to the CRE investigation

While the Conservative government faced significant criticism of its immigration control policies at the ECtHR, it also faced substantial criticism over the same policies in the domestic sphere, with the publication of the results of the CRE's investigation into the immigration control system that began in 1979. In 1985, the CRE published its report titled *Immigration Control Procedures*, which was sparked by the virginity testing controversy and then expanded to offer a broader view on the administration of immigration control in Britain.[65] The overarching question addressed by the investigation was whether the level of scrutiny given to some immigrants compared to others was justifiable or whether it was directly grounded in a racist view of what constituted a 'desirable' migrant. The CRE explained that the investigation began with the question of whether, in the Heathrow case, it was 'an acceptable procedure to ask [Mrs K] to submit to an intimate physical examination in order to test whether a passenger was genuine in her claims'.[66] The Commission took the view that the Home Office's justification of the practice, offered back in 1979 and based on its legal framework of medical examination, was inadequate. The CRE stated that 'the so-called virginity test was not solely a matter of medical practice and ethics, [and] could not be considered in isolation from immigration control procedures generally'. Further, the Commission indicated that the practice was 'a possible symptom of serious problems in the administration of immigration control'.[67]

The CRE offered the view that a harsh immigration control system would bring about inequality of treatment and unfairness of outcome, leaving out genuine applicants because of Immigration Officers' underlying assumptions about the characteristics of desirable and undesirable migrants:

> The most crucial question which arose in this respect was whether the procedures operated fairly to distinguish bogus applicants from the genuine, or whether they resulted in substantial numbers of genuine applicants being refused.[68]

The Commission recognised the 'difficult task' facing the Home Office in having to ensure that the system was consistent and fair and not disrupted by the alleged number of deceitful applicants:

> The essential argument was that attempts by the unentitled to secure settlement by fraudulent means were sufficiently numerous

and clever, and their consequences sufficiently serious, to justify causing 'inconvenience' to genuine applicants in order to detect and frustrate attempted evasion.[69]

The CRE also acknowledged the challenge of balancing the task 'between the objectives of detecting and preventing evasion and abuse on the one hand, and ensuring that genuine applicants and passengers meet the minimum delay and difficulty on the other', but highlighted that 'the balance struck has been wrong'.[70] It proposed that the act of detecting bogus migrants had been 'excessive' and 'allowed in many circumstances to override the rights of the genuine'.[71] For the Commission, 'the emphasis on the detection of the fraudulent [had] gone much further than [was] justified by evidence of evasion'.[72]

Further, the Commission noted that profiling at the border was far too influenced by a focus on particular national or ethnic groups:

> The groups most under suspicion of being likely to evade controls...included those from which there were already minority groups established in the United Kingdom....They were very likely also to be black groups.[73]

The CRE argued that the Home Office could not distance itself from these allegations of discrimination by asserting that such decisions were only taken at the lower level. For example, the Commission stated that it did 'not believe that immigration officials simply assess individuals on the basis of the group they belong to or on the grounds of their colour' based solely on individual prejudices. Rather, it claimed that the classification of countries under the label 'pressure to emigrate' and the listing of the most common countries of origin of applicants who had made previous attempts at evasion contributed to the formation of the opinion that personnel were working under instructions:

> so much of the official thinking about the procedures and the instructions and guidance to staff...[had] tended to distort the operation of the controls to the disadvantage of some racial groups.[74]

Therefore, the Commission formulated an informed opinion that the immigration officials were acting in such a manner because the Home Office had suggested 'closer attention [should be] paid to some groups than to others'.[75] This instruction had resulted in 'closer scrutiny of their motivation and incentives, while others intending to evade the controls [were] shielded by the protective colouring of their group'.[76]

A press release put out by the Commission in regard to the report stated that this 'pressure to emigrate' argument was 'used by the immigration authorities to justify the closer checks on black people', as well as 'the longer delays in granting leave to enter and the higher rejection rate'. But the CRE 'found that [the "pressure to emigrate" argument] could not be substantiated' and that the evidence available on immigration control evasion 'did not justify the "pressure to emigrate" philosophy that underlined the way in which the control procedures were operated'.[77] The Commission took the view that financial and human resources were being devoted not towards a healthy maintenance of the immigration system but towards the detection of fraudulent applicants, arguing that there is 'too great an emphasis . . . on the operation of the procedures on the detection of bogus applicants'.[78] This in turn had produced 'an unacceptable cost to genuine families and to race relations generally'.[79]

In its report, the CRE also considered possible solutions for the future, embracing the idea of 'continuous, objective review of immigration control procedures and practices to ensure that they are, and remain, fair in all aspects'.[80] Such recommendations, however, did not find a receptive ear with the Conservative government, who believed that the CRE report was unnecessary and biased. In Parliament, Home Affairs Minister David Waddington claimed that the government found 'some of its central conclusions very odd – some might say perverse'.[81] Waddington argued that most of the report's findings were borne of the 'fallacy' that 'there must be something wrong with the control because more black people are stopped than white'.[82] With regard to the scrutiny and burden of proof placed upon South Asian migrants, Waddington claimed:

> It would be absurd if one were to re-write the rules to state that anyone who made an application was presumed to have an entitlement even if he could not show it. It would be doubly absurd if we were to do that in the context of the history of applications in the

subcontinent, where there has been, regrettably, much deceit and attempts to evade the control. Every Hon. Member knows that.[83]

In a government document responding to the CRE report, this argument was developed further:

> The fact is that people from poorer countries more often attempt evasion than those from wealthy countries. This is true of parts of the Indian Sub-continent from which there has been substantial settlement in Britain since the war... [T]hese appear high on any list of countries with a higher than average proportion of refusals at the port of entry. This is not evidence of bias; it simply confirms the reality of the situation, namely that more people from these countries have an incentive to gain admission to the United Kingdom whether or not they are eligible to work or settle here.[84]

Overall, the response of the Thatcher government was that the CRE report did not recognise the importance of a strict immigration control system. In the government's response, it was argued that '[w]ithout that firm control the government would be playing into the hands of those who simply do not want good community relations and are out to make trouble. That would not be in the best interests either of the country as a whole or of the ethnic minority communities.'[85] The government did not plan to implement many (if any) of the recommendations made by the CRE,[86] and as in the case of the ECtHR judgement, Thatcher, Leon Brittan (and his successor Douglas Hurd) and the Home Office felt that a restrictive immigration and border control system was in the best interests of the British nation-state, and therefore did not accept the criticisms put by these bodies. Further amendments were made to the Immigration Act 1971 in 1986 and 1988, which placed additional restrictions on those seeking to enter the country, thereby helping to establish Britain as what Zig Layton-Henry called in 1994 the 'would-be zero-immigration country'.[87]

Conclusion

This chapter has shown that although the immigration control system was shocked by the revelations of the practice of virginity testing and the X-raying of minors in 1979, the desire of the government to maintain strict immigration controls meant that, while these practices were discontinued (either immediately or gradually over time), the discriminatory assumptions that led to these abuses remained and other forms of discrimination emerged. The chapter outlines the case of British-Pakistani woman Anwar Ditta and her children, whom the British authorities asserted were not her biological children, and the four-year battle to convince the Home Office that these were Ditta's children. It has demonstrated the unfathomable burden of proof placed upon people attempting to enter the country and the racist and sexist assumptions held by immigration officials, specifically that South Asian women are unreliable and prone to dishonest behaviour. The use of blood tests to prove that Ditta's claims were true demonstrates that the authorities relied on reading the physical body, rather than accepting her testimony. Blood tests were soon overtaken by DNA testing as a method of proving kinship between applicants, but this has more often been used to disprove kinship, rather than to help people reunite.

These intrusive measures which place an emphasis on the physical scrutiny of the migrant body were utilised while the Conservative government under Margaret Thatcher sought ways to further restrict migration, especially from the Indian subcontinent, from where the largest number of migrants originated in the 1970s and 1980s. Through the 1980 changes to the Immigration Rules and the British Nationality Act 1981, restrictions were placed upon the ability of women residing in Britain to sponsor the entry of their husbands or fiancés into the country. This move was based on the view that male migrants from South Asia had more economic value as a potential worker than as someone who reinforces the nuclear family unit in migrant communities, which was the socio-economic role deemed by the authorities to be most appropriate for South Asian women at the time. The racism and sexism of these immigration control policies were challenged at the ECtHR in 1985, which found that the Immigration Rules (and the 1981 Act) were racially and sexually discriminatory.

Alongside this critical judgement made at the international level, the Thatcher government also received strong criticism from the country's peak race relations body, the CRE, which concluded a five-year investigation into discrimination within the immigration control system in 1985. The Commission's report made significant criticisms of the system and its targeting of people from certain national or ethnic groups by immigration officials. Finding that the system placed undue attention on seeking out so-called potential bogus migrants, which meant that many genuine migrants were being unnecessarily subjected to intense scrutiny, the CRE proposed a number of recommendations. However, the Thatcher government chose to ignore most of the major recommendations presented in the Commission's report and reiterated its commitment to strict immigration control procedures. Like the restrictions placed on wives and fiancées in 1985 after the ECtHR judgement, the government responded to the criticisms of the CRE report with further restrictive amendments to the Immigration Act in 1986 and 1988. By the end of the 1980s, Britain had probably the most restrictive immigration control system in Western Europe, which provided the framework for the restrictive regime implemented in the 1990s and 2000s under John Major and Tony Blair.

Notes

1. Paul Gordon, 'Outlawing Immigrants 1: Anwar Ditta and Britain's Immigration Laws', in Phil Scraton and Paul Gordon (eds), *Causes for Concern: Questions of Law and Justice* (Harmondsworth: Penguin, 1984).
2. Ibid., p. 115.
3. Cited in Anwar Ditta Defence Committee, *Bring Anwar's Children Home: Stop the Forced Separation of Black Families* (Manchester: ADDC, 1980) p. 7, SC/C/N/27/1, Steve Cohen Collection, Race Relations Archive, University of Manchester.
4. Gordon, 'Outlawing Immigrants 1', p. 123.
5. Ibid.
6. Ibid.
7. Friends of Anwar Ditta/Manchester Law Centre, *Bring Anwar's Children Home! The Case of Anwar Ditta & Shuja Ud Din and Their Three Children Kamran, Imran & Saima* (Manchester: Friends of Anwar Ditta/Manchester Law Centre, 1980) p. 9, SC/C/N/27/2, Steve Cohen Collection, RRA.
8. Friends of Anwar Ditta/Manchester Law Centre, *Bring Anwar's Children Home!*, p. 9.
9. Ibid., p. 11.
10. Pat Fizsimmons and Kath McKay, 'One Wins, One Loses', *Spare Rib*, 98, September 1980, p. 17.
11. Gordon, 'Outlawing Immigrants 1', p. 125.
12. Cited in ADDC, *Bring Anwar's Children Home*, p. 7.
13. Gordon, 'Outlawing Immigrants 1', p. 125.

14. Cited in ADDC, *Bring Anwar's Children Home*, ADDC flyer, 1979, AD74, Tandana online archive, http://www.tandana.org/data/pg/search.php? Ref=AD74 (accessed 26 January 2013).
15. Ibid.
16. 'Anwar Ditta: Black Family Divided', *Fight Racism! Fight Imperialism!*, n.d., Tandana online archive, http://www.tandana.org/data/pg/search. php?Ref=AD106 (accessed 26 January 2013).
17. ADDC, *Bring Anwar's Children Home*.
18. Ibid.
19. Ibid.
20. Cited in ADDC flyer, n.d., p. 3, AD53, Tandana online archive, http://www.tandana.org/data/pg/search.php?Ref=AD53 (accessed 28 January 2013).
21. ADDC, *Bring Anwar's Children Home: Bulletin of A.D.D.C.*, 14 February 1981, p. 4, AD64, Tandana online archive, http://www.tandana.org/data/pg/search.php?Ref=AD65 (accessed 28 January 2013).
22. David Holmes, 'Anwar Ditta's Battle for Her Children', *New Statesman*, 22 August 1980, p. 7.
23. Draft of ADDC support letter, n.d., AD60, Tandana online archive, http://www.tandana.org/data/pg/search.php?Ref=AD60 (accessed 28 January 2013).
24. Cited in ADDC flyer, n.d., p. 3, AD53.
25. Ibid.
26. Draft of ADDC support letter, n.d., AD60.
27. Anwar Ditta, 'The Case of Anwar Ditta in Her Own Words', in ADDC, *Bring Anwar's Children Home* (ADDC: Manchester), p. 6.
28. ADDC, Press Release, 16 March 1981, AD47, Tandana online archive, http://www.tandana.org/data/pg/search.php?Ref=AD47 (accessed 29 January 2013).
29. ADDC, Press Release, 16 March 1981.
30. Letter from Timothy Raison to Joel Barnett (press release version) 19 March 1981, IRR 01/04/04/01/08/01/05, IRR Library, London.
31. ADDC, Press Release, 16 March 1981.
32. Letter from Timothy Raison to Joel Barnett (press release version).
33. Ibid.
34. Peter Evans, 'Woman Wins Fight to Reunite Her Family', *The Times*, 20 March 1981.
35. House of Lords, *Hansard*, 6 April, 1981, col. 427w.
36. Ibid.
37. Ibid.
38. Ibid.
39. Letter from Henry Yellowlees to Willie Whitelaw, 14 January 1982, HO 418/33, NA.
40. Letter from Henry Yellowlees to Willie Whitelaw.
41. Commission for Racial Equality, *Immigration Control Procedures: Report of a Formal Investigation* (London: CRE, 1985) p. 41.

42. Ibid., p. 41.
43. Anne Perkins, 'I was Robbed of my Children's Childhood', *The Guardian online*, 22 October 1999, http://www.guardian.co.uk/theguardian/1999/oct/22/features11.g24 (accessed 16 January 2013).
44. Janet M. Ihenacho, *The Effect of the Introduction of DNA Testing on Immigration Control Procedures: Case Studies of Bangladeshi Families* (Warwick: Centre for Research in Ethnic Relations, 1991) p. 38.
45. Bhabha and Shutter, *Women's Movement* (Oakhill: Trentham Books, 1984), pp. 48–50.
46. Imogen Tyler, *Revolting Subjects* (London: Zed Books), pp. 53–54.
47. *Hansard*, 4 December, 1979, col. 254.
48. Cabinet meeting conclusions, 25 October 1979, p. 1, CAB/128/66/18, NA.
49. Cabinet meeting conclusions, 25 October 1979, p. 2. Although in FCO documents given to British High Commissions in South Asia with instructions to take towards local criticisms, it was claimed that the government did 'not believe that the proposed rules are in breach of the [European] Convention [of Human Rights]' and stated that '[i]f anyone is aggrieved, they can...put their case to the European Commission on Human Rights'. Telegram no. 14, 14 February 1980, p. 2, FCO 50/681, NA.
50. 'Draft Immigration Rules', 16 October 1979, pp. 20–21, CAB/129/207/15, NA.
51. 'Draft Immigration Rules', p. 22.
52. Ibid., p. 21.
53. 'White Paper on the Immigration Rules: Memorandum by the Secretary of State for the Home Department', 16 October 1979, p. 2, CAB/129/207/15, NA.
54. See Women, Immigration and Nationality Group, *'Immigration Widows' Kit*, n.d., RC?RF/1/01/6/7, Runnymede Trust archives, BCA.
55. Robert Carr, 'Immigration: Entry of Dependants,' 22 June 1973, FCO 50/460, NA.
56. Letter from I.K. Mathers to Anthony Shepherd, 18 June 1976, FCO 50/586, NA.
57. *Abdulaziz, Cabales and Balkandali v the United Kingdom*, ECHR, 9214/80; 9473/81; 9474/81, 20 May 1985, http://hudoc.echr.coe.int/sites/eng/pages/search.aspx?i=001-57416#{%22itemid%22:[%22001-57416%22]} (accessed 10 January 2014).
58. *Abdulaziz, Cabales and Balkandali v the United Kingdom*, paragraph 75.
59. Ibid., paragraph 76.
60. Ibid., paragraph 79.
61. Ibid., paragraph 81.
62. *Hansard*, 10 July 1985, col. 425w.
63. Ibid.
64. Bhabha and Shutter, *Women's Movement*, p. 78.
65. CRE, *Immigration Control Procedures*, p. 1.
66. Ibid.
67. Ibid.

68. Ibid., p. 6.
69. Ibid., p. 9.
70. Ibid., p. 10.
71. Ibid.
72. Ibid., p. 11.
73. Ibid.
74. Ibid., p. 131.
75. Ibid.
76. Ibid.
77. CRE Press Release, 'CRE Calls for Changes in Immigration Control Procedures', 12 February 1985, pp. 3–4, RC/RF/1/01/B, Runnymede Trust archives, BCA.
78. CRE, *Immigration Control Procedures*, p. 128.
79. Ibid.
80. Ibid., pp. 132–133.
81. *Hansard*, 13 May, 1985, col. 1166.
82. Ibid.
83. Ibid., col. 1167.
84. Home Office, 'Commission for Racial Equality (CRE) Report into Immigration Control Procedures: Government Comments', December 1985, p. 3.
85. Home Office, 'Commission for Racial Equality (CRE) Report into Immigration Control Procedures', p. 4.
86. A list of the government's response to every recommendation in the report can be found in a document held in the Runnymede Trust archive at the Black Cultural Archives. See: 'General Points: Introduction to Home Office Response', December 1985, RC/RF/1/01/B, Runnymede Trust archives, BCA.
87. Zig Layton-Henry, 'Britain: The Would-Be Zero-Immigration Country', in Wayne A. Cornelius, Philip L. Martin and James F. Hollifield (eds), *Controlling Immigration: A Global Perspective* (Stanford, CA: Stanford University Press, 1994) pp. 283–296.

Conclusion

In 1985, the JCWI claimed that:

> entry clearance procedures abroad are operated on the assumption that they need to be directed towards the detection of bogus applicants even if in the process genuine applicants are refused. This licenses entry clearance officers to behave like a fraud squad, rather than as neutral officials processing applications from the wives and children of British and settled men.[1]

This quote from the JCWI gives us an understanding of the level of distrust that immigration officials, in Britain and at the British High Commissions in South Asia, harboured towards South Asian migrants and the manner in which the British immigration control system operated. As we have shown throughout this book, from the 1960s to the 1980s the British authorities saw (and still see) the strict implementation of immigration controls as necessary for 'good race relations', and discriminatory practices – with the burden of proof placed upon the applicant – as necessary for the effective implementation of these controls. The suspicion of foreigners that existed within the system and pressure to scrutinise those who fit the profile of a potentially 'bogus' migrant led to the occurrence of various physical (and mental) abuses. This is the context within which the practice of virginity testing operated.

The practice of virginity testing and other forms of intrusive examination conducted upon migrant women from the Indian subcontinent in the 1970s were informed by a mentality of postcolonial dominance. The targeting of this group of women was certainly dictated by the British colonial experience – or misconception – that the female role in South Asian society is submissive. Further, the post-imperial British government held a conviction, remaining from the colonial era, that people from the Indian subcontinent were untrustworthy. Yet, having admitted many Indian men into Britain for economic development purposes in the 1950s and 1960s, the government had to recognise the need to reunite families as a pressing point of public policy, while at the same time attempting to preserve the whiteness of British society.

The border became a space where virginity testing and other abusive treatments were justified to serve socio-economic and political aims. The increasingly restrictive conditions produced by British immigration control policy saw the authorities seek to apply a formula to create and maintain its idea of the ideal mixed society, whereby the Commonwealth migrant would be accepted on the terms of the host society. In the case of the South Asian women who came to Britain in the 1970s, they were to fulfil the purpose of joining their male family members and creating homogeneous family units in Britain's South Asian communities, thus replicating the ideals of white British society. To ensure that these women would fulfil this role, and because South Asian migrants were thought to be prone to fabrication (especially women), the body became the signifier of 'the truth' for British immigration officials. The combination of all of these elements formed the basis for the conditions under which over 120 South Asian women had to endure intrusive tests between 1968 and 1979. This practice was highly discriminatory, with a very select demographic group being the victims; it was an abuse of power and a violation of human rights.

The victims who were subjected to such practices remain mostly nameless and faceless, will never receive adequate compensation and, most importantly for the purpose of a proper healing process, have yet to receive an apology from either the past or current British governments. On this point, when the story broke again in May 2011 in *The Guardian*, and was widely reported worldwide, the Conservative government did not consider it to be a good opportunity to redress past wrongdoings:

[a] UK Border Agency spokesman said: 'These practices occurred 30 years ago and were clearly wrong. This government's immigration

policies reflect the UK's legal responsibilities and respect immigrants' human rights.'[2]

In a multi-ethnic, globalised Britain, one would assume that this matter would be taken more seriously. Redressing past wrongdoing is the foundation of restorative justice, an underpinning principle embraced by the UN to attest to the importance of acknowledging abuse and the infringement of human rights. Meaningful reparation of wrongdoings does contribute to the healing of victims, and any action in this direction ought to be encouraged.[3] In this regard, revealing is the position of a woman who underwent the virginity test, even though she was already married, and whose testimony was reported in *The Guardian* by her daughter and journalist Huma Qureshi:

> Does she want an apology from the government? 'Yes. I'd forgotten about it, because I thought it was normal. But it makes me angry remembering it. I was naive then, I went along with it. But I came here lawfully, to join my husband who was contributing to the economy. We didn't deserve that sort of humiliation.'[4]

Physical, intrusive and violent scrutiny was imposed on this woman to ascertain the truth that the authorities evidently believed could not be collected via other means and to determine whether she would fit within the British project of a compartmentalised, mixed-race society. The woman was rejected as a human being, and her human range of emotions was seen not to exist; her humiliation, if ever noted, could be forgotten because the overarching purpose of her admittance to British society was classified as more important than her integrity.

The task of discerning 'undesirable' migrants at the border was prioritised over all other economic, social and humanitarian concerns. Did ever the Immigration Officers, who used their discretionary power to argue that more intrusive examinations were needed, consider the implications of their actions? Have they ever looked back? We accept that they followed orders. We also accept that immigration officials may have agreed, up to a point, to perform their duties in a most comprehensive manner because of the government's broader vision and their background. In other areas of the world, brutalities directed at certain ethnic groups to achieve a better position for the dominant state would be framed in completely different terms. The harmful actions of the British state and its branches and personnel would not be dismissed in this way. This is why we conclude this book with a reflection on state crime. Serious harm occurred at the border during those years; this level of harm inflicted upon female migrants from the Indian subcontinent region was justified by a 'desire for order', a desire to achieve certain societal goals as a 'new paradigm of prevention'. Thorough checks at the border allow the government to identify and remove 'danger' and 'threats' before they emerge. Yet, these concepts of 'danger' and 'threats' are based upon existing racial, sexist and other prejudices, which perpetuate colonial ideals in the postcolonial society. This 'paradigm of prevention' is upheld via the violent and deviant actions of the state which can be framed under the label of state crime.

The conduct of the immigration control system as state crime

The theory of state crime is a relatively recent development in criminal justice research, particularly in relation to the discussion of the practices of governments in Western liberal democracies, where the rule of law maintains that a legitimate use of force may be wielded by the institutions of the state, and effectively 'consented' to by the people who elect the government. This relates to the idea of 'sovereignty' – that a country has the right to *solely* determine its own laws (and enforce them) within its borders – although many scholars have argued that this idea of sovereignty is a myth.[5]

Criminologists Penny Green and Tony Ward have developed this idea of state crime by questioning the concept of the liberal democratic state's legitimate use of force and arguing that the 'legal limits of legitimate force are inherently vague', and that the 'strict enforcement of what limits do exist is intrinsically difficult and will often be contrary to the interests of the enforcing agency.'[6] For Green and Ward, the concept of legitimate force derives from a state's claim to sovereignty and from 'some degree of consent', such that 'there is likely to be some tacit understanding of the limits of legitimate conduct'.[7] One of the factors these authors use to define state crime is thus when the state acts outside the limits of legitimate conduct and its actions would seem illegitimate in the eyes of the civil society that the state purports to serve. They propose that state crime 'should be restricted to the area of overlap between two distinct phenomena: (1) violations of human rights and (2) state organizational deviance'.[8] Human rights, in Green and Ward's view, are 'the elements of freedom and well-being that humans need to exert and develop ... for purposive action', while state organisational deviance is defined as:

> Conduct by persons working for state agencies, in pursuit of organizational goals, that if it were to become known to some social audience would expose the individuals or agencies concerned to a sufficiently serious risk of formal or informal censure and sanctions to affect their conduct significantly.[9]

It is taken as implicit by Green and Ward that 'passive failures to protect individuals against violations of their rights' are also included within this definition of state crime.[10]

Green and Ward also point out that there is a difference between 'individual deviant acts committed by state agents' and 'acts committed in pursuit of organisational goals',[11] with only the latter constituting state crime. Michael J. Lynch and Raymond Michalowski emphasise the term 'organisational' in the concept of state crime, proposing that often those who commit human rights abuses 'are not morally depraved', but are usually 'ordinary workers who come to accept the normalcy of an organisational culture in which these acts, even if regrettable, are understood as simply part of their jobs'.[12] We have seen this in the history of abuses within the British immigration control system, as the government has tried to refute such abuse by attributing it to an individual (or individuals), usually at the lower levels, acting outside the parameters of their job. But it is often the case that the individuals are under pressure and informed from above, which creates the opportunity for abuses to occur.

In the area of immigration control policy, with a particular focus on Australia's immigration control policy, Sharon Pickering and Michael Grewcock have both utilised the concept as developed by Green and Ward to highlight how the modern discourses that criminalise irregular migration (by refugees and asylum seekers) provide the context for state crimes to occur whereby these migrants become the victims. Grewcock states that Australia's treatment of refugees and asylum seekers has been long criticised for 'breaching human rights norms' but notes that 'few legal or formal sanctions have operated against Australian government policy'.[13] Along similar lines, Pickering points out that over the past decade and a half, 'Australia has retreated from its international human rights obligations and has sought to particularly distance itself from its international human rights obligations to refugees'.[14] However, any condemnation by the international community has been interpreted by many in Australia as 'an attempt to undermine the policies and practices of a democratically elected government'.[15] A ruling government is unlikely to prosecute itself for state crimes, even if its practices do constitute a violation of human rights, are institutionally embedded and are conducted in pursuit of the goals of the state. So what is the point of labelling these practices as state crimes? Pickering and Grewcock both argue that labelling a certain practice or act as a state crime allows a space for a challenge to be made within civil society and an alternative view of the 'refugee question' to emerge. As Pickering concludes in a 2005 article, the use of the term 'state crime' 'may assist in the deployment of alternative meanings for legitimate sovereign behaviour and the terms through which its legitimacy may be judged'.[16]

British immigration control and state crime

We see similarities between the phenomena described by Pickering and Grewcock and the abuses that we have described in this book. One of the continuous features of British immigration control since the 1970s is that there are ever-tightening restrictions placed upon non-European migration, but as mentioned earlier this has not stopped the flow of people into Britain. Liza Schuster has argued that, despite controls becoming ever tighter, people still find a way into the destination country, stating that:

> Controlled borders, let alone closed borders, are a fiction, and...the European and other governments which attempt to enforce these are involved in a symbolic battle at best.[17]

It is within this symbolic battle, Schuster claims, that there are 'very real serious costs and consequences' of the enforcement of immigration control, not only for migrants but also for the destination countries.[18] In addition to the massive financial costs of maintaining border control, hundreds of migrants die or are injured while seeking to gain entry to the destination country and there is an 'increase in racial prejudice and racial violence each time migration controls become the focus of political attention'.[19]

The figures on how many have died, been injured or been physically or mentally abused within the British immigration control process are incomplete, and only cover a much more recent period of time than that examined in this book. For example, Harmit Athwal for the Institute of Race Relations (IRR) states that, between 2006 and 2010, '77 asylum seekers and migrants... have died either in the UK or [while] attempting to reach the UK'.[20] Of these 77, 15 died 'taking dangerous and highly risky methods to enter the country', 44 died 'as an indirect consequence of the iniquities of the immigration/asylum system' (with 28 of those committing suicide), seven died in police custody, seven died 'at the hands of racists or as a consequence of altercations with a racial dimension' while out in the community and four died while undertaking work in the 'black economy' as irregular migrants who are not provided with any state assistance.[21] After the deaths of three migrants in Colnbrook Immigration Removal Centre in July and August 2011, Athwal reported on the IRR website that 14 people had died in British immigration detention centres since 1989.[22] These reported figures are most likely to be underestimates of the real size of the problem and Athwal suggests that there may be more, such as those who die while trying to enter Britain, those who are repatriated to a place where they fear for their safety and those who die while working in the 'black economy'.[23] Athwal also emphasises that these figures do not include the violence experienced by settled migrants and the next generations, at the hands of either other members of the community or institutions of the state, such as the police. Another IRR study from 2010 found that 89 people had died as a result of racial violence since 1993 (the year of Stephen Lawrence's murder),[24] while the IRR website claims that over 140 black and ethnic minority people died in police custody between December 1978 and November 2003.[25]

Can these deaths be attributed to state crime? Looking back at Green and Ward's definition, these deaths can be seen to eventuate from the pursuit of organisational goals by state personnel (such as preventing irregular migrants from entering the country, deporting unwanted migrants and ensuring that living in the UK as an irregular migrant is intolerable) or the failure to adequately protect vulnerable individuals. As Leanne Weber argues:

> The majority of border-related deaths can be attributed to the 'structural violence' of border controls – that is, to systemic effects that multiply the risks of death and injury faced by illegalised travellers.[26]

And like the Australian context, in Britain the migrant has little recourse against state crimes. Mary Bosworth and Mhairi Guild have explained that the migrant is in a 'substantially different, and far more vulnerable, position' than the domestic criminal, and the 'British immigration complex does not encounter the same [legal] constraints as the [domestic] criminal justice system'.[27] Liz Fekete has lamented that '[n]ot one of the twelve deportation deaths the IRR has documented since 1993 [to 2007] has led to a police officer or immigration official being successfully prosecuted for murder or the lesser charge of manslaughter'.[28]

The death of migrants is not the only basis on which to justify use of the term 'state crime'. Serous abuse and physical and psychological harm at the hands of the state can be classified as state crime. And the practice of virginity testing reveals that the maltreatment of vulnerable migrants is not reserved to irregular migrants. Moreover, migrants showing up at the border with documents are subjected to state abuse. This demonstrates that state crime at the border can take many forms, and more often than not goes unreported and remains unknown. However, these abuses can be explained as a consequence of attempts to achieve the organisational goals of the immigration control system: the 'desire for order' and the aim of preventing 'undesirable' migrants from entering the country.

This raises a question in relation to the cases of abuse seen in the British immigration control system and in the Australian system: can these abuses be considered 'state crimes' as defined by Pickering, Grewcock, and Green and Ward? Clearly, similar abuses have occurred in both immigration control systems. And by the definition put forward by Green and Ward, as used by Pickering and Grewcock, these abuses could indeed be defined as state crimes, pursued in the process of state organisational goals.

What is the purpose of calling these abuses state crimes? It must be to redress the balance in the discourse on how migrants are treated within the British immigration control system. The present discourse is framed by a popular assumption that migration is a transgressive act that must be responded to with the full force of the coercive powers of the state, which often surpasses the 'legal' limits of this coercion. By highlighting the actions of the state as a form of criminal activity, rather than focusing on the possibility of people entering the country under false pretences, we are hoping for a shift in the dominant discourse.

* * *

The virginity testing procedures that were conducted upon South Asian women between 1968 and 1979 were some of the gravest abuses of the powers held by immigration control officers in the history of the modern immigration control system. As attested to by the Indian representative at the UN, virginity testing was a degrading procedure which also reflected a racism fostered by the former colonialism of the British Commonwealth, and in an emerging postcolonial world cultivated a 'desire for order', which replicated the colonial stratification of society, and communicated to potential migrants their marginalisation within British society. To be allowed to enter, work and reside in Britain, potential migrants had to prostrate themselves before the authority of the state and allow themselves to be subjected to the prejudices and scrutiny of immigration officials.

The practice of virginity testing was not a mere aberration within the history of British immigration, but a severe outcome of the restrictive conditions created by the immigration control policy of successive British governments, in which the emphasis was on preventing 'bogus', non-white migrants from entering Britain. The immigration control system in Britain has focused too heavily – as it still does to some extent – on attempting to seek out the so-called bogus and undesirable migrant, at the cost of allowing the 'genuine' migrant to enter. And during this process, abuses have occurred. The archival evidence shows that the higher levels of the Home Office and the FCO knew of the abuses within the immigration control system, particularly the physical scrutiny placed upon the female body to satisfy the system's 'burden of proof', yet did nothing until it was exposed by the mainstream media. Even after the virginity testing controversy emerged and the eventual ban on the use of X-rays for age assessment purposes, other forms of discrimination and physical scrutiny were endured by South Asian women trying to enter Britain. Since the 1980s, the British immigration control system has become more restrictive and it has been an alleged aim of the current Conservative government to make the UK a 'hostile environment' for migrants.[29] To understand how this current system has been allowed to come into being, we must understand how the modern system was established. The history we have uncovered in this book reveals that the history of immigration control in Britain has long been racially and sexually discriminatory and has stressed the strict implementation of controls, rather than acknowledging the human rights of those migrants who enter the system. Although we do not know the names of most of those who suffered under the immigration control system in the 1970s and 1980s, we hope that this book helps people to acknowledge that their suffering did occur and that the British public, if not the government, will recognise this.

Notes

1. JCWI, 'Briefing on *Immigration Control Procedures: Report of a Formal Investigation* by the Commission for Racial Equality', 1985, p. 2, RC/RF/1/01/B, Runnymede Trust archive, BCA.
2. A. Travis, 'Ministers Face Calls for Apology as Extent of 1970s "Virginity Tests" Revealed', *The Guardian*, 9 May 2011, http://www.theguardian.com/uk/2011/may/08/home-office-virginity-tests-1970s (accessed 9 January 2014).
3. Much of Miriam Aukerman's analysis would apply to this context as well. See M. Aukerman (2002) 'Extraordinary Evil, Ordinary Crime: A Framework for Understanding Transitional Justice', *Harvard Human Rights Journal*, 15, pp. 39–97.
4. Qureshi, 'Passport, Visa, Virginity?'.
5. See David Garland, 'The Limits of the Sovereign State: Strategies of Crime Control in Contemporary Society', *British Journal of Criminology*, 36/4, Autumn 1996, pp. 445–471; Saskia Sassen, *Losing Control? Sovereignty in an Age of Globalization* (New York: Columbia University Press, 1996).
6. Penny J. Green and Tony Ward, 'State Crime, Human Rights and the Limits of Criminology', *Social Justice*, 27/1, 2000, p. 102.
7. Green and Ward, 'State Crime, Human Rights and the Limits of Criminology', p. 108.
8. Ibid., p. 110.

9. Ibid.
10. Ibid., p. 111.
11. Ibid., p. 110.
12. Michael J. Lynch and Raymond Michalowski, *Primer in Radical Criminology: Critical Perspectives on Crime, Power and Identity* (Mansey, NY: Criminal Justice Project, 2006) p. 186.
13. Michael Grewcock, *Border Crimes: Australia's War on Illicit Migrants* (Sydney: Institute of Criminology, 2010) p. 18.
14. Sharon Pickering, *Refugees and State Crime* (Sydney: Federation Press, 2005) p. 13.
15. Pickering, *Refugees and State Crime*, p. 14.
16. Sharon Pickering, 'Crimes of the State: The Persecution and Protection of Refugees', *Critical Criminology*, 13, 2005, p. 160.
17. Liza Schuster, 'An Open Debate on Open Borders: Reply to Stephen Castles', *Open Democracy* (29 December 2003), http://www.opendemocracy.net/print/1658 (accessed 18 November 2009).
18. Schuster, 'An Open Debate on Open Borders'.
19. Ibid.
20. Harmit Athwal, *Driven to Desperate Measures: 2006–2010* (London: Institute of Race Relations, 2010) p. 2.
21. Athwal, *Driven to Desperate Measures*, p. 2.
22. Harmit Athwal, 'Three Deaths in Immigration Detention', IRR website (4 August 2011), http://www.irr.org.uk/2011/august/ha000008.html (accessed 26 August 2011).
23. Athwal, *Driven to Desperate Measures*, p. 2.
24. Harmit Athwal, Jenny Bourne and Rebecca Wood, *Racial Violence: The Buried Issue*, IRR Briefing Paper 6 (London: Institute of Race Relations, 2010) p. 3.
25. IRR, 'Black Deaths in Custody' (19 February 2004), http://www.irr.org.uk/2002/november/ak000006.html (accessed 26 August 2011).
26. Leanne Weber, 'Knowing-and-yet-not-knowing about European Border Deaths', *Australian Journal of Human Rights*, 15/2, 2010, p. 41.
27. Mary Bosworth and Mhairi Guild, 'Governing Through Migration Control: Security and Citizenship in Britain', *British Journal of Criminology*, 48, 2008, p. 711.
28. Liz Fekete, 'Europe's Shame: A Report on 105 Deaths Linked to Racism or Government Migration and Asylum Policies', *European Race Bulletin* 66, Winter 2009, p. 5.
29. Alan Travis, 'Immigration Bill: Theresa May Defends Plans to Create "Hostile Environment"', *The Guardian*, 13 October 2013, http://www.theguardian.com/politics/2013/oct/10/immigration-bill-theresa-may-hostile-environment (accessed 14 January 2014).

Works Cited

Primary sources

Archival and collected papers

Cohen, Steve, papers, Race Relations Archive, University of Manchester
Institute of Race Relations Library, London
Joint Council for the Welfare of Immigrants archive, Hull History Centre
Runnymede Trust archive, Black Cultural Archives, London
The National Archives, London: Cabinet Papers, Foreign and Commonwealth
Office, Home Office, Prime Minister's Office
United Nations Commission on Human Rights papers, United Nations
Library, Geneva

Parliamentary debates and papers

Control of Immigration Statistics 1 July 1962–31 December 1963, HMSO, London,
1965
Control of Immigration Statistics 1964, HMSO, London, 1965
Home Office Statistical Department, *Home Office Statistical Bulletin*, 1979
House of Commons, *Hansard*
House of Lords, *Hansard*
Immigration from the Commonwealth, Cmnd. 2739, HMSO, London, 1965
Lok Sabha, *Hansard*
Select Committee on Race Relations and Immigration, *Immigration, Vol. I:
Report with Annexes and Minutes of Proceedings*, HMSO, London, 1978
Select Committee on Race Relations and Immigration, *Immigration, Vol. II:
Evidence and Appendices*, HMSO, London, 1978

Newspapers and journals

New Statesman
Spare Rib
The Guardian
The Times

Court proceedings

Abdulaziz, Cabales and Balkandali v the United Kingdom, ECHR, 9214/80;
9473/81; 9474/81, 20 May 1985
Home Office v Commission for Racial Equality, 1981, All England Law Reports
Iqbal Haque v Entry Certificate Officer, Dacca, 19 October, 1973, TH/612/73(204),
Immigration Appeals Review, vol. 3 (1974)

Secondary sources

Books

Agamben, Giorgio, *Homo Sacer: Sovereign Power and Bare Life* (Stanford, CA: Stanford University Press, 1998).

Agamben, Giorgio, *State of Exception* (Chicago: University of Chicago Press, 2005).

Alexander, Peter, *Racism, Resistance and Revolution* (London: Bookmarks, 1987).

Bailkin, Jordanna, *The Afterlife of Empire* (Berkeley, CA: University of California Press, 2012).

Ballhatchet, Kenneth, *Race, Sex and Class under the Raj: Imperial Attitudes and Policies and Their Critics, 1793–1905* (London: Weidenfeld & Nicholson, 1980).

Bevan, Vaughn, *The Development of British Immigration Law* (London: Routledge, 1986).

Bhabha, Homi, *The Location of Culture* (London and New York: Routledge, 2008).

Bhabha, Jacqueline and Shutter, Sue, *Women's Movement: Women Under Immigration, Nationality and Refugee Law* (Oakhill: Trentham Books, 1994).

Borthwick, Meredith, *The Changing Role of Women in the Bengal 1849–1905* (New Jersey: Princeton University Press, 1984).

Brah, Avtar, *Cartographies of Diaspora: Contesting Identities* (London: Routledge, 1996).

Burton, Antoinette, *Burdens of History: British Feminists, Indian Women and Imperial Culture, 1865–1915* (Chapel Hill & London: University of North Carolina Press, 1994).

Butler, David and Kavanagh, Dennis, *The British General Election of February 1974* (London: Macmillan, 1974).

Centre for Contemporary Cultural Studies, *The Empire Strikes Back: Race and Racism in 70s Britain* (London: Hutchinson, 1986).

Chaudhuri, Kirti N., *The Trading World of Asia and the English East India Company 1660–1760* (Cambridge: Cambridge University Press, 1978).

Cohen, Steve, *It's the Same Old Story: Immigration Controls against Jewish, Black and Asian People, with Special Reference to Manchester* (Manchester: Manchester City Council, 1987).

Cohen, Steve, *Immigration Controls, the Family and the Welfare State* (London: Jessica Kingsley Publishers, 2001).

Crossman, Richard, *The Diaries of a Cabinet Minister, Vol. 1: Minister of Housing 1964–66* (London: Hamish Hamilton, 1975).

Deedes, William, *Race without Rancour* (London: Conservative Political Centre, 1968).

Deleuze, Gilles and Claire, Parnet, *Dialogues* (New York: Continuum, 1987).

Deleuze, Gilles and Guattari, Felix, *Anti-Oedipus: Capitalism and Schizophrenia* (London: Continuum, 2004).

Doty, Roxanne Lynn, *Anti-Immigrantism in Western Democracies: Statecraft, Desire, and the Politics of Exclusion* (London: Routledge, 2003).

Dummett, Ann and Nicol, Andrew, *Subjects, Citizens, Aliens and Others: Nationality and Immigration Law* (London: Weidenfeld and Nicholson, 1990).

Foot, Paul, *Immigration and Race in British Politics* (Harmondsworth: Penguin, 1965).

Foucault, Michel, *Discipline and Punish: The Birth of the Prison* (London: Penguin Books, 1991).

Foucault, Michel, *Society Must Be Defended: Lectures at the College de France 1975–76* (New York: Picador, 2003).

Foucault, Michel, *The History of Sexuality, Vol. 1* (London: Penguin Books, 2008).

Foucault, Michel, *Security, Territory, Population: Lectures at the College de France 1977–78* (Houndmills: Palgrave Macmillan, 2009).

Fryer, Peter, *Staying Power: The History of Black People in Britain* (London: Pluto Press, 1984).

Gilroy, Paul, *There Ain't No Black in the Union Jack: The Cultural Politics of Race and Nation* (London: Routledge, 2002).

Gilroy, Paul, *After Empire: Melancholia or Convivial Culture* (London: Routledge, 2004).

Grewcock, Michael, *Border Crimes: Australia's War on Illicit Migrants* (Sydney: Institute of Criminology, 2010).

Grob-Fitzgibbon, Benjamin, *Imperial Endgame: Britain's Dirty Wars and the End of Empire* (Houndmills: Palgrave Macmillan, 2011).

Gupta, Rahila, *From Homebreakers to Jailbreakers: Southall Black Sisters* (London: Zed Books, 2003).

Hall, Stuart et al., *Policing the Crisis: Mugging, the State and Law and Order* (London: Palgrave Macmillan, 1979).

Hekman, Susan J. (ed.), *Feminist Interpretations of Michel Foucault* (Pennsylvania, PA: Pennsylvania State University Press, 1996).

Hiro, Dilip, *Black British, White British: A History of Race Relations in Britain* (London: Paladin, 1992).

Holdaway, Simon, *The Racialisation of British Policing* (Houndmills: Macmillan, 1996).

Holmes, Colin, *John Bull's Island: Immigration & British Society, 1871–1971* (Houndmills: Macmillan, 1988).

Hyam, Ronald, *Sexuality and Empire: The British Experience* (Manchester: Manchester University Press, 1990).

Ihenacho, Janet M., *The Effect of the Introduction of DNA Testing on Immigration Control Procedures: Case Studies of Bangladeshi Families* (Warwick: Centre for Research in Ethnic Relations, 1991).

Karatani, Reiko, *Defining British Citizenship: Empire, Commonwealth and Modern Britain* (London: Routledge, 2003).

Knowles, Caroline, *Race, Discourse and Labourism* (London: Routledge, 1992).

Kristeva, Julia, *Powers of Horror: An Essay in Abjection* (New York: Columbia University Press, 1982).

Labour Party, *Race, Immigration and the Racialists* (London: Labour Party Campaign Handbook, 1978).

Layton-Henry, Zig, *The Politics of Immigration: Immigration, 'Race' and 'Race' Relations in Post-War Britain* (Oxford: Blackwell, 1992).

Lynch, Michael J. and Michalowski, Raymond, *Primer in Radical Criminology: Critical Perspectives on Crime, Power and Identity* (Mansey, NY: Criminal Justice Press, 2006).

Mani, Lata, *Contentious Traditions: The Debate on Sati in Colonial India* (Berkeley: University of California Press, 1998).

McClintock, Anne, *Imperial Leather: Race, Gender and Sexuality in the Colonial Conquest* (New York & London: Routledge, 1995).

McNay, Lois, *Foucault and Feminism* (Cambridge: Polity Press, 1992).

Miles, Robert and Phizacklea, Annie, *White Man's Country: Racism in British Politics* (London: Pluto Press, 1984).

Moore, Robert, *Racism and Black Resistance in Britain* (London: Pluto Press, 1975).

Nicol, Andrew, *Illegal Entrants* (London: Runnymede Trust/Joint Council for the Welfare of Immigrants, 1981).

Paul, Kathleen, *Whitewashing Britain: Race and Citizenship in the Postwar Era* (Ithaca: Cornell University Press, 1997).

Phillips, Mike and Phillips, Trevor, *Windrush: The Irresistible Rise of Multiracial Britain* (London: HarperCollins, 1998).

Pickering, Sharon, *Refugees and State Crime* (Sydney: Federation Press, 2005).

Ramamurthy, Anandi, *Black Star: Britain's Asian Youth Movements* (London: Pluto Press, 2013).

Ramazanoglu, Caroline (ed.), *Up against Foucault: Explorations of Some Tensions Between Foucault and Feminism* (London: Routledge, 1993).

Rose, Eliot J.B. et al., *Colour and Citizenship: A Report on British Race Relations* (Oxford: Oxford University Press, 1969).

Said, Edward W., *Orientalism* (London: Penguin Books, 2003).

Sassen, Saskia, *Losing Control? Sovereignty in an Age of Globalization* (New York: Columbia University Press, 1996).

Sawicki, Jana, *Disciplining Foucault: Feminism, Power and the Body* (New York: Routledge, 1991).

Sherwood, Marika, *Claudia Jones: A Life in Exile* (London: Lawrence & Wishart, 1999).

Sivanandan, Ambalavaner, *A Different Hunger: Writings on Black Resistance* (London: Pluto Press, 1982).

Solomos, John, *Black Youth, Racism and the State: The Politics of Ideology and Policy* (Cambridge: Cambridge University Press, 1988).

Solomos, John, *Race and Racism in Britain* (Houndmills: Palgrave, 2003).

Spencer, Ian R.G., *British Immigration Policy Since 1939: The Making of a Multi-Racial Britain* (London: Routledge, 1997).

Spivak, Gayatri C., *A Critique of Postcolonial Reason: Toward a History of Vanishing Present* (Cambridge, MA & London: Harvard University Press, 1999).

Stoler, Ann Laura, *Race and the Education of Desire: Foucault's History of Sexuality and the Colonial Order of Things* (Durham & London: Duke University Press, 1995).

Tabili, Laura, *'We Ask for British Justice': Workers and Racial Difference in Late Imperial Britain* (Ithaca, NY: Cornell University Press, 1994).

Tompson, Keith, *Under Siege: Racial Violence in Britain Today* (London: Penguin, 1988).

Tyler, Imogen, *Revolting Subjects: Social Abjection and Resistance in Neoliberal Britain* (London: Zed Books, 2013).

Visram, Rozina, *Asians in Britain: 400 Years of History* (London: Pluto Press, 2002).

Walkowitz, Judith R., *Prostitution and Victorian Society: Women, Class, and the State* (Cambridge: Cambridge University Press, 1980).

Wilson, Amrit, *Finding a Voice: Asian Women in Britain* (London: Virago Press, 1985).

Wilson, Amrit, *Dreams, Questions, Struggles: South Asian Women in Britain* (London: Pluto Press, 2006).

Winder, Robert, *Bloody Foreigners: The Story of Immigration to Britain* (London: Abacus, 2006).

Woollacott, Angela, *Gender and Empire* (Houndmills: Palgrave Macmillan, 2006).

Book chapters

Ben-Tovim, Gideon and Gabriel, John, 'The Politics of Race in Britain, 1962–79: A Review of the Major Trends and of Recent Debates', in Charles Husband (ed.), *'Race' in Britain: Continuity and Change* (London: Hutchinson, 1982) pp. 145–171.

Bowling, Ben, Parmar, Alma and Phillips, Coretta, 'Policing Ethnic Minority Communities', in Tim Newburn (ed.), *Handbook of Policing* (Devon, UK: Willan Publishing, 2003) pp. 528–555.

Cheney, Deborah, 'Those Whom the Immigration Law Has Kept Apart – Let No-one Join Together: A View of Immigration Incantation', in Delia Jarrett-Macauley (ed.), *Reconstructing Womanhood, Reconstructing Feminism: Writings on Black Women* (London: Routledge, 1996) pp. 58–84.

Gordon, Paul, 'Outlawing Immigrants 1: Anwar Ditta and Britain's Immigration Laws', in Phil Scraton and Paul Gordon (eds), *Causes for Concern: Questions of Law and Justice* (Harmondsworth: Penguin, 1984) pp. 114–134.

'Hymen', in Vern L. Bullough and Bonnie Bullough (eds), *Human Sexuality: An Encyclopaedia* (New York: Garland Publishing, 1994) pp. 293–294.

Layton-Henry, Zig, 'Britain: The Would-Be Zero-Immigration Country', in Wayne A. Cornelius, Philip L. Martin and James F. Hollifield (eds), *Controlling Immigration: A Global Perspective* (Stanford, CA: Stanford University Press, 1994) pp. 273–295.

Levine, Philippa, 'Sexuality and Empire', in Catherine Hall and Sonya O. Rose (eds), *At Home with the Empire: Metropolitan Culture and the Imperial World* (Cambridge: Cambridge University Press, 2006) pp. 122–142.

Lunn, Kenneth, 'The British State and Immigration, 1945–51: New Light on the *Empire Windrush*', in Tony Kushner and Kenneth Lunn (eds), *The Politics of Marginality: Race, the Radical Right and Minorities in Twentieth Century Britain* (London: Frank Cass, 1990) pp. 161–174.

Parmar, Pratibha, 'Gender, Race and Class: Asian Women in Resistance', in Centre for Contemporary Cultural Studies (ed.), *The Empire Strikes Back: Race and Racism in 70s Britain* (London: Hutchinson, 1986) pp. 263–275.

Pilkington, Edward, 'The West Indian Community and the Notting Hill Riots of 1958', in Panikos Panayi (ed.), *Racial Violence in Britain in the Nineteenth and Twentieth Centuries (Revised ed.)* (Leicester: Leicester University Press, 1996) pp. 171–184.

Saggar, Shammit, 'Integration and Adjustment: Britain's Liberal Settlement Revisited', in David Lowe (ed.), *Immigration and Integration: Australia and Britain* (London: Bureau of Immigration Multicultural and Population Research/Sir Robert Menzies Centre for Australian Studies, 1995) pp. 105–131.

Sahgal, Gita, 'Secular Spaces: The Experience of Asian Women Organizing', in Gita Sahgal and Nira Yuval-Davis (eds), *Refusing Holy Orders: Women and Fundamentalism in Britain* (London: Virago Press, 1992) pp. 163–197.

Smith Wilson, D., 'Gender, Race and the Ideal Labour Force', in L. Ryan and W. Webster (eds), *Gendering Migration: Masculinity, Femininity and Ethnicity in Post-war Britain* (London: Ashgate, 2008) pp. 89–104.

Solomos, John, 'The Politics of Immigration Since 1945', in Peter Braham, Ali Rattansi and Richard Skellington (eds), *Racism and Anti-Racism: Inequalities, Opportunities and Policies* (London: Sage Publications, 1992) pp. 7–29.

Solomos, John, Findlay, Bob, Jones Simon and Gilroy, Paul, 'The Organic Crisis of British Capitalism and Race: The Experience of the Seventies', in Centre for Contemporary Cultural Studies (ed.), *The Empire Strikes Back: Race and Racism in 70s Britain* (London: Hutchinson, 1986) pp. 9–46.

Articles

Athwal, Harmit, 'Black Deaths in Custody', Institute of Race Relations (IRR), 19 February 2004, http://www.irr.org.uk/2002/november/ak000006.html.

Athwal, Harmit, 'Three Deaths in Immigration Detention', IRR website, 4 August 2011, unpaginated, http://www.irr.org.uk/2011/august/ha000008.html.

Aukerman, M., 'Extraordinary Evil, Ordinary Crime: A Framework for Understanding Transitional Justice', *Harvard Human Rights Journal*, 2002, 15, 39–97.

Aynsley-Green et al., 'Medical, Statistical, Ethical and Human Rights Considerations in the Assessment of Age in Children and Young People Subject to Immigration Control', *British Medical Bulletin*, 14 May 2012, 102, 17–42.

Bland, L., 'White Women and Men of Colour: Miscegenation Fears in Britain after the Great War', *Gender & History*, 2005, 17(1), 29–61.

Bögner, D., Brewin, C., and Herlihy, J., 'Refugees' Experiences of Home Office Interviews: A Qualitative Study on the Disclosure of Sensitive Personal Information', *Journal of Ethnic and Migration Studies*, 2010, 36(3), 519–535.

Bosworth, Mary, 'Border Control and the Limits of the Sovereign State', *Social and Legal Studies*, 2008, 17(2), 199–215.

Bosworth, Mary and Guild, Mhairi, 'Governing Through Migration Control: Security and Citizenship in Britain', *British Journal of Criminology*, 2008, 48, 703–719.

Brown, Ruth, 'Racism and Immigration in Britain', *International Socialism*, Autumn 1995, 2(68), unpaginated, http://www.marxists.org/history/etol/newspape/isj2/1995/isj2-068/brown.htm.

CARF Collective, 'Background: British Racism', *Race & Class*, 1981, 23(2–3), 232–244.

Carter, Bob, Harris, Clive and Joshi, Shirley, 'The 1951–55 Conservative Government and the Racialization of Black Immigration', *Immigrants and Minorities*, November 1987, 6(3), 335–347.

Cerwonka, Allaine and Loutfi, Anna, 'Biopolitics and the Female Reproductive Body as the New Subject of Law', *Feminists@Law*, 2011, 1(1), 1–5.

Couper, K. and Santamaria, U., 'An Elusive Concept: The Changing Definition of Illegal Immigrant in the Practice of Immigration Control in the United Kingdom', *International Migration Review*, Autumn 1984, 18(3), 947–964.

Crenshaw, Kimberle, 'Demarginalizing the Intersection of Race and Sex: A Black Feminist Critique of Antidiscrimination Doctrine, Feminist Theory and Antiracist Politics', *University of Chicago Legal Forum*, 1989, 140, 139–168.

Crenshaw, Kimberle, 'Mapping the Margins: Intersectionality, Identity Politics, and Violence against Women of Color', *Stanford Law Review*, July 1991, 43(6), 1242–1300.

Doty, Roxanne L., 'Racism, Desire, and the Politics of Immigration', *Millennium: Journal of International Studies*, 1999, 28(3), 585–606.

Ennals, David, 'Labour's Race Relations Policy', *Institute of Race Relations Newsletter*, November/December 1968, 437.

Fassin, Dider and d'Halluin, Estelle, 'The Truth from the Body: Medical Certificates as Ultimate Evidence for Asylum Seekers', *American Anthropologist*, 2005, 107(4), 597–608.

Fekete, Liz, 'Europe's Shame: A Report on 105 Deaths Linked to Racism or Government Migration and Asylum Policies', *European Race Bulletin*, http://www.irr.org.uk/pdf2/ERB_66_Europes_shame.pdf, Winter 2009, 66, 2–36.

Freeman, M.D.A. and Spencer, Sarah, 'Immigration Control, Black Workers and the Economy,' *British Journal of Law & Society*, 1979, 6, 53–81.

Garland, David, 'The Limits of the Sovereign State: Strategies of Crime Control in Contemporary Society', *British Journal of Criminology*, Autumn 1996, 36(4), 445–471.

Gilroy, Paul, 'The Myth of Black Criminality', *Socialist Register*, 1982, 47–56.

Gordon, Paul, 'Medicine, Racism and Immigration Control', *Critical Social Policy*, 1983, 3(7), 6–20.

Green, Penny J. and Ward, Tony, 'State Crime, Human Rights and the Limits of Criminology', *Social Justice*, 2000, 27(1), 101–115.

'Grunwick Strike: The Bitter Lessons', *Race Today*, November/December 1977, 9(7), 154.

Hall, Alexandra, ' "These People Could Be Anyone": Fear, Contempt (and Empathy) in a British Immigration Removal Centre', *Journal of Ethnic and Migration Studies*, 2010, 36(6), 881–898.

Hall, Rachel A., 'When Is a Wife Not a Wife? Some Observations on the Immigration Experiences of South Asian Women in West Yorkshire', *Contemporary Politics*, 2002, 8(1), 55–68.

Hayter, Teresa, 'Open Borders: The Case against Immigration Controls,' *Capital & Class*, 2001, 75, 149–156.

Jackson, Louise, A., ' "The Coffee Club Menace": Policing Youth, Leisure and Sexuality in Post-war Manchester', *Cultural & Social History*, September 2008, 5(3), 289–308.

Joshi, Shirley and Carter, Bob, 'The Role of Labour in the Creation of a Racist Britain', *Race & Class*, 1984, 25(3), 53–70.

Kelly, Mark G., 'Racism, Nationalism and Biopolitics: Foucault's *Society Must Be Defended*, 2003', *Contretemps*, September 2004, 4, 58–70.

King, Angela, 'The Prisoner of Gender: Foucault and the Disciplining of the Female Body', *Journal of International Women's Studies*, 2004, 5(2), 29–39.

Kolsky, Elizabeth, ' "The Body Evidencing the Crime": Rape on Trial in Colonial India, 1860–1947', *Gender & History*, April 2010, 22(1), 109–130.

Lindsey, Lydia, 'Halting the Tide: Responses to West Indian Immigration to Britain, 1946–1952', *Journal of Caribbean History*, 1992, 26(1), 62–96.

Marmo, Marinella and Smith, Evan, 'Is There a Desirable Migrant? A Reflection of Human Rights Violations at the Border: The Case of "Virginity Testing" ', *Alternative Law Journal*, December 2010, 35(4), 223–226.

McCulloch, J.W., Smith, N.J. and Batta, I.D., 'A Comparative Study of Adult Crime amongst Asians and Their Host Population', *Probation Journal*, 1974, 24(1), 16–21.

McManus, Nicole, 'Purging the Self: Entering the Abject in Victorian Texts of Vaginal Exploration', *Australasian Journal of Victorian Studies*, 2008, 13(1), 2–20.

Miles, Robert, 'The Riots of 1958: Notes on the Ideological Construction of "Race Relations" as a Political Issue in Britain', *Immigrants & Minorities*, 1984, 3(3), 252–275.

Miles, Robert, 'The Racialization of British Politics', *Political Studies*, 1990, 38, 277–285.

Moore, Robert, 'Labour and Colour: 1965–8', *Institute of Race Relations Newsletter*, October 1968.

Peach, Ceri, 'West Indian Migration to Britain', *International Migration Review*, Spring 1967, 1(2), 34–45.

Pickering, Sharon, 'Crimes of the State: The Persecution and Protection of Refugees', *Critical Criminology*, 2005, 13, 141–163.

Schuster, Liza, 'An Open Debate on Open Borders: Reply to Stephen Castles', *Open Democracy*, 29 December 2003, unpaginated, http://www.opendemocracy.net/print/1658.

Sivanandan, A., 'UK Commentary: Grunwick (2)', *Race & Class*, 1978, 19(3), 289–294.

Smith, Anne Marie, 'Neo-eugenics: A Feminist Critique of Agamben', Occasion: Interdisciplinary Studies in the Humanities, 20 December 2010, 2, 1–12, http://arcade.stanford.edu/sites/default/files/article_pdfs/Occasion_v02_Smith_122010_0.pdf.

Smith, Evan and Marmo, Marinella, 'Uncovering the "Virginity Testing" Controversy in the National Archives: The Intersectionality of Discrimination in British Immigration History', *Gender & History*, April 2011, 23(1), 147–165.

Trivedi, Parita, 'To Deny Our Fullness: Asian Women in the Making of History', *Feminist Review*, Autumn 1984, 17, 37–52.

Tyler, Imogen, 'Designed to Fail: A Biopolitics of British Citizenship', *Citizenship Studies*, February 2010, 14(1), 61–74.

Waters, Chris, ' "Dark Strangers" in Our Midst: Discourses of Race and Nation in Britain, 1947–1963', *Journal of British Studies*, April 1997, 36(2), 207–238.

Weber, L., 'Knowing-and-yet-not-Knowing about European Border Deaths', *Australian Journal of Human Rights*, 2010, 15(2), 35–58.

White, Melissa Autumn, 'Transnational and Intimate Crossings: The "Threatening Body" of the Migrant Sex-Worker', *Reconstructions*, 2007, 7(1), unpaginated, http://reconstruction.eserver.org/071/white.shtml.

Wray, Helena, 'An Ideal Husband? Marriages of Convenience, Moral Gatekeeping and Immigration to the UK', *European Journal of Migration and Law*, 2006, 8, 303–320.

Yuval-Davis, Nora, Anthias, Floya and Kofman, Eleonore, 'Secure Borders and Safe Haven and the Gendered Politics of Belonging', *Ethnic & Racial Studies*, March 2005, 28(3), 513–535.

Zimmermann, S., 'Reconsidering the Problem of "Bogus" Refugees with "Socio-economic Motivations" for Seeking Asylum', *Mobilities*, 2011, 6(3), 335–352.

Reports

Akram, Mohammed and Elliot, Jan, *Appeal Dismissed: The Final Report of the Investigation into Immigration Control Procedures in the Indian Sub-Continent* (London, 1977).

Athwal, Harmit, *Driven to Desperate Measures: 2006–2010* (London: Institute of Race Relations, 2010).

Athwal, Harmit, Bourne, Jenny and Wood, Rebecca, *Racial Violence: The Buried Issue*, IRR Briefing Paper 6 (London: Institute of Race Relations, 2010).

Commission for Racial Equality, *Immigration Control Procedures: Report of a Formal Investigation* (London: CRE, 1985).

Woodfield, Kandy et al., *Exploring the Decision Making of Immigration Officers: A Research Study Examining Non-EEA Passenger Stops and Refusals at UK Ports* (London: National Centre for Social Research/Home Office, 2008).

Unpublished theses

Hall, Rachel, A., 'The Interaction of Gender and Ethnicity: An Exploration of British Immigration Control, Focusing on the Experiences of South Asian Women in West Yorkshire', unpublished PhD thesis, University of Huddersfield, 2006.

Phillips, Kristen, 'Immigration Detention, Containment Fantasies and the Gendering of Political Status in Australia', unpublished PhD thesis, Curtin University, 2009.

Index

Printed and bound by CPI Group (UK) Ltd, Croydon, CRO 4YY